Hidden Debt

Hidden Debt

Solutions to Avert the Next
Financial Crisis in South Asia

Martin Melecky

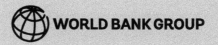 WORLD BANK GROUP

ISBN (paper): 978-1-4648-1667-3
ISBN (electronic): 978-1-4648-1668-0
DOI: 10.1596/978-1-4648-1667-3

Cover design: Sergio Andrés Moreno Tellez, World Bank Group

Library of Congress Control Number: 2021909369

Contents

Boxes

Figures

Tables

Acknowledgments

This report was prepared by a team led by Martin Melecky (Lead Economist) under the guidance of Hans Timmer (Chief Economist) and Hartwig Schafer (Vice President). Core members of the team included Matias Herrera Dappe and Burak Turkgulu (chapter 1), Katie Kibuuka (chapter 2), Siddharth Sharma (chapter 3), and Florian Blum and Pui Shen Yoong (chapter 4). Able research support and inputs were provided by Martin Brun, Mario di Filippo, Yunfan Gu, Shaheen Malik, Tom O'Keefe, Viviana Maria Eugenia Perego, Di Yang, and Kyoung Yang Kim. Tobias Akhtar Haque and Alex Sundakov contributed to the boxes on fragility, conflict, and violence country context and successful public-private partnerships in South Asia, respectively. Neelam Chowdhry provided able administrative support to the report team. The report was edited by Nancy Morrison.

We are grateful to the peer reviewers who supported the preparation of this report from the concept stage, through the authors' workshop, to the decision stage: Ila Patnaik, Ugo Panizza (both external), David Duarte, Eva Gutierrez, and Abha Prasad (all World Bank).

We thank the following colleagues for their guidance, suggestions, comments, and inputs at various stages of the report's preparation: Martin Rama, Zoubida Allaoua, and the Global Practice leadership team of Vivien Foster, Mary C. Hallward-Driemeier, Alfonso Garcia Mora, Marcello Estevão, Demetrios Papathanasiou, and Guangzhe Chen; for chapter 1: Alvaro Pedraza Morales, Fernanda Ruiz Nuñez, Diane Dorothy Menville, Deblina Saha, Reenu Aneja, Tema Alawari Kio-Michael, Cigdem Aslam, Samuel Maimbo, Shomik Raj Mehndiratta; for chapter 2: Davide Mare, Esperanza Lasagabaster, Marius Vismantas, Ilias Skamnelos, Sanket Mohapatra, and participants in the CAFRAL–World Bank Conference on "State Intervention in the Financial Sector"; for chapter 3: Ana Cusolito, Francesca de Nicola, Anoma Kulathunga, Nazmus Sadat Khan, and Dhananath Fernando; for chapter 4: Frederico Gil Sander, Manuela Francisco, Zehra Aslam, Adnan Ashraf Ghumman, Nyda Mukhtar, Rangeet Ghosh, and Fritz Bachmair; for the decision review draft: Najy Benhassine, Faris H. Hadad-Zervos, Henry Kerali, Hideki Mori, and Mercy Tembon; and for the concept review draft: Enrique Blanco Armas, Fei Deng, Jorge Jose Escurra, Alexander Anthony Ferguson, Sereen Juma, Luc Lecuit, Tatiana Nenova, Janardan Prasad Singh, and Volker Treichel.

Our thanks also go to the communications and production teams, including Elena Karaban, Yann Doignon, Diana Ya-Wai Chung, Mark McClure, Jewel McFadden, and Sergio Andrés Moreno Tellez.

We gratefully acknowledge financial support from the United Kingdom's Foreign, Commonwealth and Development Office through the Program for Asia Connectivity and Trade.

Executive Summary

The COVID-19 (coronavirus) crisis has expanded public direct interventions through state banks and enterprises to aid economies, but with possible risks to debt sustainability, long-term productivity, and equality.

The ongoing COVID-19 crisis, which has sent economies in South Asia and other parts of the world into a deep recession, has created the need for public relief efforts. It has also raised South Asia's debt levels and future contingent liabilities. This once-in-a-century shock and the subsequent vast deployment of public resources have come on the back of the debt wave that has formed over the past decade. Large amounts of debt obligations are likely to resurface for central governments as many troubled state-owned enterprises (SOEs) and state-owned commercial banks (SOCBs) will call for support through bailouts. Prematurely terminated public-private partnerships (PPPs) may require large public payments as settlements.

Increased leveraging of SOEs, SOCBs, and PPP interventions during the COVID-19 crisis must be safeguarded against possible exploitation by elites for their own benefit and must minimize misallocations of resources in the economy that could reduce productivity in the medium to long term. On balance, PPPs have yielded more successes than problems compared with SOCBs and SOEs. Some PPPs in South Asia have been highly successful in terms of both public benefits and private returns (see spotlight ES.1 at the end of this summary).

Compared with other regions, South Asia is more exposed to the risk of hidden debt and mounting contingent liabilities from SOEs, SOCBs, and PPPs because of its greater reliance on state off-balance sheet operations.
South Asia has the largest share of SOCBs in terms of banks' total assets across developing country regions, has the highest use of SOEs together with East Asia and Pacific,[1] and is among the top three regions in the use of PPPs in infrastructure (along with Eastern and Central Europe and Sub-Saharan Africa). For instance, the SOE sector in both India and Pakistan is more than twice as large as the international benchmark, controlling for size of the economy. Overall, India and Pakistan are among the biggest users of public agents such as SOEs, SOCBs, and PPPs. Other South Asian countries are prominent users of one or two of the public agents, such as Bhutan's and Sri Lanka's heavy use of SOCBs. Not only do South Asian central governments rely heavily on off–balance sheet operations to aid economic development, but so do subnational governments (SNGs).

The high degree of reliance on SOEs, SOCBs, and PPPs reflects the intention to help accelerate inclusive economic development through direct state interventions, but the negative repercussions have been largely ignored.

The strong preference of South Asian governments for direct interventions in the economy and markets comes with a price. The reality is that, on average, the efficiency of South Asian SOEs, SOCBs, and PPPs is well below the international benchmark. South Asian governments thus face a trade-off when they rebuild after the current crisis. They must balance the tension between using SOEs, SOCBs, and PPPs to maximize socially beneficial investments and minimizing the risk of large surprise liabilities due to inefficiencies and mismanagement of risks. South Asia governments must ensure that their off–balance sheet operations and their mutual interconnectedness do not become the source of the next financial crisis in the region. This report studies the trade-off between *tackling* development challenges through direct state presence in the market and *avoiding* unsustainable debt due to economic inefficiencies of off–balance sheet operations.

Financial distress of public agents is not a rare event in South Asia. Off–balance sheet operations of both national and subnational governments become distressed frequently SOCBs fare the worst.

In South Asia and globally, 8 percent of PPPs are canceled early (terminated) before their contracts expire. Railroad, treatment plant, and toll road projects under PPP arrangements appear to be the most vulnerable to distress. SOEs enter distress even more often. For instance, India's central public sector enterprises (CPSEs) are 15 percentage points to 21 percentage points more likely to enter distress than similar private firms. Other South Asian countries may confront even greater distress problems in their SOE sectors—even if those problems are seemingly well hidden because data are not available. Across Bangladesh, Pakistan, and Sri Lanka, almost half of the banks—regardless of whether private or public—could have been in state of distress between 2009 and 2018.[2] Importantly, the greater the ownership share of government in an SOCB, the higher the probability of bank distress.

Because subnational governments are constrained from borrowing autonomously, they do not experience overall distress. They do, however, experience significant shocks from triggered contingent liabilities: that is, when their own off–balance sheet operations—including subnational SOEs, SOCBs, and PPPs—go bad. Over the past two decades, a contingent liability shock has hit a South Asian subnational government about 10 percent of the time, on average.

When public agents enter distress, governments face the daunting dilemma between bailout and reduced economic activity. Typically, they resort to bailouts.

Overall, SOEs and SOCBs enjoy soft budget constraints and central government bailouts after they get into distress. The same holds for subnational governments that experience a financial shock after their own off–balance sheet operations have failed. These soft budget constraints and bailouts could be partly motivated by "guilt" stemming from the government having set unclear mandates for SOCBs and SOEs through ad hoc requests to help with economic stimulus and other political agendas. These unclear mandates hinder financial accountability, hard budget constraints, and fair monitoring of performance.

The public agents and subnational governments on one side of the social contract and the central government on the other have settled in a bad equilibrium—one that the economist would characterize as the tragedy of the commons: that is, a situation when a common pool of fiscal resources is overused for self-interest. More transparent setting of purpose and better design, incentives, and monitoring of SOEs, SOCBs, and PPPs—including a clearer definition of social versus commercial mandates—can help create a better equilibrium.

The fiscal costs of failing off–balance sheet operations are sizable and can markedly reduce the fiscal space available to South Asian governments.
This report estimates that a systemic macro-financial crisis could trigger PPP failures that would cost South Asian governments more than 4 percent of revenues—and the fallout from the current COVID-19 crisis could be even more severe. The potential fiscal costs from distressed SOEs have been even more overwhelming. In Pakistan, the total liabilities of chronic loss-makers—defined as SOEs that made a loss in three out of the five past years—have been about 8 percent to 12 percent of GDP in recent years, several times more than the country's public spending on education in FY2019/20.[3] In Sri Lanka, the liabilities of loss-making SOEs have hovered at 4 percent to 5 percent of GDP. Interestingly, in every country studied, just the top 10 loss-making SOEs account for more than 80 percent of the total losses in the SOE sector—suggesting that the problem could be managed. In India, the cumulative recapitalization of SOCBs from FY2016 through FY2020 was equivalent to almost one and a half times the country's planned public spending on health care in FY2021/22.[4] The recapitalization needs are estimated to increase markedly in FY2021/22, including due to repercussions of the COVID-19 crisis.

Distressed public agents also inflict substantial costs on the real economy and local business. When a subnational government is hit by a contingent liability shock, local investments suffer for several years. Bailouts of SOCBs can help supply credit to the economy in crises, but they also pave the way for an uneven and frail recovery—one that is especially unfair to small and medium enterprises (SMEs).
In episodes of systemic shocks—such as the global financial crisis and the COVID-19 crisis—many banks experience distress. While private banks deleverage and curtail lending, SOCBs receive capital and debt support from the state to continue (or even increase) lending. This short-term, positive stabilizing

function of SOCBs for the credit cycle, however, comes at the cost of significant credit misallocation—away from successful firms and especially SMEs. It helps unproductive zombie firms linger in the economy in the medium term and stalls needed reallocation of capital (and labor) to enable productive investments.

At the subnational level, local investments in the Indian states fall significantly in the year of a contingent liability shock, continue to decline in the year after, and remain below the trend for three years after the event. Low fiscal capacity and perhaps the greater reliance of local private investments on complementary public investments can drive the adverse impact of contingent liability shocks on total local investments. For these reasons, recklessly leveraged public capital through badly designed off–balance sheet operations of subnational governments is very costly for local economies and communities in South Asia.

How can the downside risks of leveraging public capital be mitigated and the upside benefits enjoyed? How can overleveraging and uneconomical use of public capital be prevented and thus the threat of a financial crisis minimized? Through purpose, incentives, transparency, and accountability (PITA).
Four interconnected principles form the basis of the reform agenda to ensure that public capital is leveraged responsibly in South Asia and to minimize the threat of a financial crisis originating from government off–balance sheet operations (and their interconnections):

P = Purpose. The purpose of off–balance sheet operations and leveraging of public capital through SOEs, SOCBs, and PPPs must be clearly defined by the central government or subnational government as the establisher, owner, or sponsor. This includes formulating a clear vision or mission, setting time-bound objectives, and defining corresponding key performance indicators (KPIs).

I = Incentives. Institutions, rules, and contracts must be structured in a way that creates proper incentives to perform in line with the defined purpose. The operational costs of SOEs, SOCBs, and PPPs often exceed market costs to fulfill their purpose and may thus require fiscal subsidies. The nature and extent of these operational costs and subsidies must be determined and linked to the government's budgetary and debt management frameworks.

T = Transparency. Two types of transparency are needed. *Debt transparency* and relevant data collection are critical to enabling both central and subnational governments to assess the big picture of how SOEs, SOCBs, and PPPs shape the fiscal space and contribute to the overall public debt—including direct obligations and explicit and implicit guarantees.

Economic transparency is also required. It should start with publicly disclosing the policy and purpose of SOEs, SOCBs, and PPPs, and enforcing the requirement that each public agent publish its theory of change for fulfilling its objective and purpose.

A = Accountability. The electorate, civil society organizations (CSOs), industry associations, media, and financial markets must support reforms to enact the principles of purpose, incentives, and transparency (PIT) so that off–balance sheet operations of governments cannot be used for political self-interest or side deals—or at least make it harder to do so. Once the reforms are implemented, the electorate, CSOs, industry associations, and financial

---

BOX ES.1 **Applying the Purpose, Incentives, Transparency, and Accountability (PITA) Recommendations in Fragile and Conflict-Affected Contexts**

Fragility, conflict, and violence (FCV)-afflicted countries and jurisdictions are characterized by weak institutions and thus present challenging contexts for effectively operating, reforming, or privatizing state-owned enterprises (SOEs) and state-owned commercial banks (SOCBs), as well as structuring successful public-private partnerships (PPPs).

In FCV countries such as Afghanistan, persistent security and governance constraints on the effective delivery of central government functions and services can prompt the local private sector or communities to provide these services instead. Further, the state may be unable to provide the institutional underpinnings of markets—such as property rights and contract protections—as well as basic infrastructure and services. State institutions are often captured by political elites to extract rents rather than to serve the public interest because proper accountability mechanisms are missing, among other problems.

At the same time, in response to disrupted social networks and formal structures during periods of

conflict, the informality of the private sector rises. This response and the state's various inabilities can lead to the development of a "gray" economy, in which private sector activity is irregular and largely opportunistic and operates without regulation. In financial markets, beyond local short-term traditional lending markets based on family or kinship, credit is provided at either steep rates or is confined to the individuals and businesses best-connected to officials controlling SOCBs.

Regularly using public funds to bail out or recapitalize inefficient SOEs and SOCBs creates tension because it competes against other and higher priorities by the use of public money. This tension may propel efforts by the state to divest or fully privatize state enterprises, banks, and other assets, as occurred in Bosnia and Herzegovina and Mozambique during past periods of fragility and conflict. This generally positive move is, however, not without risk. For instance, the privatization of SOCBs and the licensing a private banks to recapitalize a failing banking system have sometimes been highly

(Box continues on next page)

BOX ES.1   **Applying the Purpose, Incentives, Transparency, and Accountability (PITA) Recommendations in Fragile and Conflict-Affected Contexts** *(continued)*

nontransparent—especially when initiated during wartime. In the former Yugoslavia, this process resulted in large asset transfers to war criminals. By contrast, with a lag of several years following the cessation of civil war, Mozambique was able to privatize its commercial banks by bringing in foreign partners.

Development agencies are increasingly conscious of the ways that development interventions—including public sector reforms (such as privatization of SOEs and civil service reforms), major infrastructure projects, and community-level decentralization programs—can "do harm" and contribute to tensions in already fraught situations unless they are well at tuned to knowledge of local context and political economy.

The four-pronged reform agenda advanced by this report and centering around purpose, incentives, transparency, and accountability (PITA) also pertains to FCV contexts in South Asia when sensitized to the local context and political economy. Sensitizing proposed concrete actions is perhaps even more important in Afghanistan than in other countries of the region. Some of the challenges that set Afghanistan apart involve (1) political systems dominated by patronage that can reduce the effectiveness of transparency measures; (2) weak

rule of law and weakly enforced contracts; (3) binding capacity constraints, including for the governance and management of SOEs, SOCBs, and PPPs; and (4) fragmented and dysfunctional financial markets lacking the capacity to price risk and exert market discipline.

In FCV areas, it is challenging to identify and carefully align the appropriate reform path with the country context. In contexts in which markets are distorted and dysfunctional, reforms should not rely on unrealistic assumptions that exposure to market discipline is possible—even via full or partial privatization. In contexts in which policy makers are not necessarily held accountable by citizens, reforms should reflect a realistic assessment of how and through which channels increased transparency can change incentives. Planned reforms should be informed by analyses of the broader context of the political economy as well as the specific incentives affecting decision makers and how these can be influenced using the available policy levers. International development organizations can play a key role in creating incentives for reform, enabling sustained change leadership, and providing required technical assistance over the medium to long term.

Source: World Bank.

markets must remain vigilant and active. These actors need to keep testing the justifications for continuing the off–balance sheet operations—such as the existence of SOEs and SOCBs, as well as the use of PPPs for the right (socially beneficial) purpose and with desirable results.

These PITA principles must be based on realistic assessments of the national and subnational contexts and available policy levers. With care, they can be applied to a variety of

contexts, including areas affected by fragility and conflict (see box ES.1).

In closing, while the government must lead in reform, it takes a concerted effort by society to ensure that the off–balance sheet operations of government serve the right socioeconomic purpose and responsibly leverage public capital for the sake of more rapid and more equitable development. Falling short of this task, South Asian countries face the threat of possible financial crises soon.

Spotlight ES.1: Examples of Highly Successful PPPs in South Asia

Public-private partnerships (PPPs) that are highly successful allocate risk between the public sector and the private sector in a sustainable way. These transactions should instill confidence, so that the private capital is mobilized for a particular project and further private participation is encouraged. From the government's viewpoint, a highly successful PPP project must not only be fiscally sustainable, but must also ensure delivery of the demanded infrastructure services—avoiding situations of expensive, unnecessary "white elephant" projects. A PPP project can be partially successful if it meets some but not all the criteria for a high degree of success. For example, the government may succeed in protecting its fiscal position by transferring risk to the private sector, but the project could be a financial failure for the private investors, causing loss of confidence in a PPP program. The four examples that follow, ranging from the local to the national level, illustrate features of highly successful PPPs in four South Asian countries.

Sri Lanka

The South Asia Gateway Terminal (SAGT) is a 30-year build-operate-transfer (BOT) container terminal project within the Port of Colombo signed in September 1999. The project was conceived when the government recognized that the Port of Colombo—then fully operated by the Sri Lanka Ports Authority (SLPA)—was performing poorly. In addition, SLPA did not have access to financing to enable additional dredging and other investment required to handle the largest container vessels. By the mid-1990s, projections indicated that trans-shipment business would start diverting to ports outside Sri Lanka.

To remain competitive, the government of Sri Lanka sought private expertise and the private operation of one of the port terminals. The PPP included extending the quay, repairing and upgrading existing facilities, and purchasing new equipment to (1) quadruple capacity, from 250,000 twenty-foot equivalent units (TEUs) to 1.1 million TEUs per year; and (2) improve efficiency in terms of the number of containers handled per hour and the average waiting time for container vessels.

South Asia Gateway Terminals (Private) Limited (SAGT partnership) won the 30-year BOT contract. The SAGT partnership has financed infrastructure improvements and leases the terminal from SLPA, which also earns income as a minority equity holder. While the partnership is majority-owned by domestic entities, an international terminal operator (APM Terminals) provides key operational expertise. The increased traffic to the Port of Colombo also provides additional benefits to SLPA through port fees charged directly to vessels that use the terminal.

SAGT handled 2 million TEU throughput in 2018, and productivity increased greatly. Time spent loading, offshoring, and repositioning cargo rose from 12 gross gantry moves per hour in 1998 to 30 by 2003. Waiting time for vessels in berth decreased from 6.9 hours in 1997 to 0.9 hours by 2003. SAGT has invested in advanced terminal handling equipment and tracking technology.

During recent, and somewhat controversial, attempts to secure PPP contracts for other terminals at the Port of Colombo, public debate identified SAGT as an undoubted success and centered on whether new PPPs were sufficiently closely modeled on the SAGT approach.

Nepal

The Khimti I Hydropower Project (Khimti) is the first power sector PPP and the first foreign-owned and foreign-operated power project in Nepal, developed using a build-own-operate-transfer (BOOT) contract. Khimti is a run-of-the-river hydroelectric power generation plant with an installed capacity of 60 megawatts. The project is located about 100 kilometers east of Kathmandu along a tributary of one of Nepal's major rivers.

Khimti is owned and operated by Himal Power Limited (HPL), a special purpose company. The government of Nepal and HPL entered into both a project agreement and a power purchase agreement (PPA) in January 1996. The government issued HPL a 50-year project license that gives it the right of uninterrupted water flow of the Khimti River. At the end of the 50-year period, HPL will transfer the project to the government. The Nepal Electricity Authority (NEA) and HPL also entered into a 20-year PPA from the commercial operation date, which was in July 2000. At the end of the PPA period (July 2020), HPL was to transfer 50 percent ownership to NEA. The remaining 50 percent will be transferred at the end of the 50-year project license period. However, the initial transfer process remains delayed due COVID-19 issues, and the project is operating under an interim agreement.

HPL was established on February 21, 1993, by one of Nepal's leading private companies—Butwal Power Company Limited—and three Norwegian companies: Statkraft SF; ABB Energi AS (now ABB Kraft); and Kvaerner AS (now GE Hydro). The World Bank Group's Multilateral Investment Guarantee Agency (MIGA) issued a US$32.8 million guarantee in 1996 to the Norwegian investors to insured their equity against currency transfer limitations, expropriation, and war risks. The construction was financed half by debt and half by equity, with the World Bank Group's International Finance Corporation (IFC) among the parties providing project finance.

The project was successful in transferring construction cost risks associated with such hydropower projects to the private sector. The Khimti project had an unusually large tunneling component, with an 890-meter access tunnel and 7,620-meter headrace tunnel. Despite this, it was completed on time and on budget. Participation by highly capable international specialist firms was a key element of success. The project remained fully operational following an earthquake in April 2015. A recent review by IFC concluded that the project is well positioned to take adaptive measures to address climate change risks.

India

The Hyderabad Rajiv Gandhi International Airport (Hyderabad Airport) was the first greenfield PPP airport in India. It is primarily owned and operated by the GMR Group, one of India's largest listed infrastructure companies, through a 30-year concession agreement with the government of India (through the Ministry of Civil Aviation). The concession was signed in December 2004, and the Hyderabad Airport was inaugurated in March 2008.

HIAL, the project company for the Hyderabad Airport PPP was a joint venture between the GMR Group (63 percent); the government of India (13 percent); the government of Telangana (13 percent); and Malaysia Airports Holding Bhd (11 percent). Under the PPP contract, HIAL was responsible for designing, financing, building, commissioning, operating, maintaining, and managing the Hyderabad Airport. HIAL won the concession by promising to pay the highest concession fee as well as by assuming all commercial and financing risks.

The Hyderabad Airport PPP was conceived to replace an existing airport in Hyderabad. In return for the government's equity share, the concession agreement required the government to (1) close the existing airport to commercial operations and pay any resulting costs or claims; (2) not allow a new or existing airport to be developed within 150 aerial kilometers of Hyderabad Airport within a certain period; (3) not provide other major airports with an unfair competitive advantage; and (4) allow HIAL to propose amendments to the concession agreement, should a change in law lead to an increase in costs or impair the financial position of HIAL exceeding a certain amount.

The concession agreement capped the aggregate liability of the government of India in respect to any breach, default, or change in law to approximately US$14 million (Rs 100 crore).

Hyderabad Airport was commissioned in a record time of 31 months. The airport's initial capacity was 12 million passengers per year, but before the onset of the COVID-19 pandemic, the airport was handling more than 21 million passengers. In March 2021, the government of India announced its intention to sell its stake in the Hyderabad Airport (among others) as part of its ambitious program to monitize assets.

Bangladesh

Khulna is the third-largest city in Bangladesh. It is connected to Bangladesh's capital, Dhaka, and other regional cities through rail, road, water, and air transport. Improved transport links have resulted in a large influxes of people from nearby cities, affecting the city's liveability and putting pressure on the city's infrastructure and services. Within the city, major roads and urban landscaping are constructed by the Roads and Highways Department (RHD) and the Khulna Development Authority (KDA).

As is common, the city budget for roads and related infrastructure tends to be allocated for new construction projects, with limited funds available for maintenance. As a result, roads and road medians tend to deteriorate, reducing traffic safety and urban amenities.

In 2016 and 2017, the Khulna City Corporation (KCC) entered into a series of innovative agreements with multiple private parties to take over responsibility for maintaining 4.6 kilometers of city road medians in return for the right to install advertising billboards on the section allocated to each private party. The objectives of these small-scale PPPs are to ensure that landscaping and maintenance make road crossing safer as well as to improve the attractiveness of the streetscape. The positioning and size of the permitted billboards are specified, to be consistent with those objectives.

Various sections of the road are maintained by private companies—such as the mobile operator Grameen, Banglalink, and the stainless steel manufacturer KSRM—that would otherwise be renting advertising space on the sides of private buildings.

Public opinion surveys indicate more than 80 percent satisfaction with the outcomes. This simple PPP model enables KCC to ensure maintenance that would otherwise not have happened.

Lessons Learned

Successful PPPs can range in size from micro solutions to local problems to large-scale, transformative infrastructure projects. Common features of successful PPPs involve realistic and clear delineations of responsibilities between the public and private sectors, careful selection of private sector counterparts (including appropriate combinations of international skill and capability with local capital), and transparency regarding the risks and rewards allocated to the private sector.

Bibliography

Sri Lanka

ADB (Asian Development Bank). 2020. "Democratic Socialist Republic of Sri Lanka: National Port Master Plan." Technical Assistance Consultant's Report prepared by Maritime & Transport Business Solutions B.V. (MTBS), February. https://www.adb.org/sites/default/files/project-documents/50184/50184-001-tacr-en_7.pdf.

Bisbey, J. "Public-Private Partnerships for Sustainable Port Development." UNESCAP (United Nations Economic and Social Commission for Asia and the Pacific). https://www.unescap.org/sites/default/files/1.4%20PPP%20for%20sustainable%20port%20dev_Jyoti%20Bijbey_ESCAP.pdf.

SAGT website: https://www.sagt.com.lk/about-us/journey-of-sagt.html.

UNDP (United Nations Development Programme). 2012. "Colombo, Sri Lanka Case Study (Port Expansion)." November. https://www.esc-pau.fr/ppp/documents/featured_projects/sri_lanka.pdf.

Nepal

Bhatta, S. "Public Private Partnership in Nepal." National Planning Commission. https://www .unescap.org/sites/default/files/Nepal%20PPT .pdf.

Himal Power Limited website:
https://hpl.com.np/projects/khimti-power -plant/
https://hpl.com.np/projects/project-license -agreement-2/
https://hpl.com.np/projects/project-license -agreement-2/power-purchase-agreement-ppa/
https://hpl.com.np/projects/project-license -agreement-2/project-generation-and-cost/

MIGA website:
https://www.miga.org/project/himal-power -limited
https://www.miga.org/project/himal-power -limited-0

India

Hyderabad Airport PPP Concession Agreement. Downloadable from World Bank PPP Legal Resource Center website: https://ppp .worldbank.org/public-private-partnership library/concession-agreement-development -construction-operation-and-maintenance -hyderabad-internatio.

Bangladesh

Haque, M. N., M. Saroar, M. A. Fattah, and S. R. Morshed. 2020. "Public-Private Partnership for Achieving Sustainable Development Goals: A Case Study of Khulna, Bangladesh." *Public Administration and Policy* 23 (3): 283–98.

Notes

1. Regions are as defined by the World Bank. Regional comparisons of SOEs are difficult. This study uses the database of SOEs maintained by the Organisation for Economic Co-operation and Development (OECD) for several regions outside South Asia. Yet in that database, for instance, East Asia and Pacific is represented only by China and Eastern and Central Europe by Poland.

2. That is, their interest coverage ratio (ICR)—a measure used to determine how easily a company can pay interest on its outstanding debt—lingered below 1, on average. A ratio of 1.5 is considered healthy. The ratio is calculated by dividing a company's earnings before interest and taxes (EBIT) by its interest expense during a given period.

3. Pakistan's public expenditure on education as a percentage of GDP is estimated at 2.3 percent for FY2019/20, making it the lowest in the region.

4. Recapitalization of public banks entailed a cumulative capital infusion of Rs 3.16 lakh crore from FY2016 through FY2020. By contrast, the Union Budget 2021–22 proposed a significantly smaller outlay of Rs 2.23 lakh crore toward health and well-being. For FY2020/21, the Indian credit rating agency ICRA estimates that the budgeted capital of Rs 20,000 crore, along with the external equity raised of around Rs 7,500 crore by a few public sector banks, will be sufficient for public banks.

Abbreviations

AG	Auditor General
AIC	Akaike information criterion
BIC	Bayesian information criterion
CPSE	central public sector enterprise
CRAR	capital to risk-weighted assets ratio
CSO	civil society organization
DFI	development financial institution
EU	European Union
FB	foreign commercial bank
FCV	fragility, conflict, and violence
FY	fiscal year
GDP	gross domestic product
GFCF	gross fixed capital formation
ICR	interest coverage ratio
ICT	information and communications technology
IMF	International Monetary Fund
KPI	key performance indicator
LGD	loss given distress
M&E	monitoring and evaluation
MRPK	marginal revenue product of capital
MRPL	marginal revenue product of labor
MRPM	marginal revenue product of material inputs
MSMEs	micro, small, and medium enterprises
NHAI	National Highways Authority of India
NPA	nonperforming asset
NPL	nonperforming loan
NPV	net present value
OECD	Organisation for Economic Co-operation and Development
OLS	ordinary least squares
PCB	privately owned commercial bank
PH	proportional hazards

PITA   purpose, incentives, transparency, and accountability
PO   proportional odds
PPI   Private Participation in Infrastructure
PPP   public-private partnership
PSB   public sector bank
PVTB   domestically owned private bank
R&D   research and development
ROA   return on assets
RRB   regional rural bank
SBI   State Bank of India
SCB   scheduled commercial bank
SFA   stock-flow adjustment
SFB   small finance bank
SMEs   small and medium enterprises
SNG   subnational government
SOCB   state-owned commercial bank
SOE   state-owned enterprise
TFPR   revenue total factor productivity
UNDP   United Nations Development Programme
WDI   World Development Indicators

Overview

The recent COVID-19 (coronavirus) pandemic, a once-in-a-century global shock, has sent economies in South Asia and the rest of the world into a deep recession. It has also cloaked future developments in a deep cloud of uncertainty. Governments have deployed numerous relief measures to buttress the economy and livelihoods. The indirect measures have come through regulatory forbearance, while the direct ones have involved hefty social transfers and financial support programs.

This big shock and deployment of public resources have come on the back of the latest global debt wave. Since 2010, emerging market and developing economies have experienced the largest, fastest, and most broad-based increase in debt in the past 50 years (Kose et al. 2020). Many of the debt increases have been pushed by the activation of contingent liabilities—obligations incurred by governments off their balance sheets that have triggers for payment. Such indirect (hidden) debt has been historically large in South Asia.

At the heart of the rising debt wave and pandemic response have been state-owned commercial banks (SOCBs), state-owned enterprises (SOEs), and public-private partnerships (PPPs) as well as other off–balance sheet operations by national and subnational governments. They have helped governments address important development challenges and rapidly deliver relief measures. However, because of their inefficiencies, they have been an important way in which public debt has accumulated. Over time, part of the debt generated by off–balance sheet operations is revealed as it hits the central government budget and debt stock, but at a given time, a large part remains hidden under the radar of the existing financial disclosure standards.

Because of the economic importance that hidden debt carries for South Asia and beyond, this report studies the trade-offs between addressing development challenges directly through a state presence in the markets and the risk of accumulating unsustainable debt through the economic inefficiencies of off–balance sheet operations.

This report offers some insights regarding the ongoing COVID-19 crisis. Specifically, the crisis is likely to exacerbate problems many SOCBs, SOEs, and PPPs confronted even before the COVID-19 shock because of their opaque contracts and distorted incentives, operational inefficiencies, and substandard management of risks. As a result, large amounts of debt obligations are likely to resurface for central governments. PPPs in South Asia and around the world are likely to terminate early as the COVID-19 crisis strains partnerships and project viability; many private partners can exploit force majeure clauses as expected project revenues plunge. SOCBs and SOEs will require injections of liquidity through debt and equity bailouts to sustain their operations. This fiscal cost may be well justified to help SOEs continue to invest and SOCBs continue to lend. However, adverse side effects are likely. For instance, SOCBs' positive countercyclical lending in the short term is likely to trigger capital (and labor) misallocation in the medium term, and in turn, create conditions for inequitable and unproductive recovery. Similar strains are likely to resurface at the level of subnational governments (SNGs) due to triggered contingent liabilities. Central governments will be obliged to come to the rescue with bailout loans and tax transfers. However, this may not be enough to sustain SNG expenditures, including public investments. As SNG expenditures shrink, local investments (both public and private) are likely to contract significantly for several years. On the positive side, by exposing vulnerabilities and the urgency for reform, the COVID-19 crisis can also help policy makers push for change in the key areas that this report highlights.

In general, governments run operations off their balance sheets for two main reasons. The first is to address market failures and help create markets by encouraging (crowding in) the private sector to make investments with positive spillovers that benefit the public. The second is to expand the pool of public finance by turning direct debt obligations into a larger pool of indirect debt obligations that may or may not have to be met, depending on future events (contingent liabilities).[1] Jointly, the two approaches aim to leverage public capital financially and economically to advance development. For financial reasons, governments leverage public capital off their balance sheets to mobilize greater resources from the private sector and foreign savings—extra resources they typically de-risk through explicit or implicit guarantees. For economic reasons, governments aim to leverage public capital off their balance sheets to maximize the development impact of those resources.

Three prominent agents through which governments leverage public capital in South Asia are SOCBs, SOEs, and, more recently, PPPs. This leveraging of public capital through off–balance sheet operations can happen at the level of both central and subnational governments. As decentralization increases in India and Pakistan, and more recently in Bhutan, Maldives, and Nepal, subnational off–balance sheet operations could grow considerably. For instance, as of 2020, India had three times as many subnational SOEs than it had federal SOEs—and the financial performance of SOEs is much worse at the subnational level.

South Asian countries use direct interventions in the markets through off–balance sheet operations more heavily than the international benchmark. India and Pakistan are among the biggest users of all three public agents considered in this report (SOCBs, SOEs, and PPPs). Other countries stand out in using one or two of the agents, such as Bhutan and Sri Lanka for SOCBs. Figure O.1 shows how the use of SOCBs, SOEs, and PPPs depends on the size of the economy as measured by the real GDP (in logs). It sheds some light on whether governments that develop public policies for bigger markets tend to utilize direct tools more heavily—in addition to utilizing indirect interventions, such as regulations.

The use of SOCBs increases with the size of the economy (figure O.1, panel a). India, Bhutan, Sri Lanka, and, to a lesser extent, Bangladesh are outliers compared with the international average marked by the trend line. Interestingly, there is no significant codependence between how many SOEs governments deploy and the size of the economy (figure O.1, panel b). However, even here India and Pakistan stand out, exceeding the international benchmark (the trend line).

The use of PPPs increases only marginally with the size of the economy (figure O.1, panel c).

PPPs may have advantages for both smaller and larger economies. De-risking may be needed in small markets. Bigger markets present more opportunities for risk pooling, but also can experience bigger coordination failures that governments may need to resolve—including through de-risking. Pakistan has a large share of PPPs compared with the benchmark, while India has only marginally more. However, given India's—and Bangladesh's—large pipelines of infrastructure PPPs, the two countries can be expected to increase their shares significantly in the near future.

Overall, it seems that South Asian governments have a strong preference for direct intervention in the economy and markets, but it comes with a price. The reality is that the efficiency of South Asian SOCBs, SOEs, and PPPs is well below the international benchmark, on average. Some notable examples of inefficiencies and surprise liabilities include the following:

- In 2013, the Pakistan government cleared the circular debt of energy companies that stemmed from arrears between enterprises in an attempt to clear hidden debt once and for all. The cost was estimated at 1.5 percent of GDP (Bova et al. 2016)—but the problem continues today. In 2014, the Sri Lankan government had to inject about 1.2 percent of GDP (SL Rs 123 billion) from the budget into its strategic SOEs (Government of Sri Lanka 2014). The SOE sector then generated net losses in two out of the next three years.
- Recapitalization of SOCBs has been an ongoing issue over the last two decades in most South Asian countries, including Afghanistan, Bangladesh, India, Nepal, and Sri Lanka. In Bangladesh, for instance, a single branch of Sonali Bank (an SOCB) extended loans valued at about $454 million based on fraudulent documents. The massive fraud led to a nonperforming loan ratio of 37 percent at the SOCB in 2014. These loans have invariably defaulted and have created a big hole in the bank's capitalization (World Bank 2020b).

FIGURE O.1   Some South Asian Governments (India, Pakistan) Use State-Owned Commercial Banks, State-Owned Enterprises, and Public-Private Partnerships More Commonly Than the Global Benchmark While Others (Bangladesh, Sri Lanka) Are Catching Up

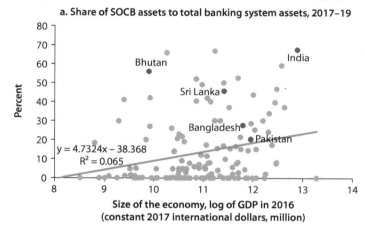

a. Share of SOCB assets to total banking system assets, 2017–19

$$y = 4.7324x - 38.368$$
$$R^2 = 0.065$$

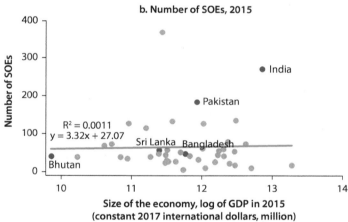

b. Number of SOEs, 2015

$$R^2 = 0.0011$$
$$y = 3.32x + 27.07$$

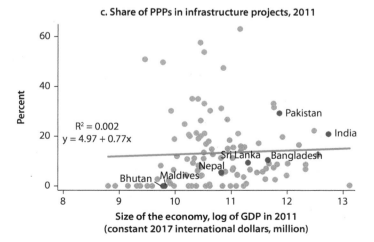

c. Share of PPPs in infrastructure projects, 2011

$$R^2 = 0.002$$
$$y = 4.97 + 0.77x$$

Sources: Original figures for this report. Data for panel b are from the Organisation for Economic Co-operation and Development (OECD) and World Bank World Development Indicators.
Note: The diagonal lines (trend lines) in each panel indicate the international average at varying levels of real GDP (in logs). In panel b, the number of SOEs for India does not include subnational SOEs. PPPs = public-private partnerships; SOCBs = state-owned commercial banks; SOEs = state-owned enterprises.

- Overoptimistic bidding on PPP contracts has led to many cancellations in the PPP portfolio of the National Highways Authority of India. In turn, these cancellations have increased the level of nonperforming assets in India's banking sector. The State Bank of India, which holds the greatest nominal amount of debt related to Indian highways, reported that about 20 percent of loans to ports and highways were in nonperforming status by the end of 2016, with the trend increasing throughout 2016 (ADB et al. 2018).
- At the subnational level, to resolve the problems of long-running underperformance and overindebtedness at power distribution companies (subnational SOEs), Indian states unexpectedly increased their debt stock by about 5 percent, on average, between FY2015 and FY2018 through the Ujwal DISCOM Assurance Yojana (UDAY) scheme, according to Reserve Bank of India data. In 2017 alone, India's state public sector enterprises—the SOEs owned by subnational governments—lost an amount equal to 0.5 percent of GDP. In FY2018, eight Indian states provided farm loan waivers amounting to 0.32 percent of GDP.

As these experiences highlight, South Asian governments face a trade-off between using PPPs, SOCBs, and SOEs to maximize socially beneficial investments and minimizing the risk of large surprise liabilities due to inefficiencies and mismanagement of risks. Specifically, through PPPs, the governments try to minimize the inefficiency of project execution and leverage public capital, but potentially at the cost of assuming too much risk—and at times allowing for moral hazard on the part of the private sector. Through SOCBs, the government tries to reach the financially underserved and finance the economy even when big shocks hit, but potentially at the cost of mismanagement of risks by SOCBs and misallocation of capital in the economy. Through SOEs, the government addresses market failures related to risky, long-term investments, or underinvestment in externalities and natural monopolies, but potentially at the cost of exposure to large financial risks and potential surprise liabilities. At the level of SNGs, the trade-off concerns the tension between offering rewards for good performance and providing bailout support in bad times: that is, increasing the fiscal autonomy of SNGs with good fiscal performance to boost the efficiency of local public spending (including through subnational SOEs and PPPs), while limiting bailout support from the central government to exceptional cases and retracting some fiscal autonomy if a subnational government systematically underperforms in normal times.

These and similar tensions have led economists to formulate three complementary views about the character of SOCBs, SOEs, and PPPs and the challenges for managing their performance (World Bank 2020b):

- **Social view.** Public agents (SOCBs, SOEs, and PPPs) are created by government to address market failures and improve social welfare, mixing profitability goals with social objectives. These mixed objectives create challenges for monitoring outcomes and performance.
- **Agency view.** Because of the inability to monitor public agencies, an agency problem emerges involving a discrepancy between the objectives of managers (the agents) and owners (the principals). While governments (principals) may seek to maximize social welfare, their agents (and private partners) may lack the incentive to maximize the use of resources toward this end.
- **Political economy view.** Social objectives might be corrupted by politicians who pursue their personal interests. That is, in some cases, the public agents can become mechanisms for politicians to pursue their individual goals, often at the cost of economic distortion or inequitable distribution of resources.

These views explain the high operational inefficiencies, reckless risk management, and problematic governance and political economy issues that can be the leading reasons behind the financial underperformance of public agents (SOCBs, SOEs, and PPPs). The problems can occur at the level of public agents, but also at the level of the political government (the principal of these agents).

For instance, SOEs are often promised subsidies to run costly government programs—such as advancing access to electricity to underserved populations and small enterprises—that are not received on time. SOCBs are asked to run government programs—such as to advance financial inclusion or lend to underserved and riskier micro, small, and medium enterprises (MSMEs)—but without receiving the subsidy for the expected and unexpected losses that private markets avoid. They are also asked to help stimulate economies during downturns or financially support large PPPs with concentrated risks: that is, take risk that they cannot diversify away. They are often asked to perform these functions in an ad hoc fashion and without prior consideration of costs and risks—for which fiscal transfers (subsidies, extra capitalization) must be arranged and delivered. They are often tasked with the impossible: to cross-subsidize the related losses from the profits on their commercial portfolio and activities.

In so doing, the government (the principal) becomes part of the problem. Governments at the national and subnational levels originate frictions that complicate effective financial management of the public agents (among others) by being unclear about the purpose(s) that the agents should serve and by being inconsistent over time when confronting political and systemic shocks.

As a result of financial underperformance due to various tensions and shocks, South Asia's SOCBs, SOEs, and PPPs face periodic financial distress. At such times, they need to adjust—with more or less help from the government (the owner or sponsor). These adjustments can inflict fiscal and wider economic costs. The latter, through lower economic activity and tax revenues, among others, come back to weaken the government's fiscal stance and increase public indebtedness. To investigate financial distress among public agents, trace the fiscal costs and costs to the real economy of such distress, and better understand the implications for public policy reform, this report has devised an analytical framework.

Analytical Framework

If governments run off–balance sheet operations through SOCBs, SOEs, and PPPs that financially underperform or are otherwise financially vulnerable, these operations are likely to experience periodic distress. The SOCBs, SOEs, and PPPs will be forced to adjust—including with the help of financial bailouts or by curtailing their activity. In turn, these adjustments will generate adverse impacts on the fiscal stance by triggering contingent liabilities and/or adverse impacts on the real economy by depriving the firms and individuals of some services delivered by SOCBs, SOEs, or PPPs. Figure O.2 traces these pathways through an analytical framework that the report adopts and follows in its analysis.

Distress

A public agent enters distress when its financial condition has worsened to the point that it cannot perform some of its common functions. For instance, an SOCB in distress cannot lend to its clients at the same amount as before, or an SOE in distress cannot continue investing in new infrastructure to reach underserved population. In empirical analyses, the state of distress can be determined using a threshold for financial ratios computed from accounting data. In situations of adequate financial transparency, this approach is the preferred way of measuring distress—mostly because of its simplicity and equal treatment across similar types of agent, such as SOCBs and SOEs.

FIGURE O.2   **Analytical Framework: Links from Distress to Adjustments to Impacts**

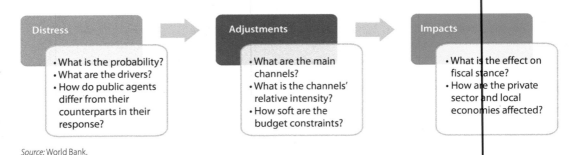

Source: World Bank.

As an indicator of financial distress for SOCBs and SOEs, this report uses the interest coverage ratio (ICR) along with alternatives that serve as robustness checks. The ICR reveals whether the revenue that the agent generates suffices to cover the interest payments on its debt. When the ICR falls below 1, an SOCB or SOE is considered to be distressed.

Some PPP projects could be hard to compare with SOCBs or SOEs because they can enter distress early in their investment cycle before they start operating, that is, performing their functions. This distress could occur because the public and private partners disagree and engage in a dispute that cannot be resolved; in such instances, the PPP is canceled or terminated before the PPP contract expires. As the measure of distress for PPPs, this report uses early terminations of PPPs. The empirical data to capture PPP distress is retrieved from the Private Participation in Infrastructure (PPI) database of the World Bank.[2]

When financial transparency is impaired and accounting data are unavailable or unreliable, econometric methods can be used to determine the distress events empirically. This report uses such an econometric approach to empirically define distress—such as triggering of major contingent liabilities—for SNGs. Because the financial transparency of SNGs—especially concerning their off–balance sheet operations—is inadequate, the report associates SNG distress with an unexpected increase in SNG debt. Here the expected debt dynamics are determined by past levels of SNG debt and planned fiscal balances. While indirect, this identification by econometric association has been successful and validated by some publicly recognized distress events, such as the unexpected increase in the debt of Indian states through the UDAY scheme.

With respect to distress, the analyses in the report tackle questions such as the following: What is the *probability of distress* for a given public agent? Which factors can help predict nearing distress? How do public agents differ from their private counterparts?

Adjustment in Times of Distress

A public agent becomes distressed because its financial situation becomes unsustainable. Something needs to change—and usually several things. These changes concern the public agent's financials and business operations. They must adjust to resolve the unsustainable financial situation and exit distress. The adjustments could be fast—such as instant recapitalization of the distressed SOCB, SOE, or PPP. Or they can be protracted—such as if the resolution depends on the result of an investigation of a committee tasked with deciding on behalf of the public how to proceed and what adjustments to make. Unresolved and protracted distress may require bailouts and/or adjustments that are ultimately more costly and/or severe.

The adjustments in times of distress can occur through various channels. Typically, the public agent uses a combination of channels rather than a single channel. For instance, even if recapitalization is promised, it may not be instant. The distressed SOCB may need to curtail its lending for some time. The report considers the following five adjustment channels:

1. Request a bailout by injection of public equity or debt financing from the central government.
2. Approach financial markets to raise new private debt or equity, or mobilize additional deposits.
3. Reallocate or forgo planned expenditure—such as postponing investment to cover unexpected expenditures or curtailing lending to meet unexpected needs for liquidity.
4. Sell assets to cover unexpected expenditures.
5. Enter bankruptcy and/or liquidation or cancel the partnership and/or the project.

This list is by no means exhaustive; it focuses on the main adjustments observed in practice. For instance, the first channel could include less transparent forms of bailout, such as bailout purchases from the central government against delivery of services in the future, overinvoicing and underinvoicing of transactions among SOEs, and overpricing of assets purchased by central government entities. Under the second channel, the extreme case could be outright privatization—including through conversion of private debt into private equity and ownership. Under the third channel, the reallocated or foregone expenditures often involve maintenance expenditure that can severely impair the quality of core assets and of service provision by the public agent—generating a second round of distress pressure—or reduced wage expenditures also resulting in firing of employees. Under the fourth channel, the sale of noncore assets could be revitalizing because it can cleanse the public agent from unfit and distracting business lines. By contrast, the sale of core assets could impair the bottom line of the business and service provision by the public agent, including by decreasing its economies of scale and productivity. Under the fifth channel, the

public agent could seek help and time to recover under the bankruptcy protections and/or be liquidated—including if it fulfilled its purpose and there is no rationale for its further existence.

With respect to adjustments, the analyses in the report tackle questions such as the following: What are the main *adjustment channels* that public agents in South Asia use when resolving situations of distress? How intensively are these different channels used? How soft (binding) are the budget constraints that public agents in South Asia face?

Impacts

The forced adjustment in times of distress inflicts losses on the central government and/or the economy. Hence, the report considers and studies two main impacts of SOCB, SOE, and PPP distress. The first is the direct impact on the fiscal stance (that is, the fiscal deficit or public debt). The second is the impact on the economy (that is, the macroeconomy, industrial activity, and/or local economic activity), which in turn affects the fiscal stance indirectly, for example, through lower tax revenues because of lower economic activity. We consider these two impacts at the levels of both the central and subnational governments.

If the central government or a subnational government decides that the SOCBs, SOEs, or PPPs need to recover from distress with the help of a bailout, its fiscal expenditures or debt will increase and its future fiscal space will shrink. By issuing new public debt, governments may discourage (crowd out) private sector investment by increasing borrowing costs for private borrowers and/or shrinking the limited pool of funding in the economy. For instance, Huang, Pagano, and Panizza (2020) find that in China, increasing local public debt crowded out the investment of private firms by tightening their funding constraints. Importantly, such increases in government expenditure and debt cover only the accumulated losses of the public agent and are not new investments or purchases of any kind. They merely help restore the functioning of the public agent, restructure it, or liquidate it.

One type of restructuring is full privatization, which turns the public agent into a private entity, essentially ceases its noncommercial social functions (that is, the public production of socially beneficial externalities), and, in principle, releases the central or subnational government from any official exposure to this entity. Here, two observations are warranted. First, even after full privatization, the government may not be completely released from exposure because of perceived reputation risks if the privatized entity gets into distress or otherwise fails soon after privatization. The government may still extend support to privatized firms. Second, while forced adjustment involving liquidation or privatization may impose short-term costs on the economy, it could have positive long-term effects if the public agents had been distorting private markets—such as by crowding out private activity, pursuing undue competitive advantage, or mispricing production inputs or final goods and services.

If the central government decides not to bail out (or only partially bail out) the PPPs, SOCBs, or SOEs in distress—including for reasons of limited fiscal space—the agents must financially adjust by themselves. They can do so in two broad ways: increasing their liabilities by raising equity or debt financing from the private sector; or limiting their activities or asset growth.

The first way can crowd out private financing available for the private sector because investors might prefer to allocate funds to public agents with their (perceived) implicit government guarantee—even if those agents are distressed. The uncompetitive advantage on the better risk-adjusted return can cause the crowding out of private financing even if the central (or subnational) government itself does not issue new debt. Of course, SOEs and other public agents also borrow when they are not distressed—possibly inducing some crowding out as well. However, their borrowing in times of distress can have more adverse effects for two reasons. First, the public agents may be in distress because of a systemic risk event (such as the global financial crisis or the COVID-19 pandemic) when most private firms in the same tier of creditworthiness are trying to raise funds as well. Second, this crowding-out effect can occur in a segment of financial markets other than government securities markets—a segment in a lower creditworthiness tier to which the distressed SOEs and other public agents rightfully migrate. This segment—involving banks as well as private debt and equity—also serves small and medium enterprises (SMEs), whose access to finance can worsen. Hence, such a crowding-out effect may be even more detrimental for equal access to opportunities.

The second way—by limiting activities or assets—could also be costly for the economy if public agents help create markets (through positive supply side effects, such as spillovers in investment in research and development) or perform socially beneficial functions that help sustain or stimulate the demand side of markets—such as connecting buyers to information and communication technology (ICT) infrastructure and e-commerce or providing credit after disasters. Consider the example of PPPs. If PPPs are terminated early (canceled), not only is the government likely to lose directly because it will have to compensate the private partner, but the project will not be realized or will be realized under full public ownership and operations. When the needed project is not realized, the cost is apparent. However, even if the government decides to finish the project on its own—as the sole financier and overseer—the efficiencies that the private sector could generate by managing the project implementation through PPP will also be lost.[3] For instance, highways will be of lower quality, thereby increasing the maintenance expense, and will be inefficiently operated. Another example of costly adjustment for the economy is curtailed lending by SOCBs. When SOCBs in distress adjust by decreasing their lending, the economy will be deprived of credit and businesses will decrease their activity (investments, production, and purchase of inputs).

Again, the distributional effect can more adversely hit the segments that are riskier to lend to, such as MSMEs.

With respect to impacts, the report examines such questions as the following: What *impact* does the distress experienced by public agents have on the fiscal stance? How are the private sector and local economies affected by the forced adjustment of public agents in times of distress?

Empirical Findings

Figure O.2 and the previous discussion frame some key questions addressed by this report. This section highlights some answers to these questions based on the in-depth analyses presented in the report's chapters. Key findings

> In South Asia, off–balance sheet operations by governments are common, but produce mixed results and may cost societies too much.

are summarized around the topics of distress of public agents (SOCBs, SOEs, PPPs); their adjustment in times of distress; and fiscal and economic impacts. Highlights of the main findings are presented in figure O.3, in line with the report's framework. The respective chapters on SOCBs, SOEs, and PPPs as well as the chapter on the off–balance sheet operations of SNGs provide the full analysis and detail.

FIGURE O.3 **Highlights of the Report's Findings on Distress, Adjustments, and Impacts**

Distress
- About 4% to 10% of the time, PPPs, SOCBs, and SOEs enter distress, including at the SNG level.
- About 92% of PPP projects survive until the end of their contract period. For their success, macrofinancial stability is fundamental, as is contract design and structuring.
- The main drivers are operational inefficiency; weak governance, institutions, and contracts; and poor risk management.
- SOCBs and SOEs do not take more risk than private firms. SOCBs manage credit risk worse, and SOEs overemploy. Their conditions are likely worse at the subnational level.

Adjustments
- SOCBs and SOEs tend to get bailed out with access to new debt and equity in times of distress. Hence, they mostly keep their business running as usual, while private firms and banks in distress must deleverage, decrease activity, or curtail lending.
- PPPs in distress can terminate early. Because PPP contracts are individually structured, adjustments in distress can be based on distorted incentives that are unexpected and nontransparent.
- SNGs hit by triggered off–balance sheet commitments reduce their fiscal spending but also receive bailouts through tax allocations from the central government.

Impacts
- The liabilities of chronically distressed federal SOEs could account for up to 5% of GDP in India. The cost of recapitalizing SOCBs is increasing in India, trending beyond $50 billion over 2019–20.[a] A macrofinancial crisis could trigger fiscal losses from PPPs of around 4% of government revenue in Pakistan, Bangladesh, and India.
- Successful SMEs with high sales growth suffer the most from impaired access to finance when linked with SOCBs.
- In Indian states that experienced triggering of contingent liabilities, the local investment activity is depressed for the next four years, on average.

Source: World Bank.
Note: The highlights follow the analytical framework for the report presented in figure O.2. PPPs = public-private partnerships; SNGs = subnational governments; SMEs = small and medium enterprises; SOCBs = state-owned commercial banks; SOEs = state-owned enterprises.
a. *The Economic Times*, https://economictimes.indiatimes.com/news/economy/policy/indian-banks-may-need-20-50-bn-capital-over-next-1-2-years-as-bad-loans-set-to-rise/articleshow/76043255.cms?from=mdr.

Distress of Public Agents

Distress is not a rare event in South Asia. The off–balance sheet operations of government examined by this report enter distress frequently. There is an 8 percent likelihood that PPPs in the region and beyond will terminate early—meaning that the partnership will be canceled before its contract expires. In other words, only about 92 percent of PPP projects survive until the end of their contract period. Railroad, treatment plant, and toll road projects under PPP arrangements appear the most vulnerable to distress.

SOEs enter distress more often, especially India's central public sector enterprises (CPSEs), which are majority owned by the federal government. Regression analysis for this report estimates that a CPSE is 15 percentage points to 21 percentage points more likely to enter distress than similar private firms. CPSEs in the manufacturing sector are significantly more vulnerable to distress. Pakistan has an even larger SOE sector than India judging by the sector's total liabilities as a share of GDP. Similarly, based on SOE debt as a share of GDP, Bhutan has a larger SOE sector than India, with Bangladesh and Sri Lanka following not far behind India. However, the lack of data prevents deeper analyses for South Asian countries other than India. Nevertheless, the dearth of data and lower transparency suggest that other South Asian countries may confront even greater distress problems in their SOE sectors than India—even if those problems seem well hidden.

As for banks, our analysis indicates that in Bangladesh, Pakistan, and Sri Lanka, half of the banks—regardless of whether they are private or public—could have been in distress between 2009 and 2018, that is, have an interest coverage ratio (our baseline indicator of distress) lingering below one, on average. The situation appears significantly better in India. While India's SOCBs are likely to be in distress 25 percent of the time, old private banks fare progressively better and new private banks even more so. Overall, SOCBs in South Asia are about 11 percentage points more likely to experience distress than private banks, on average (controlling for bank characteristics). Moreover, compared with an average SOCB, an SOCB with majority government ownership share (of more than 70 percent) is about 24 percentage points more likely to experience distress than a similar private bank.

Because SNGs are constrained from autonomous borrowing, they do not experience overall distress. But they do experience significant shocks from triggered contingent liabilities—that is, when their own off–balance sheet operations, including subnational PPPs, SOEs, and SOCBs—go bad. A contingent liability shock hits a South Asian SNG about 10 percent of the time (based on results for Indian states). Fiscally weaker states, such as India's special category states,² are shocked even more often—about 13 percent of the time.

Adjustments in Times of Distress: Bailouts versus Reduced Activity

How do SOCBs and SOEs adjust in times of distress compared with private banks and firms? Do they raise new equity and debt to cover unexpected losses? How big is the bailout that the central government provides? How big is the adjustment on the business and investment side of SOCBs and SOEs?

The adjustment of SOCBs in times of distress differs significantly from that of private banks (figure O.4). If private banks get into distress, they reduce lending much more than state banks in distress, which continue lending at the same or marginally higher rate—compared with healthy SOCBs or private banks (compare the long blue negative "lending" bar for distressed private banks with the shorter positive orange bar for distressed SOCBs). When in distress, SOCBs enjoy softer budget constraints and readily obtain state equity and debt support (compare the positive orange "capital" and "debt" bars for distressed SOCBs with the negative blue bars for distressed private banks).

The softer budget constraint, as well as conditions of government recapitalization, enable SOCBs to sustain investments in times of distress. However, the soft budget constraints impose substantial fiscal costs and erode market discipline. The policy question is whether this costly insurance and risk-absorption function of SOCBs pays off in terms of wider economic benefits, such as sustained investment by firms that bank with and borrow from SOCBs.

For SOEs, the report finds that distress does not restrain these public agents from investing and acquiring new fixed assets to the same extent as it does private firms. As a condition of their recapitalization or other bailouts, SOEs could also be required to expand their investment and stimulate the economy. Focusing on some of the shocks triggering distress, this report finds that private firms confronting a negative revenue shock reduce investments, debt, and paid-in capital. Naturally, the availability of funds to finance asset growth is sensitive to revenue shocks because, for banks and investors, revenue shocks are indicative of repayment capacity. However, for SOEs, the access to financing—whether through equity or debt—is much less sensitive to revenue shocks than for private firms. Therefore, SOEs do not need to adjust to such shocks by reducing their activity to the same extent that private firms do. Private firms infer a negative shock as a market signal to slow down their borrowing and investment, but SOEs can largely ignore such market signals. For this reason, during 2015–17, government support to SOEs in India and Pakistan averaged between 1.2 percent and 1.7 percent of GDP per year (figure O.5).

The adjustments of distressed PPPs are less clear because the contracts that uphold such partnerships are not standardized or transparent. Often their details and the contractual clauses that create various obligations for the government are not disclosed or adequately shared—even with the public debt managers. And when PPPs are renegotiated, the fiscal implications are rarely reported. When the parties do not reach an agreement to

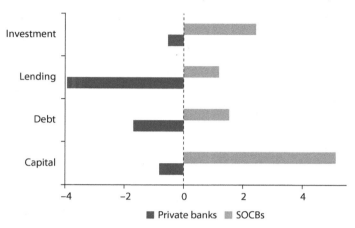

FIGURE O.4 State-Owned Commercial Banks Adjust Differently from Private Banks in Times of Distress, 2009–18

Source: Original calculations for this report.
Note: The bars depict the t-score of the estimated adjustment coefficients. Like the z-score for the population average, the t-score for a regression coefficient helps illustrate the "economic" significance of the estimate by combining its magnitude and associated degree of uncertainty. That is, longer bars in the figure denote that the estimates are generally large and certain, while small bars denote that the estimate is small or uncertain. For instance, the two top bars show that, on average, one can be confident to expect that SOCBs will receive a sizable capital injection (bailout) in times of distress, while private banks in distress will not be able to raise capital and will have to write off some capital. SOCBs = state-owned commercial banks.

renegotiate the PPP, the government often needs to fully compensate the private partners for the debt, equity, and foregone earnings from the failed PPP project. The government can decide to form another PPP to implement the project, implement the project on its own, or not implement the project at all. These adjustments are potentially very costly both fiscally and economically in terms of essential infrastructure that the PPP projects aim to build and operate and that is supposed to reach the most vulnerable firms and communities.

At the subnational level, contingent liability shocks due to distressed off–balance sheet operations have direct budgetary impacts. They require unplanned expenditures if not adequately provisioned for; increase SNG indebtedness; raise their borrowing costs; and shrink their overall fiscal space. The shocks necessitate a fiscal policy adjustment. This adjustment can involve reducing expenditure or increasing revenue or both. SNGs may also receive assistance from the central government, through either increased transfers or loans. Our estimations reveal that after a

FIGURE O.5 Annual Government Support for South Asian State-Owned Enterprises Could Account for More Than 2 Percent of GDP, on Average, Depending on the Country, 2015–17

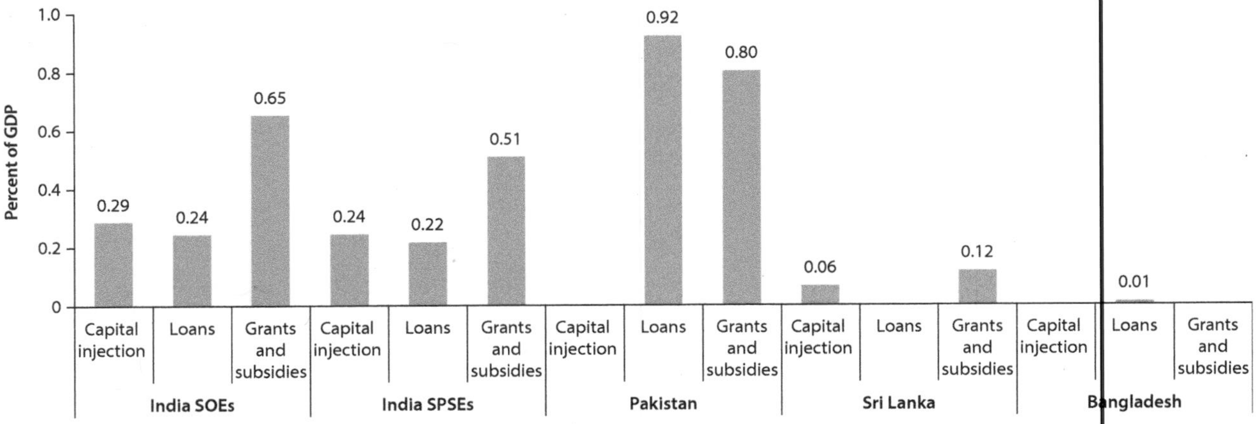

Source: Data from government reports, averaged over 2015–17.
Note: Indian state-owned enterprises (SOEs) include both central public sector enterprises (CPSEs) and state public sector enterprises (SPSEs).

contingent liability shock, state governments in India reduce expenditures—split approximately equally between capital and revenue expenditures—and increase revenue through taxes in the subsequent year. Moreover, the states receive assistance from the central government in the form of loans and increased tax devolution.

Overall, SOCBs, SOEs, and SNGs enjoy soft budget constraints and central government bailouts after SOCBs or SOEs get into distress or SNGs experience a financial shock after their own off–balance sheet operations have failed. These soft budget constraints and bailouts could be partly motivated by the government's "guilt" stemming from unclear mandates it sets for SOCBs and SOEs through ad hoc requests to help with economic stimulus and other political agendas. Given this pattern, accountability, hard budget constraints, and fair monitoring of performance are often not possible together. The public agents and SNGs on the one side of the social contract, and the central government on the other, have settled in a bad equilibrium—one that the economist would characterize as the tragedy of the commons: that is, a situation when a common pool of fiscal resources is overused for self-interest. How fiscally costly

are the distresses of public agents and their adjustments? What are the costs for the real economy and local economic activity? These impacts are explored next.

The Fiscal Impacts of Distress in Public Agents

The fiscal implications of failing off–balance sheet government operations are sizable and could notably reduce the fiscal space available to South Asian governments. For instance, the report estimates the likely fiscal costs from PPP projects that are terminated early by simulating the effect of a profound macroeconomic crisis in 2020—combining a large depreciation of local currency with banking and debt crises. Such a profound macrofinancial crisis would dramatically increase the fiscal costs from early termination of PPPs, particularly in 2021. The estimated fiscal costs over the 2020–21 period could reach 1.0 percent to 4.3 percent of government revenues. Specifically, they could be as high as 4.3 percent of government revenues in Pakistan, 3.9 percent in Bangladesh, and 3.7 percent in India (figure O.6). In Nepal, early termination of PPPs could require up to 3.3 percent of government revenues, while in

FIGURE O.6 **A Profound Macrofinancial Crisis Could Trigger Failures among Public-Private Partnerships That Would Cost South Asian Governments up to 4 Percent of Revenues**

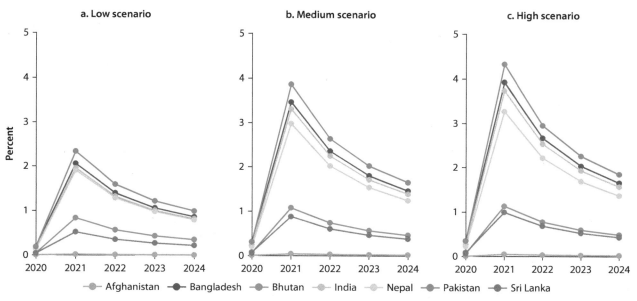

Source: Original figures for this report.
Note: Estimated fiscal costs as a percentage of government revenues from early termination of public-private partnership portfolios assuming a profound macrofinancial crisis.

> The huge problem of SOE losses can
> be addressed by focusing on the
> largest, chronic loss-makers.

Bhutan and Sri Lanka, it could require around 1 percent of government revenues. These simulations underestimate the effect of the crisis because government revenues are kept constant—even though they would contract during such a profound macrofinancial crisis.

The potential fiscal costs from distressed SOEs are even more overwhelming. Unfortunately, due to the unavailability of data, the report cannot measure SOE-level distress based on the interest coverage ratio for South Asian countries other than India. However, it examined the total liabilities of loss-making SOEs using the limited SOE-level data available for Pakistan and Sri Lanka (figure O.7). In Pakistan, the total liabilities of loss-making SOEs have ranged from 12 percent to 18 percent of GDP in recent years—a remarkably high percentage.

If a more conservative measure is adopted and only chronic loss-makers—defined as SOEs that made a loss in three out of the five past years—are considered, this number remains between 8 percent and 12 percent of GDP. In Sri Lanka, the liabilities of loss-making SOEs have hovered between 4 percent and 5 percent of GDP. If these percentages are deducted from the calculations of available fiscal space, the debt sustainability picture for South Asian countries notably deteriorates. Interestingly, in every country studied, the top 10 loss-making SOEs account for more than 80 percent of the total losses in the SOE sector. Focusing on these heavy loss-makers means that this huge problem can be addressed!

The Economic Impacts of Distressed Public Agents

One key measure of economic development is the rate at which firms and the local economy invest. The report focuses on such a measure when estimating the economic impact of

FIGURE O.7 **The Liabilities of Loss-Making State-Owned Enterprises in India, Pakistan, and Sri Lanka Have Been Huge, but More Than 80 Percent of Losses in Each Country Have Occurred in Only the Top 10 Loss-Makers**

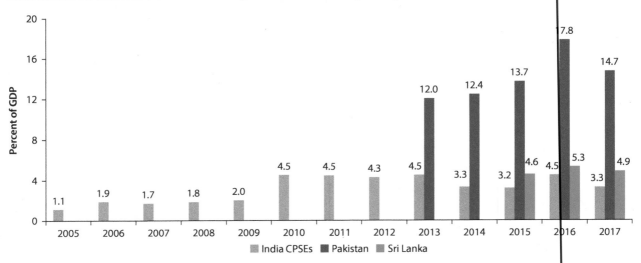

Source: Data from Prowess and government reports, various years.
Note: Total liabilities of loss-making state-owned enterprises in India, Pakistan, and Sri Lanka (as percentage of GDP). CPSEs = central public sector enterprises.

> Recklessly leveraged public capital by subnational governments has been very costly for local communities and must be remedied.

frequent distress at public agents and failing off–balance sheet operations of governments.

For instance, the report finds that when firms start borrowing from SOCBs (as opposed to private banks), they systematically invest less. Even firms with high growth of sales and greater investment potential invest less when engaging with SOCBs. The implications of banking with SOCBs are particularly strong for SMEs. Using the Indian Chamber of Commerce definition of SMEs, the report finds that the SMEs that started banking with SOCBs invest much less than other SMEs. This negative SME effect is more significant than the effect of firm size or age. Even more than average SMEs, SOCBs hinder successful SMEs with high sales growth from realizing their investment potential. It seems that SOCBs are particularly challenged by screening the creditworthiness of opaque SMEs and enabling their potential for investment.[5,6] This finding is in line with the existing

literature that shows that SOCB lending induces credit misallocation and does not generally serve credit-constrained SMEs.[7] Our findings therefore suggest that in episodes of systemic shocks—such as the global financial crisis or the COVID-19 pandemic—when many banks experience distress simultaneously, private banks deleverage and curtail lending, while SOCBs receive capital and debt support from the state to continue (or even increase) lending. This short-term, positive stabilizing function of SOCBs for the credit cycle, however, comes at the cost of significant credit misallocation—away from successful firms and especially SMEs. This short-term positive effect makes for an unequal and unfair recovery and helps unproductive, zombie firms linger in the economy in the medium term. It stalls the necessary reallocation of capital (and labor) to enable productive investments.[8]

At the subnational level, how does the distress of off–balance sheet operations and the resulting contingent liability shocks affect local investments in South Asia? Such shocks reduce public capital expenditure and decrease public investment. Consequently, private investment that relies on the execution of public investment and is typically crowded in by public investment also declines. Moreover, contingent liability shocks dampen local investments indirectly: for instance, by raising the tax burden and thus discouraging private investment or by reducing the viability of investment projects, firm creditworthiness, and local lending by banks. The report confirms that local investments in Indian states fall significantly in the year of a contingent liability shock, continue to decline in the year after, and remain significantly below the trend for three years after the event (figure O.8). Interestingly, low fiscal capacity and possibly greater reliance on the crowding-in effect of public investments can drive the adverse impact of contingent liability shocks on local investments. For instance, in India's general category states, local investments contract only marginally after the shock. However, in special category states, investments contract by more than 60 percent in the year after a contingent liability shock. Therefore, recklessly leveraged public capital through badly designed off–balance sheet operations of SNGs is a very costly affair for local economies and communities in South Asia. This practice must be urgently remedied by informed policy reforms.

Factors That Can Help Explain Distress, Inform Policy Reform, and Improve Outcomes

What are some of the main factors that can predict distress and help inform policies to mitigate distress of public agents in South Asia?

- *PPPs.* Larger PPP projects are more prone to distress (figure O.9). The exception is the largest projects—which could perhaps benefit from more checks and balances of more stakeholders. Distress is more likely in certain sectors, particularly railroads, treatment plants, and toll roads. Preserving macroeconomic stability—in particular, preventing the occurrence of local currency devaluations and banking and debt crises—can significantly increase the probability

FIGURE O.8   Local Investments in Indian States Fall Significantly with a Contingent Liability Shock, Keep Dropping the Year After, and Stay Well Below the Trend for Three Years

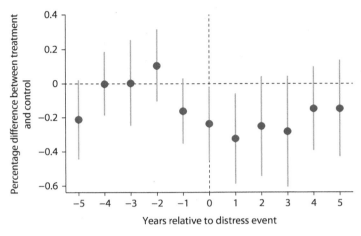

Source: Original calculations for this report.
Note: The figure plots decreases in subnational governments' gross fixed capital formation following contingent liability shocks. The blue dots in the figure mark the value of the estimated effect (regression coefficients) of the occurrence of a contingent liability shock on gross fixed capital formation in the state (in logs). The orange line intersecting each dot marks the 80 percent confidence interval associated with the estimated effect. The underlying regression controls for the confounding effect of business cycle shocks by using common time dummies.

that PPPs will not fail. Institutionalized checks and balances on the decision-making powers of chief government executives reduce PPPs' vulnerability to expropriation by the government, such as through a change in policy or direct political interference. Direct government support to PPPs—involving capital and revenue subsidies as well as in-kind transfers—lowers the probability of distress, perhaps thanks to more effective de-risking of the underlying projects.

The analysis in the report shows that PPPs executed by subnational governments are less likely to face early termination than PPPs with central governments. Perhaps local authorities understand local problems better or oversee projects better because they are nearby. By contrast, national governments may engage in riskier projects because they can bear the termination risk from an individual PPP project thanks to their more diversified PPP portfolio and greater fiscal resources.[9] In terms of contract design, PPP contracts based on

FIGURE O.9   **Checks and Balances on Government Executives Help Prevent Distress of Public-Private Partnerships**

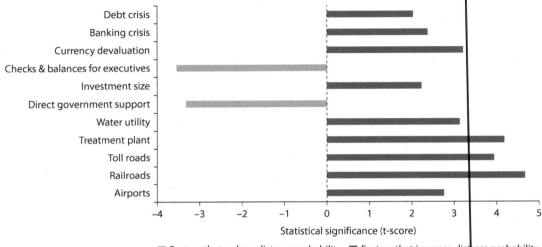

Source: Original calculations for this report.
Note: The bars depict the t-scores of the estimated adjustment coefficients. Like the z-score for the population average, the t-scores for the estimated regression coefficient help illustrate the "economic" significance of the estimate by combining its estimated magnitude and associated degree of uncertainty. That is, longer bars in the figure denote that the estimates are generally large and certain, while small bars denote that the estimate is small or uncertain.

premium payments to government may create an unsound incentive structure and provoke overly optimistic bids from the private sponsor to win a PPP contract.

- **SOCBs.** The extent of government ownership matters in the frequency of distress at SOCBs. SOCBs with a government share of between 50 and 70 percent can be less prone to distress than SOCBs in which government has more than 70 percent ownership. SOCBs can be more fragile by design (Calomiris and Haber 2014). That is, the overall governance around and at SOCBs can expose them to more or greater shocks, such as directed lending, directed support of government programs, political interference in management, forced overemployment, and unqualified employment (Cole 2009; Ashraf, Arshad, and Yan 2018; Richmond et al. 2019). The likelihood of distress increases as bank size decreases. Therefore, smaller SOCBs with more concentrated business models are the most prone to distress. Banks—and SOCBs in particular—that are not able to intermediate the volume of deposits they mobilize are less efficient

and more vulnerable to distress. Credit risk culture and management can help explain the more frequent distress at SOCBs. Interestingly, SOCBs do not appear to take on more risk than private banks. The organizational culture, possibly from formative experiences in sheltered markets, explains the patterns of slower adoption of credit scoring technology and inferior risk management among India's SOCBs relative to new private banks (Mishra, Prabhala, and Rajan 2019). But this report's findings also implicate broader governance issues and political economy influences as important factors in shaping the structures and decisions underpinning credit risk management in SOCBs.

- **SOEs.** South Asia's SOEs do not engage in inherently more risky activities than private firms. For instance, India's SOEs do not have more volatile sales or profits than comparable private firms, nor are the SOEs concentrated in sectors that have lower profit margins. So, what factors explain SOE underperformance and recurring distress? SOEs overemploy capital and labor. Controlling for size, age, and sector, the revenue-to-wage bill ratio of SOEs is 85.8 log points lower, and their revenue-to-fixed-assets ratio is 21.5 log points lower than comparable private firms. Thus, SOEs earn less per unit of labor cost and per unit of capital than their private sector comparators. This is despite the SOE's higher debt-to-asset ratio and financial leverage.[10] It has long been argued that SOEs underperform due to various internal management problems.[11] Our findings support the argument that SOEs are constrained from adjusting labor use. Based on the idea that corporate governance reforms could improve SOE performance, such reforms have emerged in South Asian countries. However, this report finds that a higher corporate governance rating for an SOE does not significantly correlate with better SOE performance. Hence, improvements in corporate governance must be complemented by broader reforms in the governing environment around SOEs. One aspect of this environment are soft loans and implicit guarantees that distort the incentives of SOEs to monitor debt levels and act early to improve performance.

- *SNGs.* At the subnational level, when off–balance sheet operations of governments go bad, they trigger contingent liabilities that shock the government fiscal stance. These shocks do not have a purely external origin; they are induced endogenously as a response to political incentives. The report finds that during the run-up to state elections,[12] SNGs assume debt from off–balance sheet operations, such as debt of subnational SOEs, to secure jobs in the short term. At the same time, SNGs delay recognizing some other debt shocks until after elections because the required adjustments and the impact on the local economy may cause political fallout. The contingent liability shocks can be mitigated through increased transparency, such as through the publication of debt-related information. Such measures take time to become effective, but once they do,

> The negative risks of leveraging public capital can be mitigated and the possible benefits enhanced through four principles: purpose, incentives, transparency, and accountability (PITA).

they permanently reduce the likelihood of contingent liability shocks. In addition, financial markets do not help exert discipline on the states by effectively using the disclosed information in their pricing. Although fiscal rules have immediate mitigating effects, these effects are short lived and more significant in fiscally weaker states (such as the special category states in India). Because contingent liability shocks have triggered support from the central government in the past, the states engage in some moral hazard by failing to optimize their efforts to properly manage the risk from contingent liabilities.

Overall, the report finds ample evidence of issues related to unclear objectives of off–balance sheet operations, distorted incentives, weak transparency, and lack of monitoring or faulty monitoring. These and other issues can be addressed by the recommendations that follow.

Policy Recommendations

The report's findings suggest that the reform agenda to leverage public capital responsibly in South Asia can be framed through four principles: purpose, incentives, transparency, and accountability (PITA).

- *Purpose.* The purpose of off–balance sheet operations and leveraging of public capital through SOCBs, SOEs, or PPPs must be clearly defined by the central government or subnational government as the establisher, owner, or sponsor. This includes formulating a clear vision or mission, setting time-bound objectives, and defining corresponding key performance indicators (KPIs). For example, when a government council formulates the vision and mission for SOCBs and SOEs, the government entity/unit representing the state as the owner of SOCBs and SOEs in turn can formulate the objectives for each SOCB and SOE (or for each cluster by similar purpose)—such as advancing financial inclusion in rural areas or access to electricity by SMEs. The government ownership entity/unit can further define the corresponding measurable or verifiable KPIs. The KPIs can combine commercial indicators (such as the return on equity) and development outcomes (such as accelerated growth in newly opened and actively used payment accounts by the adult population in rural areas).

• *Incentives.* Institutions, rules, and contracts must be structured in a way that creates proper incentives to perform in line with the defined purpose. The operational costs of SOCBs, SOEs, and PPPs often exceed market costs in order to fulfill their purpose. The nature and extent of these operational costs need to be determined and linked to the government's budgetary and debt management frameworks. For example, expanding connective infrastructure—energy, transport, and ICT—to underserved areas may generate very low commercial returns or losses over the time horizon during which the typical private firm would maximize profits. The length of the horizon over which the activity would become profitable, or the inability to secure all the returns from the activity, may require an ongoing budgetary subsidy. This subsidy must be assigned in the budget and specified in the medium-term fiscal framework. The boards of directors for SOCBs and SOEs must be properly staffed to deliver a skill mix to effectively guide the SOCBs and SOEs in fulfilling the twin objectives of generating both profitability and developmental impact—possibly over longer horizons than commercial private firms. Likewise, PPP contracts must be structured in a way that encourages competitive and responsible bidding as well as fair restructuring of PPPs in distress—rather than their early

termination—and most important, delivers efficiency gains in the construction and operation of the infrastructure. Fiscal rules for SNGs must be binding and their adherence or breach reflected in the degree of fiscal autonomy the central government awards the SNG. For example, on the back of limited transparency, SNGs have used off–balance sheet operations and contingent liabilities to escape from fiscal rules.

• *Transparency.* Two types of transparency are needed. *Debt transparency* and relevant data collection are critical to enable both central governments and SNGs to pull together the big picture of how SOCBs, SOEs, and PPPs shape the fiscal space and contribute to the overall public debt—including direct obligations and explicit and implicit guarantees. Of importance, a meaningful system for setting the probabilities that guarantees are triggered (conversion probabilities) and become direct obligations of the government must be developed, regulated, and enforced. This will require that the accounting and other back office systems of SOCBs, SOEs, PPPs, and SNGs can communicate with the central government's back office systems for debt management. Further, South Asia should move from the cash-based fiscal accounting standards toward accrual accounting to disclose debt and contingent liability risks when they accrue, not when they materialize, to allow for adequate budgeting, decision making, and market response.

Economic transparency is also required. It should start with publicly disclosing the policy and purpose of SOCBs, SOEs, and PPPs and enforcing the requirement that each public agent publish its theory of change for fulfilling its objective and purpose. Furthermore, monitoring and evaluation (M&E) frameworks (central, cluster-based, or individual) need to be developed to inform the necessary data collection and to demonstrate economic (development) impact. M&E processes and outcomes should be periodically audited.

For both the financial and economic (development) impact audits, the auditor general of the government and the fiscal council have a crucial role to play in ensuring the thoroughness and quality of these audits and proper functioning of the monitoring system.

South Asian countries—and many other nations—are in the early stages of developing financial and debt transparency. The availability and *quality* of data on SOEs and PPPs—especially subnational ones—and the data quality for SNGs is very low in South Asia. In Pakistan, for example, neither the provinces nor the Ministry of Finance publishes a time series of the provinces' debt that is harmonized, unified, and centrally audited. The total liabilities of subnational SOEs are generally not known and could be in some cases even greater than those of the federal SOEs. While the quality of financial data for SOCBs is slightly better than that of SOEs, the economic transparency of SOCBs is often murkier. For the sake of transparency, the government's medium-term fiscal framework—at both the central and subnational levels—should account for contingent liabilities from PPPs, SOCBs, and SOEs by assessing the public agent's debt trajectories and their sensitivity to shocks as well as keep track of likely government commitments in case of distress.

- *Accountability.* The electorate, civil society organizations (CSOs), industry associations, media, and financial markets must take action to support reform that implements the PIT principles so that off–balance sheet operations of governments cannot be used for political self-interest (such as increasing reelection prospects) or side deals ("I'll scratch your back if you scratch mine")—or at least make it harder to do so. Once the reforms are implemented, the electorate, CSOs, industry associations, and financial markets must remain vigilant and active. The actors need to keep testing the justifications for

continuing the off–balance sheet operations—such as the existence of SOCBs and SOEs as well as the use of PPPs for the right purpose and with desirable results. These actors must periodically ask and demand public answers to questions such as the following:

- CSOs, for example, can question whether SOCBs and SOEs expand the reach of public and commercial services to undeserved households and businesses (MSMEs). CSOs can also ask whether it is time for the public agents to gradually exit some market segments and give way to the private sector to ensure that the quality of service is improved on a commercial basis.
- Industry associations must ask whether SOCBs and SOEs can help stabilize the market, set the strategic direction for the industry to decrease investment uncertainty, or generate positive spillovers for the rest of the industry (such as through their R&D investments). Industry associations can point out that market distortions, such as in funding and pricing, as well as product and service competition are becoming so harsh that streamlining or the exit of state ownership from the industry is warranted.
- Financial markets need to have enough information to differentiate good performers from bad ones among SOCBs, SOEs, PPPs, and SNGs, for example, by pricing the debt of worse performers higher than that of good performers. Along with necessary transparency and disclosure, various other steps could help, including developing markets for project bonds to ensure pooled, local-currency funding and market monitoring of PPPs; requiring listing on stock exchanges and public trading of the debt and equity of the agents; issuing of debt (and bail-in instruments) by SOCBs and SOEs; and improving markets for subnational bonds to price the risk of SNG financial performance.

TABLE O.1   Implementing the High-Level Policy Recommendations for Public-Private Partnerships, State-Owned Commercial Banks, State-Owned Enterprises, and Subnational Governments

The PITA principles	Public-private partnerships	State-owned commercial banks	State-owned enterprises	Subnational governments
Purpose	To create efficiency in public projects through well-incentivized private sector participation. Should not be used primarily to expand fiscal space (public funding) because infrastructure PPPs are ultimately funded through tax revenues or user fees, which could have been collected by the government if the infrastructure were publicly provided.	To help create markets for financial services by addressing market failures. Typically combine social and commercial objectives. Purely commercial SOCBs could be used to expand government capacity to generate revenue.	To help create markets and provide an alternative to ineffective regulation of natural monopolies in some sectors. Typically combine social and commercial objectives. Purely commercial SOEs could be used to expand government capacity to generate revenue.	To expand the local efficiency of SNG operations and help create local infrastructure, markets, and public services using off–balance sheet operations at the SNG level. Experience suggests caution in expanding these operations rapidly at the SNG level.
Incentives	Improve de-risking of projects and risk sharing between the government and private sector. Risk must be addressed by the government and efficiently assigned between the public and private partners, not simply passed on to the private partner. Establish checks and balances on the powers of executives to mitigate expropriation risks and corruption and strengthen governance around PPPs. Ensure that the contract design encourages competitive but responsible bidding.	Establish fiscal provisions to cover the above-market operating costs and risk taking needed to pursue legitimate objectives. Avoid using commercial operations to cross-subsidize social functions. Couple assurances that fiscal transfers will cover legitimately higher losses with binding rules and hard budget constraints. Ensure proper supervision by an independent regulator.	Include fiscal provisions in medium-term expenditure and debt management frameworks to cover the above-market operating costs needed to pursue legitimate objectives. Ensure that the distribution of transfers is timely to keep incentives aligned. Couple assurances that fiscal transfers will cover legitimately higher losses with binding rules and hard budget constraints.	Make the ability to run sizable off–balance sheet operations through PPPs, SOCBs, and SOEs an earned privileged that responsible SNGs obtain with greater autonomy. So far, the incentive for off–balance sheet operations has largely been the escape from subnational fiscal rules. Consider empirical evidence that subnational PPP projects have been more successful—thanks to more efficient local supervision—than subnational SOCBs and SOEs because of their more concentrated geographic and industry risks, as well as weaker governance of subnational SOCBs and SOEs.
Transparency	South Asian governments should move from cash-based fiscal accounting standards toward accrual accounting to disclose debt and contingent liability risks when those risks accrue, not when they materialize, to allow for adequate budgeting, decision making, and market response.			
	Disclose and gradually standardize contracts for PPPs. Link all contingent liabilities from PPP contracts to medium-term expenditure and debt management frameworks. Publicly disclose the entire compensation of private partners in case of success or failure. Publish private bids to enable monitoring by the public and competitors to enforce bidding that is both competitive and responsible.	Publicly disclose SOCB lending to and funding from SOEs, together with the policy/directed lending share of the SOCB loan portfolio, within the audited financial statements of SOCBs. Shift SOE investment borrowing from SOCBs to capital markets through the issuance of SOE corporate bonds or government bonds.	Better assess and monitor the fiscal risks from SOEs. Incorporate them into fiscal planning and debt management frameworks. Improve collection of financial data of subnational SOEs so that, for example, the total liabilities of all SOEs are disclosed. Ensure adequate provisions to meet each contingent liability, and all contingent liabilities, without disrupting public spending plans.	Collect and consolidate information on debt and other contingent obligations through a single entity at the subnational level, such as a specialized debt management unit within the Finance Department. Further consolidate data at the central government level to disclose the big picture. Audit, analyze, and publicize the data on consolidated debt and contingent obligations through an independent national agency, such as the fiscal council, to ensure the consistency and accuracy of the data.
Accountability	The electorate, civil society organizations, industry associations, media, and financial markets must take action to support reform that implements the PIT (purpose-incentives-transparency) principles so that off–balance sheet operations of governments cannot be used for political self-interest or side deals—or at least make it harder to do so. Once the reforms are implemented, all these actors must remain vigilant and active and keep testing the justifications for continuing off–balance sheet operations.			

Source: World Bank.
Note: PITA = purpose, incentives, transparency, accountability; PPPs = public-private partnerships; SNGs = subnational governments; SOCBs = state-owned commercial banks; SOEs = state-owned enterprises.

In closing, while public policy must lead, it takes a concerted effort by society to ensure that the off–balance sheet operations of government make sense and responsibly leverage public capital for the sake of more rapid and more equitable development. Table O.1 summarizes the high-level policy recommendations discussed in this report and organizes them into a matrix with the PITA principles in the rows and the types of public agents in the columns. The report chapters discuss these recommendations in detail.

Notes

1. Note that contingent liabilities can originate from many sources, such as potential bailouts of systemically important banks, unexpected costs from litigation against the government, natural disasters, and schemes that the government may run (pensions and health insurance obligations or social transfers in recessions). For instance, Bova and others (2016) estimate that the largest average fiscal cost of contingent liability realizations for 80 countries sampled came from financial sector support and bank bailouts in financial crises, followed by the unexpected litigation costs. This report focuses on a narrower set of potential contingent liabilities related to PPPs, SOEs, and SOCBs, including at the subnational government level.

2. See the PPI Data page at https://ppi .worldbank.org/en/ppidata.

3. When the government finishes the project on its own as the sole financier and overseer, it may either use SOEs or contract private firms to build, operate, and/or maintain the infrastructure. Because the government is unable to manage the project implementation as efficiently as the private sector, a large part of the implementation efficiencies will be lost even if the government contracts private firms to build, operate, and/or maintain the infrastructure.

4. Special category status is a classification given by India's central government to assist in the development of states that confront geographical and socioeconomic disadvantages, such as hilly terrains, strategic international borders, economic and infrastructural backwardness, and nonviable state finances.

5. It is not clear whether this finding might be due to SOCBs not lending enough to SMEs overall or their willingness to lend to SMEs only for working capital needs. Future research could examine this.

6. Anecdotal evidence suggests that SOCBs focus more on meeting lending quotas for the volume of extended credit than they focus on the quality of project screening. These quotas are more easily met by serving larger firms—including SOEs implicitly backed by a government guarantee—than opaque and risker SMEs. Therefore, the combination of more frequent distress with the inability to take informed risks and manage them makes SOCB operations problematic for private sector development (Mishra, Prabhala, and Rajan 2019).

7. For example, studies for India (Cole 2009), Pakistan (Khwaja and Mian 2005), and Brazil (Carvalho 2014) show that SOCBs induce significant credit misallocation in the economy. Besides being more politicized and inefficient, the lending of SOCBs may not reach more credit-constrained economic agents such as SMEs (see Berger et al. 2008; Ongena and Sendeniz-Yüncü 2011).

8. However, this is not to deny the successes of SOCBs in mobilizing deposits, advancing financial inclusion in digital payments, or facilitating relief after disasters (World Bank 2020a).

9. Highway projects in India provide an interesting example: All the highway projects that were canceled between 2012 and 2015 were PPPs with the central government. At the same time, however, state governments continued to form successful PPPs for road construction and operation.

10. Interestingly, CPSEs compensate for the overuse of labor by "underusing" other inputs. For example, SOEs could be using more manual processes that consume less power.

11. It is harder to align the incentives of management and owners in the public sector (Ehrlich et al. 1994). The compensation of managers is weakly linked to the SOEs' market performance (Borisova, Salas, and Zagorchev 2019), and SOE managers are prevented from making optimal choices, for example, because of a government mandate leading to excessive hiring (Shleifer and Vishny 1994).

12. We focus on the state legislative assembly (Vidhan Sabha) elections, which largely determine the state-level governments, which hold fiscal authority.

References

ADB, DFID, JICA, and World Bank (Asian Development Bank, UK Department for International Development, Japan International Cooperation Agency, and the World Bank). 2018. *The WEB of Transport Corridors in South Asia*. Washington, DC: World Bank.

Ashraf, B. N., S. Arshad, and L. Yan. 2018. "Do Better Political Institutions Help in Reducing Political Pressure on State-Owned Banks? Evidence from Developing Countries." *Journal of Risk and Financial Management* 11 (3): 1–18.

Berger, A, L. Klapper, M. Martinez Peria, and R. Zaidi. 2008. "Bank Ownership Type and Banking Relationships." *Journal of Financial Intermediaries* 17 (1): 37–62.

Borisova, G., J. M. Salas, and A. Zagorchev. 2019. "CEO Compensation and Government Ownership." *Corporate Governance: An International Review* 27 (2): 120–43.

Bova, E., M. Ruiz-Arranz, F. Toscani, and H. Elif Ture. 2016. "The Fiscal Costs of Contingent Liabilities: A New Dataset." IMF Working Paper WP/16/14, International Monetary Fund, Washington, DC.

Calomiris, C. W., and S. H. Haber. 2014. *Fragile by Design: The Political Origins of Banking Crises and Scarce Credit*. Princeton, NJ: Princeton University Press.

Carvalho, D. 2014. "The Real Effects of Government-Owned Banks: Evidence from an Emerging Market." *Journal of Finance* 69 (2, April): 577–609.

Cole, S. 2009. "Fixing Market Failures or Fixing Elections? Agricultural Credit in India." *American Economic Journal: Applied Economics* 1 (1): 219–50.

Ehrlich, I., G. Gallais-Hamonno, Z. Liu, and R. Lutter. 1994. "Productivity Growth and Firm Ownership: An Analytical and Empirical Investigation." *Journal of Political Economy* 102 (October): 1006–38.

Government of Sri Lanka. 2014. *Department of Public Enterprises–Performance Report 2014*. Department of Public Enterprises.

Huang, Y., M. Pagano, and U. Panizza. 2020. "Local Crowding-Out in China." *Journal of Finance* 75 (6): 2855–98.

Khwaja, A. I., and A. Mian. 2005. "Do Lenders Favor Politically Connected Firms? Rent Provision in an Emerging Financial Market." *Quarterly Journal of Economics* 120 (4): 1371–411.

Kose, A. M., P. Nagle, F. Ohnsorge, and N. Sugawara. 2020. *Global Waves of Debt: Causes and Consequences*. Washington, DC: World Bank.

Mishra, P., N. Prabhala, and R. G. Rajan. 2019. "The Relationship Dilemma: Organizational Culture and the Adoption of Credit Scoring Technology in Indian Banking." Johns Hopkins Carey Business School Research Paper no. 19-03, Johns Hopkins University, Baltimore, MD.

Ongena, S., and I. Sendeniz-Yüncü. 2011. "Which Firms Engage Small, Foreign, or State Banks? And Who Goes Islamic? Evidence from Turkey." *Journal of Banking & Finance* 35 (12): 3213–24.

Richmond, C. J., D. Benedek, E. Cabezon, B. Cegar, P. A. Dohlman, M. Hassine, B. Jajko, P. Kopyrski, M. Markevych, J. A. Miniane, F. J. Parodi, G. Pula, J. Roaf, M. Song, M. Sviderskaya, R. Turk Ariss, and S. Weber. 2019. "Reassessing the Role of State-Owned Enterprises in Central, Eastern and Southeastern Europe." IMF Departmental Paper 19/11, European Department, International Monetary Fund, Washington, DC.

Shleifer, A., and R. W. Vishny. 1994. "Politicians and Firms." *Quarterly Journal of Economics* 109 (4): 995–1025.

World Bank. 2020a. *South Asia Economic Focus, Spring 2020: The Cursed Blessing of Public Banks*. Washington, DC: World Bank.

World Bank. 2020b. *State Your Business! An Evaluation of World Bank Group Support to the Reform of State-Owned Enterprises, FY08–18*. Washington, DC: World Bank, Independent Evaluation Group.

Public-Private Partnerships in South Asia: Managing the Fiscal Risks from Hidden Liabilities While Delivering Efficiency Gains

1

Since the early 1990s, public-private partnerships (PPPs) to provide infrastructure have been expanding around the world, including in South Asia. Well-structured PPPs can unleash efficiency gains in the provision of infrastructure, but PPPs can also create liabilities for governments, among them contingent liabilities: that is, liabilities triggered by a specific event. Providing infrastructure through PPPs is preferred to public provision if the efficiency gains offset the higher cost of private financing and the public liabilities that PPPs may create. This chapter assesses the fiscal risks from contingent liabilities assumed by South Asian governments through their current stock of PPPs in infrastructure. First, it analyzes the drivers of PPP distress. Second, it simulates scenarios of possible fiscal costs for South Asian governments that could stem from risky PPPs. Third, it studies specific PPP contract designs and their relationship to early termination in South Asia to draw lessons for structuring future PPP contracts.

The Need to Carefully Manage the Fiscal and Economic Risks of PPPs

Worldwide, nearly 1 billion people lack electricity, 1 billion live more than 2 kilometers from an all-season road, and many are unable to access work and educational opportunities because transport services are not available or are too costly. In South Asia, estimates of the annual investment needs to close the infrastructure gap range from 7.5 percent of GDP (Rozenberg and Fay 2019) to 8.8 percent of GDP (ADB 2017). To meet these investment needs, infrastructure spending will have to increase by 3.5 percent to 4.3 percent of GDP from its current level.[1]

Different approaches can be used to provide infrastructure services. In the traditional, public provision approach, line ministries, government agencies, or state-owned enterprises directly procure the infrastructure. In the private provision approach, regulated or unregulated private companies that own the infrastructure assets provide infrastructure. Infrastructure provision through PPPs

Note: This chapter draws on the background research paper: Herrera Dappe, M., M. Melecky, and B. Turkgulu. 2020. "PPP Distress and Fiscal Contingent Liabilities in South Asia." Background paper for *Hidden Debt*. World Bank, Washington, DC.

falls in between the public and private approach. In a PPP, the private party controls the rights to the infrastructure during the contract term and returns the infrastructure to the government when the contract term expires.

PPPs can help emerging market economies and developing countries expand their infrastructure stock, build required infrastructure more efficiently, and maintain infrastructure better in the long term. The potential efficiency gains can be seized through an appropriate design of PPP contracts that bundle various aspects of the infrastructure project and allocate risks according to the partners' ability to manage them. Economies such as Brazil, China, India, South Africa, and Turkey have used PPP arrangements extensively to boost their infrastructure investments.

Infrastructure PPPs are no free lunch. They create liabilities for governments, including contingent (hidden) ones. To share risk appropriately between the public and private parties, governments tend to provide *explicit* guarantees to the private party, such as revenue or credit guarantees. The government, as the ultimate guarantor of the public infrastructure service, also provides an *implicit* guarantee to backstop the fiscal and economic consequences of any failures by the partnership.

At the center of the PPP approach rests a trade-off between the efficiency of execution and the efficiency of financing. The private partners bring the efficiency of execution because they can better monitor the project. However, governments can achieve a greater efficiency of financing because they can finance a project at cheaper (sovereign) rates than the private partners in PPPs, which need to pay a funding premium on top of the sovereign rate to cover extra risk.[2] If the efficiencies in project execution are systematically overestimated or the contingent liabilities due to risk and uncertainty are underestimated, the government may be better off executing investments through conventional contracting of the private sector or even state-owned enterprises.

The rising popularity of PPPs, and thus the increase in the contingent liabilities associated with them, warrant careful management of the fiscal and economic risks they pose. The

> It is important not to overestimate the efficiency gains or underestimate the risks and liabilities of a PPP.

opacity of financial records, confidentiality of most PPP contracts, and prevalence of cash rather than accrual accounting systems in emerging markets and developing economies hide the fiscal risks for government finances until the contingent liability materializes.

This chapter assesses the fiscal risks South Asian governments assume when an infrastructure PPP is terminated early. There are three major reasons for early termination of PPPs: the government's default or voluntary termination of the project; the private partner's default or breach of contract; or force majeure (unforeseen circumstances). For the assessment, the study adopts the value-at-risk methodology (see annex 1A). The expected loss from a PPP project is gauged using the probability of distress, exposure of the government in the event of distress, and the loss given distress. Using data from the World Bank Private Participation in Infrastructure (PPI) database, World Bank World Development Indicators (WDI), the Polity IV Project, and the banking crises data set of Laeven and Valencia (2018), the study identifies systematic contractual, institutional, and macroeconomic factors that can help predict the probability that a PPP project will be terminated early (see annex 1B).

Factors that contribute to the early termination of PPPs. The analysis finds that PPPs in developing countries have a lower probability of early termination when they are contracted by subnational entities. Direct support from the government—whether capital grants, revenue subsidies, and/or in-kind transfers—decreases the financing risk of the project. The probability of early termination is also lower for PPP contracts in countries with greater constraints on executive power in government. Large physical investments and macrofinancial shocks increase the likelihood of early terminations. In particular, unexpected currency depreciations, and incidences of debt and systematic banking crises, increase the rate of project cancellation.

The analysis also derives lessons on ways to structure contracts for better results by examining the PPP highway sector in India, for which rich data are available. PPPs for national highways are more likely to terminate early if, through their contractual obligations, they put the private sponsor under larger financial commitments—namely, higher payments to the government and a larger share of debt financing. The pattern of higher payments to the government might reflect a perverse incentive structure that encourages private partners to make overoptimistic bids on payments to the government in order to win tenders on PPP contracts, which have been financed largely by public banks.

Balancing the Efficiency Gains from PPPs against Their Risks and Liabilities

A PPP is an organizational arrangement that enables public and private institutions to cooperate in providing a public project—which in the context of this chapter is an infrastructure project. As Grimsey and Lewis (2017) point out, a PPP is an enduring and relational partnership, with each partner bringing something of value (money, property, authority, reputation) to the partnership.[3] A key defining feature of a PPP is the sharing of responsibilities and risks of outcomes between the partners. Underpinning the partnership is a framework contract that sets out the "rules of the game" delineating each partner's rights and obligations. Because of uncertainties inherent in long-term projects, PPP contracts are incomplete: that is, they do not cover all possible scenarios, and they leave room for renegotiation (Guasch 2004).

PPPs can offer numerous efficiency gains. Well-structured PPPs have the potential to provide infrastructure services at a relatively low cost to society. This can increase a country's capacity to invest in infrastructure, given that some investments would potentially be feasible only under a PPP arrangement (Iossa and Martimort 2012). PPPs aim to efficiently allocate among the partners the risks and responsibilities associated with different stages of the project to maximize the value for money. Outsourcing of responsibilities to the private sector and bundling of investment and service provision can yield efficiency gains. Outsourcing allows the public sector to leverage private sector expertise and gain organizational efficiency in service provision. The potential of knowledge and technology spillovers from foreign sponsors may be better harnessed by the host country within a PPP relationship (ITF 2018). Competitive procurement to select the private partner can also drive the cost down compared to in-house public sector provision.

PPPs bundle investment and service provision—that is, financing, design, construction, rehabilitation, operation, and maintenance—into a single long-term contract. This contrasts with traditional procurement practices, in which the government separates the contractual relationships for each phase of the infrastructure investment and operation. The idea behind bundling is to combine the two major stages of a typical infrastructure project (investment and service provision) to achieve efficiency gains. When these two stages are bundled, the private party has the incentive to adopt improvements during the design and construction stages that reduce operation and maintenance costs or increase the quality of services and revenues during operation, as long as the additional construction costs are offset by higher returns in the latter stage.[4]

Efficiency gains from PPPs may also arise from mobilizing private finance. Private finance may provide outside expertise in valuing risks and monitoring effort that public finance lacks. Hence, when private creditors that are specialized in project finance are involved in financing, private finance may resolve uncertainty and agency problems faced by the government (Iossa and Martimort 2012, 2015).[5] By providing incentives for efficient termination, private finance may also resolve soft budget constraints (privileged access to additional financing due to the implicit guarantee of unconditional government support) through which governments can keep bad projects alive (de Bettignies and Ross 2009).[6]

The funding structure in a PPP affects the allocation of risks and costs and the quality of service provision. Demand risk—the risk that demand for the infrastructure services will fall short of a forecast and hence so will revenues—is a major risk of infrastructure PPPs. The allocation of demand risk affects the financing cost of the project and the operator's incentives to ensure adequate service under conditions of imperfect monitoring and regulation. The funding structure determines the allocation of demand risk between the government and the private sponsor (operator). A contract funded purely by user fees collected by the operator allocates the entire demand risk on the private sponsor. In contrast, the government assumes the demand risk under an availability payment scheme (committing to provide a fixed payment to the private provider/operator as long as the performance of the project meets agreed performance metrics). The operator in a user fee scheme would face higher costs of capital than in an availability payment scheme because creditors would require compensation for the extra risk. The operator in the former case would have an incentive to attract more users through better services to increase its revenues, while in the latter case the public partner would have to monitor the quality of service to ensure a certain level of service. Intermediate arrangements—whereby the government guarantees a minimum revenue from user fees or provides some availability payments and allows the operator to charge reduced user fees—are common.

PPPs have the potential to weed out a bad project when it is funded by user fees and the government commits not to fund it through public sources (tax revenues). When the demand risk is effectively transferred to the private party, the project will only attract private sponsors and external creditors if the project is financially profitable. This means that bridges to nowhere would not be built under a PPP arrangement funded by user fees. However, this market test is less useful than it appears. It fails to indicate whether projects, even if they are unprofitable, yield benefits to society.

Private finance still poses a fiscal burden on government. Sometimes policy makers and development practitioners claim that a benefit of mobilizing private finance is that it allows governments to invest in infrastructure when the government has no fiscal space (budgetary room that allows a government to provide resources for public purposes without undermining fiscal sustainability). This argument is based on confusion between funding and financing. Private financing, by itself, does not reduce the fiscal burden on the government because either through future availability payments or foregone user fees, the government ends up directly or indirectly funding the provision of the infrastructure service over the lifetime of the project (Grout 1997; Hart 2003; Engel, Fischer, and Galetovic 2013). It could be argued that in a developing economy when the government is facing temporary credit constraints but must invest in critical infrastructure needed right away, mobilizing private financing could be beneficial—if international private sponsors with well-diversified portfolios and good credit ratings can obtain financing at a low cost (de Bettignies and Ross 2010; Yehoue 2013).

A better framework is needed for valuating and reporting the liabilities created by PPPs. PPPs can create liabilities for governments based on how risks are shared with the private partner. A good way to categorize these liabilities is to use a fiscal risk matrix, which categorizes the government's liabilities as direct or contingent and explicit or implicit (Polackova 1998; Budina, Polackova Brixi, and Irwin 2007). *Direct explicit liabilities* created by PPPs are contractual or legal promises by the government in the event that all stages of the project go according to the schedule foreseen in the contract. Availability and capacity payments, shadow tolls, and energy payments in power purchasing agreements where the public party has no control over energy generated[7] are examples of direct explicit liabilities for the government.[8]

Contingent liabilities can be explicit or implicit. *Explicit contingent liabilities* created by PPPs are the contractual or legal guarantees by the government contingent on the occurrence of an exogeneous event. For example, the government may commit to a minimum revenue guarantee for a toll road or for an independent power producer in the PPP contract. *Implicit contingent liabilities* created by PPPs are the noncontractual liabilities that the partnership and incomplete contracts create in various states of the world. For example, even though the government might not contractually promise any guarantees to the private party in the event of a default, given that the government is the ultimate guarantor of public services in most societies, the government might have to bail out the private party or assume the remaining debt and service obligations of the private party to avoid service disruption. This means that when a PPP contract is agreed upon, the government assumes the ultimate insolvency risk (Irwin 2007). The most common implicit contingent liabilities of PPPs stem from renegotiation and early termination. Renegotiations can lead to additional fiscal

burdens that could not be foreseen at the beginning of the contract. If the renegotiation process fails, the contract may be terminated as a last resort, and the government may be left to settle the claims of the creditors and the private sponsors at a rate beyond what is specified in the termination clauses.

The current public sector accounting principles do not provide an adequate framework for valuating and reporting the liabilities created by PPPs. This uncertainty exacerbates the fiscal risks from PPPs (see box 1.1). Cash-based accounting practices, which are still popular in many developing countries, do not provide a way to include the liabilities in government finances. Even the financial accounting frameworks recommended by the International Monetary Fund (IMF) and the European Union (EU) limit their inclusion based on assessment of the risks and control borne by the government (Heald and Georgiou 2010; de Vries 2013). Furthermore, governments facing fiscal constraints tend to increase their levels of PPP investments as a percentage of GDP without instituting proper institutional mechanisms to deal with the liabilities they create (Reyes-Tagle and Garbacik 2016).

BOX 1.1   The Hidden Debt of National Highways in India

The annual funding needs of the National Highways Authority of India (NHAI) are approved by the Ministry of Road Transport and Highways and the Ministry of Finance through the Union Budget. This includes a contribution from the Central Road and Infrastructure Fund (CRIF) and approval for market borrowings (with implicit or explicit sovereign guarantee). However, debt service for market borrowings and the payment obligations under the hybrid annuity model are also part of the annual funding needs of NHAI. Thus, NHAI, as a national authority, raises debt and undertakes long-term liabilities (PPP hybrid annuity model payment obligations) not on the strength of its financials, but on the assurance of government of India

support through budgetary transfers. In short, the Ministry of Finance covers full debt service and payment obligations throughout the government's public-private partnerships (PPPs), but such debt and liabilities are not explicitly stated on the government's balance sheet—and thus become part of the "hidden debt." This arrangement differs from other state-owned enterprises (SOEs), which are corporatized and have independent balance sheets.

Source: World Bank staff, based on inputs from World Bank experts.
Note: Under the hybrid annuity model, the project company is entitled to receive from the NHAI both semi-annual availability payments during the operation of the road and a capital grant during the construction phase. The project company is responsible for the construction and the maintenance of the road, but it is the authority's responsibility to collect tolls.

Booming Infrastructure PPPs, Their Country and Sector Distribution, and Signs of Distress in South Asia

PPPs have grown rapidly in South Asia. The use of PPPs in infrastructure in the region grew exponentially from the early 1990s to the early 2010s, but has slowed down since 2012. PPP investments accelerated between 2005 and 2012, increasing the value of the active portfolio by more than five-fold, from $45 billion to $267 billion, or from 3.9 percent to 11.4 percent of the region's GDP (figure 1.1, panel a). After 2012, investment growth slowed, falling behind GDP growth, as indicated by the decline in investments as percentage of GDP observed in the same panel. At the end of 2018, cumulative investment in the active portfolio of PPP projects was just over $320 billion,[9] according to the World Bank PPI Database,[10] which corresponds to 8.9 percent of the region's total GDP.

The number of active projects in South Asia increased exponentially between the early 1990s and early 2010s, but slowed down after 2012 (figure 1.1, panel b). The increase in the number of projects was slower between 2005 and 2012 than the increase in investment volumes, which indicates that the countries in the region

increased the number of projects as well as their average size.

India has the most infrastructure PPPs in South Asia, by far. India accounted for more than three-quarters of the 1,232 infrastructure PPPs in South Asia. Pakistan and Sri Lanka implemented 81 and 79 PPPs, respectively, followed by Bangladesh with 45 and Nepal with 38 during 1990–2018. Afghanistan and Bhutan implemented only 2, while Maldives had 1 PPP in infrastructure. In terms of value, PPP investments in India—amounting to $283 billion—account for more than 85 percent of the $328 billion in aggregate investment in PPPs in the region. India is followed by Pakistan and Bangladesh with total investments of $31 billion and $6.9 billion, respectively. Sri Lanka's PPP program had investments of $3.4 billion and Nepal's had $2.9 billion. The PPP programs of Maldives, Bhutan, and Afghanistan have been the smallest, with investments of $469 million, $240 million, and $39 million, respectively (figure 1.2, panel a).

Most PPPs in South Asia are in the energy and transport sectors. Of the 1,232 PPP projects in infrastructure with financial closure in the region since 1990,[11] 97 percent are in the energy or transport sectors (figure 1.2, panel a). The remaining 38 projects are in the water and sewerage sector and the

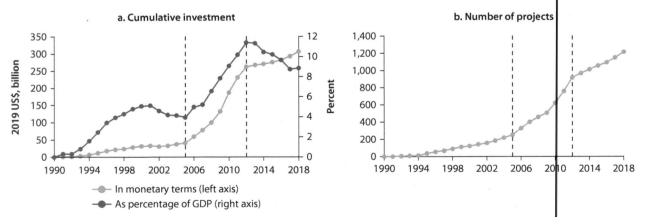

FIGURE 1.1   **Active Portfolio of Public-Private Partnerships in Infrastructure in South Asia, 1990–2018**

a. Cumulative investment

b. Number of projects

— In monetary terms (left axis)
— As percentage of GDP (right axis)

Sources: Private Participation in Infrastructure database; World Development Indicators.
Note: Dashed lines indicate the start (2005) and the end (2012) of the boom period of PPP investments.

Source: Private Participation in Infrastructure database.
Note: Dashed lines indicate the start (2005) and end (2012) of the boom period of PPP investments.

FIGURE 1.2   Sectoral Distribution of Public-Private Partnership Projects with Financial Closure in South Asia, by Country and Number of Cancellations, 1990–2018

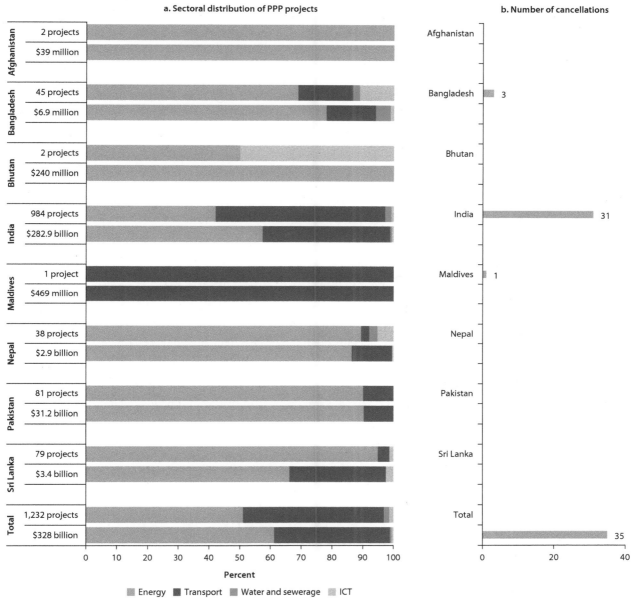

Source: Private Participation in Infrastructure database.

Note: Investment totals are in 2019 US$, million. ICT = information and communications technology; PPP = public-private partnership. See also annex 1C.

information and communications technology (ICT) sector. The composition by country shows that aside from India, Bhutan, and Maldives, the country programs are dominated by investments in the energy sector. In

India, there are 543 PPPs in the transport sector and 414 in the energy sector.

While the share of cancellations in South Asia is low and similar to the global share, the transport sector in India has a disproportionate number of cancellations (figure 1.2, panel b). Only 2.8 percent of the infrastructure PPPs initiated in South Asia have been canceled. This share is similar to the global share, which is 3.7 percent. The cancellations in South Asia have mostly been in the Indian transport sector, particularly national highways, which accounts for 27 of the 35 canceled PPPs in South Asia (figure 1.2, panel b, and table 1C.1). Even though the highest number of cancellations occurred in the transport sector, the sector with the largest share of canceled PPPs is the ICT sector, with 19 percent.

The PPP national highways program in India showed signs of distress in 2013 and 2014. Twenty-four of the 27 cancellations in the Indian national highways sector occurred in 2013 and 2014. At that time, there were about $7 billion of highway PPPs in operation and roughly $34 billion of highway PPPs under construction. About one-third of the PPPs under operation and two-thirds of those under construction showed signs of distress. Infrastructure developers and banks (mainly public) that financed highway PPPs were also stressed. As a result, the national highways development program experienced a sudden stop in 2013 and 2014 after a period of rapid growth between 2010 and 2012 (figure 1.3).

The distressed projects in India also coincide with the slowdown in PPP investments in South Asia, as can be seen in figures 1.2 and 1.3. Although it can be argued that it is coincidental, there is evidence that the cancellations led to more caution in initiating new PPPs. For example, a federal statute that came into effect in 2014 set the requirement that a PPP seeking to acquire land must obtain the consent of at least 70 percent of the affected persons and made compensation more generous—and thus more costly for the project. Earlier projects were undertaken with as little as 30 percent of the land having been secured (Pratap and Chakrabarti 2017). Furthermore, after 2010 in India, traditional procurement of infrastructure became the preferred choice at an increasing rate (figure 1.4).

Fiscal Risks from Contingent Liabilities Due to Early Termination of PPPs

This section analyzes the fiscal risks from contingent liabilities that are realized when an infrastructure PPP project is distressed. In this analysis, distress refers to early termination of the PPP project. The fiscal costs estimated in this section are the costs that a government incurs in the event that a project

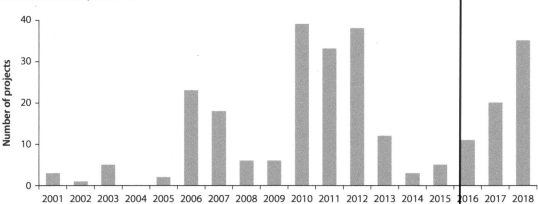

FIGURE 1.3   Number of National Highway Public-Private Partnership Projects in India, by Year of Financial Closure, 2001–18

Source: Private Participation in Infrastructure database.
Note: Year of financial closure refers to the year in which the sponsor secured financing for the project. PPP = public-private partnership.

FIGURE 1.4   **Traditional versus Public-Private Partnership Procurement of Infrastructure in India, 2001–17**

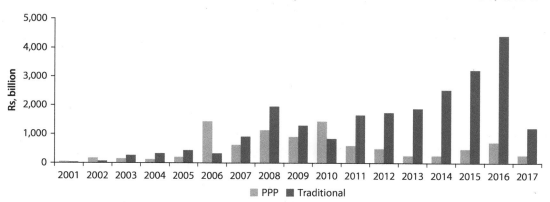

Sources: Department of Economic Affairs, Ministry of Finance, India; Private Participation in Infrastructure database.
Note: For PPPs, year is the year of the concession agreement, financial closure, or the appointed date, whichever is available, in that order. For traditional procurement, the year is the project award year. PPP = public-private partnership.

is terminated early. To value the fiscal risks, the study adopts a value-at-risk methodology (see annex 1A for details).

Predicted Probabilities of Distress for Active PPP Projects in South Asia

Data come from four sources: the World Bank Private Participation in Infrastructure Project (PPI) database;[12] the Polity IV Project;[13] the World Bank's World Development Indicators (WDI);[14] and the Systemic Banking Crises data set of Laeven and Valencia (2018) (see annex 1B).

The PPI database includes data on project characteristics as they were agreed at the time of the signing of the PPP contract or at the time of financial closure. These characteristics include the type of project, sector, contract period, government level (national or subnational) granting the contract, identities of the sponsors, types of government support, amount of investment commitments, and financing information. The PPI database also provides the current status of the project as active, concluded, distressed, or canceled.

The PPI database is sourced from publicly available information, such as press reports. As a result, some projects might not be captured in the database, and a considerable number of projects in the database lack the data for all characteristics. For the variables essential for the analysis—namely, contract period and the level of government that granted the contract—missing data were added for all projects using the individual project descriptions provided in the database, if available. The institutional characteristics of a country are drawn from the Polity IV data, using variables on yearly executive recruitment, the concept of constraints on the executive, and the concept of political competition. From the WDI, annual series of per capita growth rate and nominal exchange rates are used to create series of detrended and demeaned series of per capita growth rates and exchange rate shocks using the filter suggested by Hamilton (2018). The data on financial crises come from the Systemic Banking Crises data set of Laeven and Valencia (2018).

The econometric estimation uses the data on all PPP projects in low- and middle-income countries. After estimating equation (1A.2), in annex 1A, predicted probabilities of distress are obtained for the PPP projects in South Asia using the predictions implied by the survival analysis.[15]

The PPI database records 7,979 projects in emerging markets and developing countries, encompassing 127 economies, with financial closure dates from 1990 to 2019. The sample includes projects from five sectors: ICT, energy, transport, water and sewerage, and municipal solid waste. Because the municipal solid waste data have been a recent addition to the database, and only cover the currently active projects with financial closures starting in 2009, they were dropped from the sample to make all projects comparable. ICT projects, merchant and rental greenfield projects,[16] management and lease projects, and divestitures were also excluded from the sample because they are not PPPs as this study defines them.

In the analysis, distress is defined as early termination of a project. The PPI database labels any project "canceled" if the private party has exited by selling or turning over its shares back to government or has ceased operations. The database labels any project "distressed" if it is in international arbitration or either the government or the private party has requested that the contract be terminated. Using news articles and other public online sources, the current status of each distressed project was determined and all projects were relabeled as "canceled," "concluded," or "active." When no definitive information about the resolution of the distress could be found, the project was dropped from the sample.

The contract periods of some projects in the PPI database have been completed although they are labeled as still active. Possible reasons are that successfully concluded projects have gone unnoticed because they are not covered in the news or that project companies have obtained contract extensions after fulfilling the terms of their initial contract. The projects with completed contract periods but still labeled as active are kept in the analysis and relabeled as concluded.

Figure 1.5 shows the distribution of the percentage of contract period elapsed within the estimation sample. It includes 3,977 projects, of which 167 were canceled.

An overwhelming majority of the projects included in the sample have not passed the halfway mark in their contract periods. One reason is that PPPs have been originated in larger numbers only recently compared to the median contract period of a PPP in the sample, which is 25 years. Another reason is that some of the older projects in the PPI database are missing crucial information, such as the contract period and level of contracting government; hence they were dropped from the sample used for the econometric estimation.

Estimation Results: When Are Projects Most Likely to Fail?

PPP projects are most likely to fail during the early portion of their contract periods, and risks accumulated during their contract periods are not trivial, non-parametric estimates show (figure 1.6). The risk of early termination for a project increases rapidly until around 20 percent of the project's contract period elapses. It plateaus at this level and declines slightly until it reaches 50 percent. Beyond 50 percent of the contract period, except for a small increase at around the 80 percent mark, the risk of early termination decreases until the project approaches the end of the contract period.

The cumulative hazard curve shows that the accumulated probability of distress increases steadily, but its pace decreases after reaching around 50 percent of the contract

FIGURE 1.5   Distribution of the Percentage of Contract Period Elapsed, 1990–2018

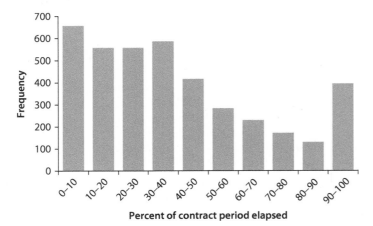

Source: Private Participation in Infrastructure database.

period (figure 1.7, panel a). The survival curve estimate mirrors the profile and implies that the probability of an average project has a 92 percent likelihood of surviving until the end of its contract period (figure 1.7, panel b).[17]

Estimation Results: What Factors Determine the Likelihood of Distress?

The estimation examines the explanatory power of project-level variables, institutional variables, and macroeconomic variables. Details on selection of the econometric model are contained in annex 1E. Figure 1.8 presents the results from estimating the econometric model in equation (1A.2). Positive coefficients indicate factors that increase the cumulative hazard and ultimately the probability of distress. Negative coefficients indicate factors that decrease the cumulative hazard and ultimately the probability of distress.

Project-Level Factors

Brownfield versus greenfield projects. *The probability of distress from a brownfield project is not statistically different from that of a greenfield project,* the estimation results suggest.[18] Private sponsors tend to express a preference for brownfield projects over greenfield projects because the returns of the latter projects are uncertain. The results show that ex ante uncertainty about the return of projects is not associated with higher risk of distress.

Sector. *Natural gas, railroad, toll road, treatment plant, and water utility projects are associated with higher hazard rates relative to electricity projects.* PPPs in water utility and treatment plant projects experienced high rates of early termination because of difficulties in adapting the contracts to changing conditions, contract designs that were not viable, and a bidding process that led to unrealistic financial conditions. For example, a concession in Cochabamba (Bolivia) required substantial tariff hikes to make the large investment required from the private operator viable—which proved socially unsustainable and

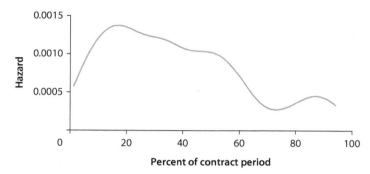

FIGURE 1.6   Distribution of Failures of Public-Private Partnerships over the Contract Period, 1990–2018

Source: Herrera Dappe, Melecky, and Turkgulu 2020.
Note: The figure shows the smoothed hazard function estimate over the percentage of the contract period completed, using a Gaussian kernel with optimal bandwidth. PPPs = public-private partnerships.

brought about the rapid demise of the contract (Marin 2009).

Large versus small projects. *Larger projects are associated with a higher probability of distress, except for the largest PPP projects.* Increases in the committed investment in physical assets are associated with higher probability of distress as long as the investment is less than $3.4 billion. For investments in physical assets above $3.4 billion (about 1 percent of the sample), the higher the investment, the lower the probability of distress.

Direct versus indirect government support. *Government support that reduces financing risk is the most effective in preventing distress.* Direct government support, which includes capital and revenue subsidies and in-kind transfers, is associated with lower probability of distress. Indirect government support, which includes various guarantees to the sponsors and support from multilateral organizations, also reduces the likelihood of distress—but the coefficients are not statistically significant at the 10 percent level.

Subnational versus national governments. *PPPs with subnational governments are less likely to face early termination than PPPs with central governments.* This finding could be related to better project selection at the local level because the local authorities may understand the local problems better or oversee the project better because it is nearby.

FIGURE 1.7   **Estimates of Survival and Cumulative Hazard for Public-Private Partnership Projects**

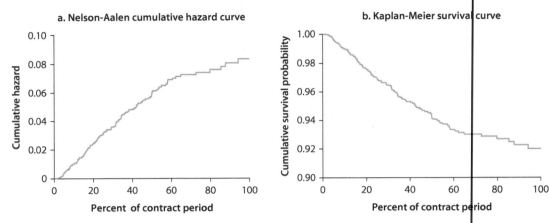

a. Nelson-Aalen cumulative hazard curve

b. Kaplan-Meier survival curve

Source: Herrera Dappe, Melecky, and Turkgulu 2020.

FIGURE 1.8   **Factors That Predict the Likelihood of Public-Private Partnership Distress**

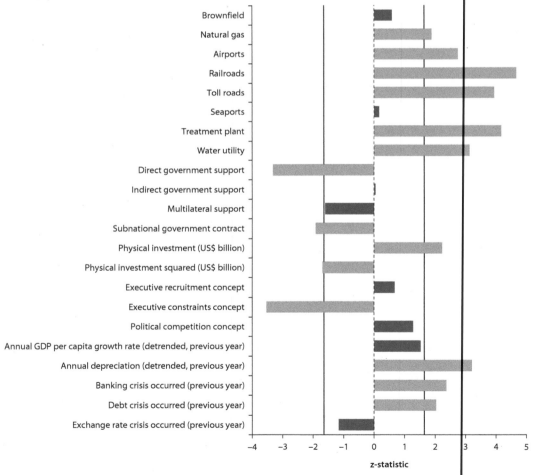

Source: Herrera Dappe, Melecky, and Turkgulu 2020.
Note: Vertical lines indicate the thresholds for significance at the 90 percent confidence level. Blue color indicates significance at the 10 percent level. The base category for sectoral indicators of projects (natural gas, airports, railroads, toll roads, seaports, treatment plant, water utility) is the electricity sector.

It could also be the case that national governments tend to engage in risky projects as they can bear the termination risk from an individual PPP project because they have a more diversified PPP portfolio and fiscal resources. The highway projects in India provide an interesting example: all the highway projects that were canceled between 2012 and 2015 were PPPs with the central government. At the same time, state governments continued to enter into successful PPPs for road construction and operation.

Institutional Factors

Constraints on the executive branch of government. *Greater constraints on the executive are associated with lower probability of distress.* When the government can exercise authority without adequate checks and balances, it leaves PPPs vulnerable to expropriation by the government through a change in policy or direct interference. Hence, the project becomes susceptible to policy and political risks (Irwin 2007; Grimsey and Lewis 2017). More generally, when the constraints on the executive are not stringent enough, the contract loses its value in mediating the relationship between the government and the private party, making the project more susceptible to distress.

Macroeconomic Factors

Unexpected currency depreciation. *A surprise depreciation in the local currency—a deviation of the annual depreciation rate from its long-term average—is associated with a higher risk of distress.* Exchange rate risk affects infrastructure investment in two ways, as Irwin (2007) notes. First, many infrastructure PPPs, such as those in power generation, use inputs priced in foreign currency. Second, given the insufficient local savings and underdeveloped local currency markets in most low- and middle-income economies, financing of long-term infrastructure projects most often relies on debt denominated in foreign currency, but the revenues of the operators are in local currency. The currency mismatch between revenues and costs can push the project company to insolvency very quickly if the local currency depreciates sharply.

Systematic banking and debt crises. *The occurrence of systematic banking and debt crises are associated with higher hazard rates for PPP projects.* A systematic banking crisis undermines the ability of financial institutions to provide the financing that is necessary to sustain long-term infrastructure projects. A debt crisis can limit the government's ability to fund PPP projects according to the terms of the contracts. It may also hinder the ability of a local private party to secure debt financing through the market and increase the cost of its outstanding debt, leading to early termination of PPP projects. Because of the long-term nature of PPPs and the high transaction costs of preparing, procuring, and awarding them, both parties try to negotiate changes to the contract or some kind of compensation in response to macrofinancial shocks. Early termination happens only if the parties cannot reach an agreement, which explains the lag in the impact of macrofinancial shocks.

Predicting the Probabilities of Distress for Currently Active PPPs in South Asia

Probabilities of distress for currently active projects in the PPI database in South Asia have been predicted using equation (1A.9), in annex 1A, assuming all active projects have survived until the end of 2019. Missing values for project-specific variables essential for prediction were collected. When such efforts proved fruitless, values were imputed using the characteristics of similar projects. The details of the imputation process for all variables are presented in annex 1D.

Active projects in South Asia are far from being riskless. Figure 1.9 shows the distribution of the predicted probability of distress at the 99th percentile (that is, the maximum loss with 99 percent confidence) of active projects over the remainder of their contract periods after 2020. The predictions assume that no banking or debt crisis occurs and that the local currency does not depreciate beyond its trend against the US dollar. In addition, institutional variables are assumed to remain at their 2018 levels. The median probability of distress is 0.03 and the mean is 0.049.

FIGURE 1.9   **Distribution of Predicted Probabilities of Distress for Public-Private Partnerships in South Asia, from 2020 to the End of Contractual Period**

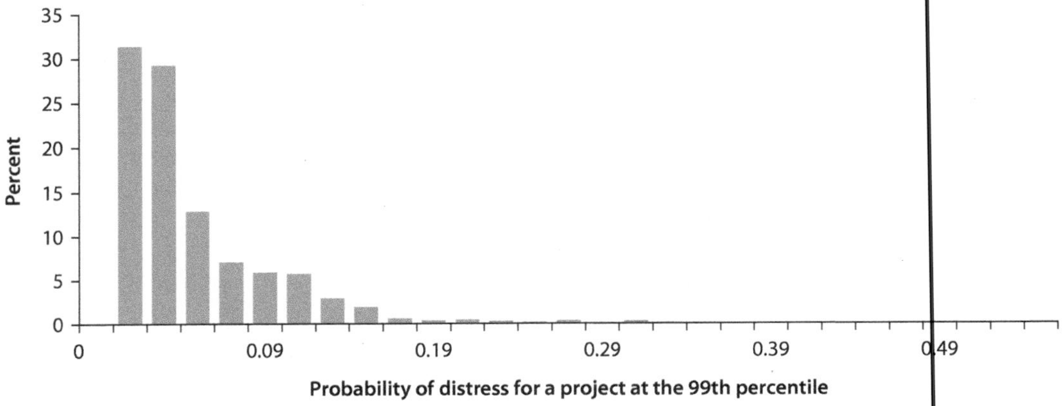

Source: Herrera Dappe, Melecky, and Turkgulu 2020.
Note: The 99th percentile refers to the confidence level with which the computed loss is not exceeded.

What Are the Fiscal Risks to South Asian Governments If PPPs Terminate Early?

Calculating Exposure at Distress

In general, governments are exposed to obligations from the debt and equity financing of an infrastructure project when the PPP is terminated. As the ultimate guarantor of the public infrastructure service, the government steps in to resolve the matter. As indicated in World Bank's Guidance on PPP Contractual Provisions, the market practice in the event a PPP contract is terminated is that both the lenders and the equity owners must be compensated if distress occurred without any fault of either party (World Bank 2019). Without such explicit or implicit guarantees, especially in emerging market economies and developing countries, private finance cannot be effectively mobilized.

The PPP portfolio captured by the PPI database is used to value the fiscal risk from early termination of PPPs for each country, and the exposure at distress due to each project is calculated using the debt and equity data in the PPI database. The PPI database provides the shares of the physical investment that have been financed through debt, equity, or capital grant from the government. In the case of missing values, data were collected. When information could not be found, the missing values were imputed as discussed in annex 1D. It is important to note that the analysis can be underestimating a country's exposure at distress if some PPPs are not captured in the PPI database.

The total debt used to finance the currently active 1,056 greenfield and brownfield PPP projects in energy, transport, and water and sewerage in South Asia is estimated to be $218 billion, and the total equity financing is estimated to be $77 billion.[19] The average leverage ratio, at the time of financial closure, among the active PPP projects in South Asia is 3.22. Debt financing makes up more than 70 percent of total physical investments in India, Nepal, and Pakistan, while it is between 60 percent and 70 percent of total physical investment in Bangladesh, Bhutan, and Sri Lanka (figure 1.10). Capital grants from government play a larger role in Afghanistan than in the other countries in South Asia.

Calculating Value at Risk

The losses from debt and equity obligations in the event of distress depend on the causes of distress. In the case of government default or voluntary termination of the project, the market practice is for the government to compensate the private party for the full amount invested in the project (debt and equity)

FIGURE 1.10   **Composition of Public-Private Partnership Financing for Active Projects in South Asia, by Country, 1990–2018**

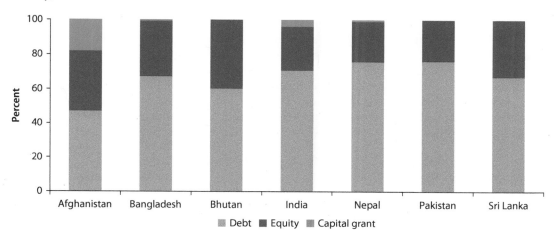

Sources: World Bank staff calculations; Private Participation in Infrastructure database.
Note: PPP = public-private partnership.

plus the equity return it had forecasted (World Bank 2019).

In the case of termination due to the private partner's default or breach of contract, the market practice is to provide some amount of compensation. The justification for compensation is that if there is no compensation, the government might be seen as enjoying windfall gains unfairly and would have a hard time attracting lenders and investors for PPP projects in general (EPEC 2013; World Bank 2019). Even if a private partner defaults, the private partner may legally allege government responsibility, so the government becomes liable to compensate the private party or otherwise incur additional legal costs (World Bank 2019).

In the case of force majeure, because the event triggering distress is outside both parties' control, the risk should be shared between both parties. As such, the government is liable for less than full compensation and has the right to take over the relevant asset, while the private partner loses any return on its invested equity and possibly some of the invested equity (EPEC 2013; World Bank 2019).

Only limited data are available on losses incurred by governments in cases of early termination of PPPs. The data on the recovery rates of bank loans to PPP projects, mainly in

developed countries, collected by the Data Alliance Project Finance Consortium show that the average ultimate recovery rate is 79.3 percent (Moody's Investors Service 2019; see box 1.2).[20] This might be a low estimate in the context of South Asia because the model PPP concession agreements in the road sector in India guarantee as much as 90 percent of the debt financing, even in the cases of the project company's default or force majeure.

The data on compensation of private equity are even scarcer than data on recovery rates of bank loans. The government's loss involving private equity in the event of distress depends on the reason for termination, the explicit clauses in the contract, and— potentially—the negotiation at the time of termination. Road concession agreements in India offer a range of possibilities depending on the source of termination of the contract. If the project company defaults, the concession agreements do not foresee any compensation on equity, but if the public authority defaults, the contract entitles the private sponsor to 150 percent of its equity. If a force majeure event that is indirectly caused by a political event occurs, the private party is entitled to 110 percent of the equity it invested in the project. Anecdotal evidence also suggests that no matter the cause for termination, governments might pay a premium on the

---

BOX 1.2   Low-, Medium-, and High-Risk Scenarios for Computing Losses to the Government from Contingent Liabilities of Public-Private Partnerships

In the event that a project is terminated, it is safe to assume that the government will lose the entire public equity. Based on the considerations discussed so far in this chapter, equation (1A.1) in annex 1A can be written as follows, assuming that three scenarios—low, medium, and high risk—are considered for the loss given distress:

$$EL_{i,99\%} = PD_{i,99\%} \left(Debt_i \, LGD_{Debt} + Public \; Equity_i + Private \; Equity_i \, LGD_{Equity} \right). \quad \text{(B1.2.1)}$$

In the low-risk scenario, the loss on debt given distress of the government from a project (LGD_{Debt}) is assumed to be the recovery rate estimated by Moody's Investors Service (2019): ($LGD_{Debt} = 0.793$). Assuming this, the government does not cover the loss of private equity and only loses its own equity in the PPP, ($LGD_{Equity} = 0$).

In the medium-risk scenario, the loss on both debt and equity given government distress from a project is assumed to be 1 ($LGD_{Debt} = 1$; $LGD_{Equity} = 1$). That is, the government guarantees the total financing of the project, but does not compensate the private party for the foregone return.

In the high-risk scenario, in addition to compensating for all the debt ($LGD_{Debt} = 1$), the government compensates the private party 150 percent of the equity it invested in the project ($LGD_{Equity} = 1.5$), in line with the aforementioned contract terms for India's road sector.

The expected losses from contingent liabilities due to PPPs in country c, reported with 99 percent confidence—that is, with 99 percent confidence that the maximum annual loss will not exceed the calculated amount—are the sum of the expected losses within the set of all active projects in the country, I_c:

$$EL_{c,99\%} = \sum_{i \in Ic} EL_{i,99\%}. \quad \text{(B1.2.2)}$$

Note: In the calculation of $EL_{i,99\%}$ for each project, correlations across projects in the same country are taken into account via both the distress probabilities, which control for country-specific factors, and their standard errors, calculated using the delta method. The delta method uses the variance-covariance matrix of the regression analysis, in which the observations have been assumed to be correlated within the country (clustered at the country level).

---

equity to compensate the private party for the loss of expected return on its investment.

Estimating Fiscal Costs of Active PPPs in South Asia

India, Pakistan, and Bangladesh have the highest estimated fiscal costs from early termination of active PPPs in the region, while Afghanistan and Bhutan have the lowest. The estimated fiscal cost from early termination over the remainder of the contract periods of the PPPs ranges from $9.7 billion to $18.5 billion in India; $1 billion to $2 billion in Pakistan; and $379 million to $730 million in Bangladesh (see table 1F.1 in annex 1F). Even though Sri Lanka's current PPP portfolio is about half the size of Bangladesh's portfolio in terms of the number of projects, and almost 50 percent larger than Nepal's portfolio in terms of total investments, the fiscal cost estimates in Sri Lanka are less than one-sixth of the estimates in Bangladesh and less than 80 percent of the estimates in Nepal. The main reason is that the PPPs in Sri Lanka have mostly passed 40 percent of their contract period, while the portfolios in Bangladesh and Nepal are younger.[21]

In most South Asian countries, about 39 percent to 50 percent of the fiscal costs from early termination of active projects are due to the risks of early termination during the 2020–24 period. Nepal is the exception to this trend because the costs increase at a slower pace. In the low scenario, for India the fiscal cost due to the risk from PPP cancellations is estimated not to exceed $853 million (8.8 percent of total costs) in 2020, with 99 percent confidence. In the 2020–24 period, the estimated fiscal cost (value at risk

FIGURE 1.11 Estimated Total Fiscal Costs from Early Termination of Public-Private Partnership Portfolio in South Asia, as a Percentage of GDP, 2020–24

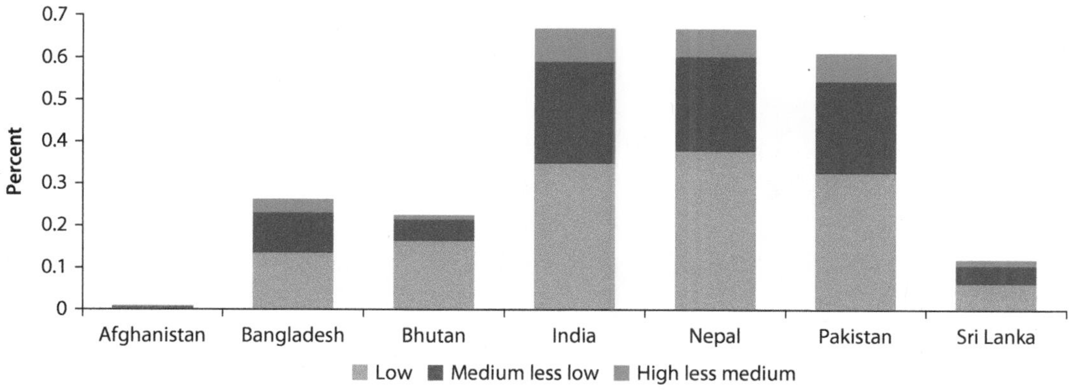

Source: Herrera Dappe, Melecky, and Turkgulu 2020.
Note: The estimated fiscal costs are based on the value at risk at 99 percent over the entire contract period and are expressed as percentage of GDP of a single year. The 99th percentile refers to the confidence level with which the computed maximum loss is not exceeded during the relevant period. PPP = public-private partnership.

at 99 percent) is about $3.8 billion (39 percent of total costs).

Nepal, India, and Pakistan have the highest estimated fiscal costs from early termination of active PPPs as a share of GDP (figure 1.11). The cumulative fiscal costs estimated for the entire lifetime of the PPP portfolio in Nepal (based on the value at risk at 99 percent) ranges from 0.38 percent to 0.67 percent of annual GDP; in India, from 0.35 percent to 0.67 percent; and in Pakistan, from 0.33 percent to 0.61 percent. Bangladesh, Bhutan, and Sri Lanka follow, with estimated fiscal costs from early termination of active PPPs ranging from 0.14 percent to 0.26 percent, 0.16 percent to 0.22 percent, and 0.06 to 0.12 percent of annual GDP, respectively. These estimates give an idea of the resources that would be needed in case of early termination of the PPP portfolio relative to the size of the economy.

South Asian governments are quite different in terms of their revenue mobilization capacity, which helps determine their ability to absorb the fiscal costs from early termination of PPPs in infrastructure. The government of Bangladesh's revenues represent only 9.6 percent of GDP, while the government of Pakistan's revenues represent 15.6 percent of GDP, and the government of

India's revenues represent 20.5 percent of GDP.[22] *Pakistan faces the most significant fiscal challenge from early termination of PPPs in South Asia—slightly less than 4 percent of the government's annual revenues.* Even though Bangladesh's estimated fiscal costs are low relative to the size of its economy, they are high compared to the annual government revenues (figure 1.12), posing a significant fiscal challenge to the country, if only the revenues of a single year are available to absorb the costs of early termination of PPPs.

The probability that an entire PPP portfolio is terminated in a single year is very low. Hence, a more realistic analysis is to compare the estimated fiscal costs over a period of time with an estimate of the government revenues over the same period of time. The estimated fiscal costs from early termination of PPPs as a percentage of government revenues tend to decrease over the 2020–24 period. Figure 1.13 presents the estimated fiscal costs for different periods, all starting at the beginning of 2020, as the ratio of government revenues of that period.[23] The estimated fiscal costs decline for most countries because active projects get older and some reach the end of their contract periods.

FIGURE 1.12   **Estimated Total Fiscal Costs from Early Termination of the Public-Private Partnership Portfolio in South Asia, as a Percentage of Government Revenues for a Single Year**

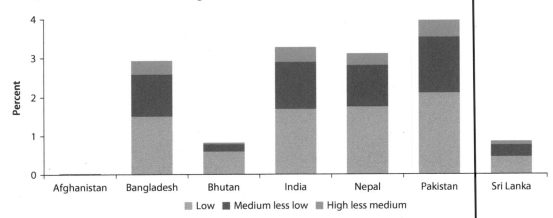

Source: Herrera Dappe, Melecky, and Turkgulu 2020.
Note: Low, medium, and high correspond to the three scenarios. The estimated fiscal costs are based on the value at risk at the 99th percentile and are over the entire contract period and are expressed as percentage of government revenue of a single year. The 99th percentile refers to the confidence level with which the computed maximum loss is not exceeded during the relevant period. PPPs = public-private partnerships.

FIGURE 1.13   **Estimated Fiscal Costs from Early Termination of the Public-Private Partnership Portfolio in South Asia over Different Periods as a Percentage of Expected Government Revenues, 2020–24**

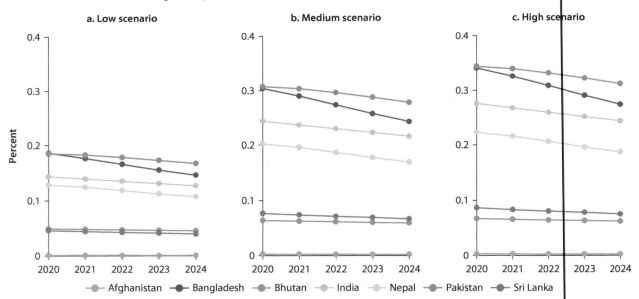

Source: Herrera Dappe, Melecky, and Turkgulu 2020.
Note: Each data point represents the estimated fiscal costs from early termination of the PPP portfolio based on the 99 percent value at risk over the period starting at the beginning of 2020 and ending at the end of the corresponding year, as a percentage of the government revenue over the same period. The analysis assumes that annual government revenues during the 2020–24 period are the same as in 2019. PPP = public-private partnership.

Estimating the Effects of Adverse Macrofinancial Shocks

Multiple types of macroeconomic shocks have significant effects on the probability of early termination (figure 1.8). The estimated fiscal costs presented so far assume there will be no macrofinancial shock, such as depreciation of local currency or a stress in the banking sector.

This section simulates the results of a macrofinancial shock. The Systematic Banking Crises data set of Laeven and Valencia (2018) identifies 104 banking crisis episodes among the countries included in the PPI data set, of which 13 also involved both sovereign debt and currency crises. In the episodes of banking, debt, and currency crises, the maximum yearly deviation in the depreciation rate from its long-term average ranged between 15.1 percentage points and 116 percentage points, with an average of 48.3 percentage points.[24] The simulation assumes a 48.3 percentage-point currency depreciation shock and the occurrence of

a banking and a debt crisis in 2020.[25] Such a profound macroeconomic crisis is similar to some crises in emerging market economies and developing countries that led to early termination of many PPPs.

A profound macroeconomic crisis in 2020 would significantly increase the estimated fiscal costs from early termination of PPPs, particularly in 2021. The estimated fiscal costs over the 2020–21 period could be as high as 4.3 percent of government revenues in Pakistan, 3.9 percent in Bangladesh, and 3.7 percent in India (figure 1.14). In Nepal, early termination of PPPs could require up to 3.3 percent of the government revenues under a scenario of severe macrofinancial crisis, while in Bhutan and Sri Lanka, it could require around 1 percent of government revenues. These estimates underestimate the effect of the crisis because government revenues are kept constant—even though they would contract in such a profound economic crisis.

FIGURE 1.14 **Estimated Fiscal Costs from Early Termination of the Public-Private Partnership Portfolio Assuming Profound Macrofinancial Shocks, as a Percentage of Government Revenues, 2020–24**

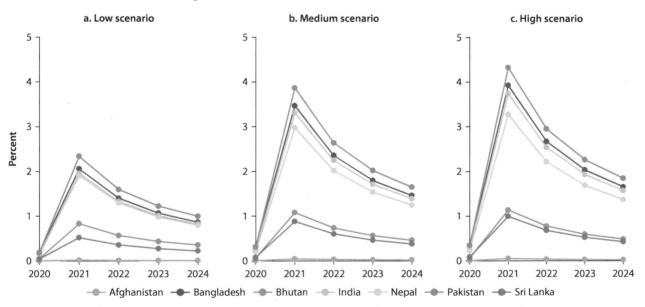

Source: Herrera Dappe, Melecky, and Turkgulu 2020.
Note: Each data point represents the estimated fiscal costs from early termination of the PPP portfolio based on the 99 percent value at risk over the period starting at the beginning of 2020 and ending at the end of the corresponding year, as a percentage of government revenue over the same period. The analysis assumes that government revenues during the 2020–24 period are each year the same as in 2019. PPP = public-private partnership.

Features of Contract Design That Matter: Exploring the Link between PPP Contract Design and Early Terminations of Highway PPPs in India

PPPs for national highways in India experienced several early terminations between 2013 and 2015. Anecdotal evidence points to the incentives created by some contract designs as a potential reason for early termination (ADB et al. 2018; Pratap and Chakrabarti 2017). This section takes advantage of the existence of different contract designs for national highway PPPs in India during the early 2010s to identify contract features that can help explain the large number of early terminations. Narrowing the sample to national highway PPPs in India allows the analysis to examine contract features that are not available for the global and cross-sectoral sample used in previous sections. The analysis in this section can help improve the design of road PPPs and their contract structure and inform the design of PPPs in other sectors with similar incentive structures.

The analysis uses those national highway PPPs in India with financial closure or concession agreement years from 2010 to 2014 included in the PPI database. Of the 125 projects, 26 were canceled, and 24 of those cancellations occurred between 2013 and 2014. One cancellation occurred in 2015 as a result of a lengthy court process over the terms of termination after the project company decided to withdraw from the project in 2014. The time frame allows the analysis to compare canceled projects with contemporaneous active projects.

Data on the investment amount, the project status, the length of the road to be constructed, and the data on financing mix were extracted from the PPI database. When the data for a project were missing in the PPI database, the data were collected from the concession agreements published on the National Highways Authority of India (NHAI) website, and in the case of financing data, from online news articles or private sponsors' annual reports.

During this period, two types of PPP contracts were mainly initiated by NHAI: toll-based and annuity-based projects. *Toll-based projects* entitled the project company to charge tolls. *Annuity-based projects* entitled the project company to semi-annual availability payments from the NHAI after the road was built or rehabilitated.

All contracts were awarded through competitive auctions. For toll-based projects, the outcome of the auction could be either an annual *premium payment* from the private sponsor to the government, which would escalate at 5 percent yearly, or an upfront *capital grant* from the government for the PPP project through a scheme known as Viability Gap Funding—based on the expected profitability of the roads. Sponsors would bid either the highest premium they would pay or the lowest capital grant they would require. For annuity-based projects, the sponsors would bid the lowest annuity payments they require.[26]

The procurement process ends in three types of contracts, each of which presents a different set of risks. While both types of contracts for toll-based projects expose the project company to demand risk, *capital-grant contracts* alleviate the financing risk. *Annuity-based contracts* insulate the project company from the demand risk, but the company is still exposed to the full financing risk.

In 2012, an unusually high number of PPP contracts were awarded based on premium payments, and about half of them were canceled (figure 1.15). This increase occurred partly because the NHAI decreased the development of annuity-based projects after 2011, and private sponsors started bidding more aggressively for toll-based contracts. The decrease in the capital-grant contracts indicates that private sponsors were more optimistic about the projects offered in 2012 compared to the earlier toll-based projects.

A logistic regression model was estimated to identify the contract characteristics affecting early termination of national highway PPPs. The contract characteristics are introduced in the regression in three different ways. First, they are introduced as indicator variables for each type of contract. Second, the net present value (NPV) of payments to the government is introduced as a continuous

FIGURE 1.15 **Number of Indian Highway Projects Canceled versus Not Canceled, by Contract Type and Financial Closure Year, 2010–14**

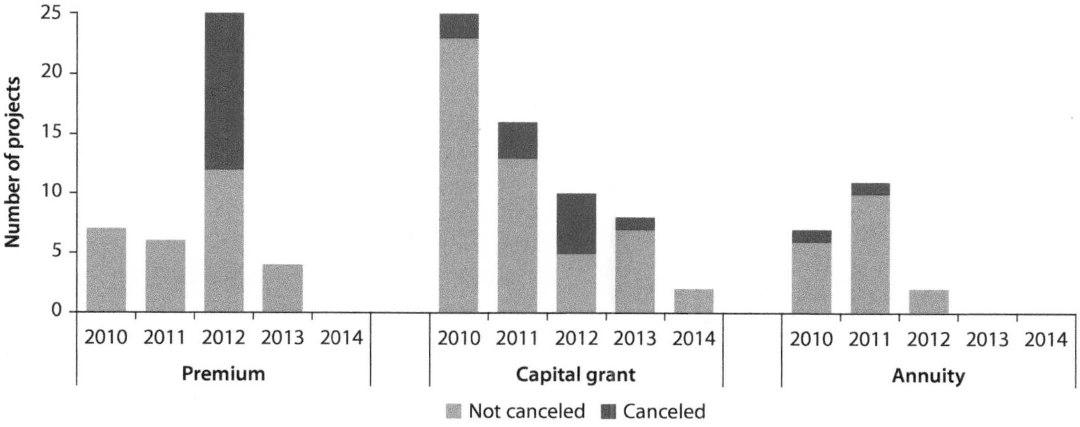

Sources: Private Participation in Infrastructure database; National Highways Authority of India.
Note: The concession agreement year is used if financial closure had not been achieved by the time of cancellation.

indicator of the net cost of the contract to the sponsor.[27] Third, the net present value of payments is rescaled by the amount of investment. Two additional variables are introduced in all cases: road length and fraction of the total investment financed by debt. The debt variable only applies to projects that secured financing. Table 1F.2 in annex 1F presents the regression results.

The size of premium payments and tender payments matters. The larger the tendered premium payments to the government, the higher the probability that national highway PPPs were later canceled. Similarly, the smaller the tendered payment from the government to the sponsor as capital grant or annuity payment, the higher the probability that national highway PPPs were later canceled. Premium-payment contracts are more likely to be canceled than annuity-based contracts when no other project characteristics are included (column 1 in table 1F.2). However, the relationship is not statistically significant when controlling for the length of the road (column 2). When using the net present value of the premium payments to government, either by itself or as a share of investment in the project, the coefficient again turns statistically significant—even when controlling for road length and fraction of

the total investment financed by debt (columns 4–9). The findings indicate that as the sponsor and the project company's financial burden increases, the likelihood of cancellation of the project increases. Alternatively, the premium-payment contracts may create an unsound incentive structure that encourages overoptimistic bids from the private sponsor to win the PPP contract in order to access funds that can be channeled to other construction companies in the same financial group (ADB et al. 2018; Pratap and Chakrabarti 2017).

The likelihood of cancellation increases with the share of the investment financed through debt. This finding is important from a fiscal risk perspective because roughly 80 percent of the debt to finance the NHAI portfolio has come from public sector banks in which the government owns more than 50 percent of capital shares. The large number of cancellations in the NHAI portfolio have contributed to the rising number of nonperforming assets in India's banking sector. The State Bank of India, which holds the greatest nominal amount of Indian highway-related debt, reported that about 20 percent of loans to ports and highways were nonperforming by the end of 2016, with the trend increasing in 2016 (ADB et al. 2018).

The likelihood of cancellation increases with the length of the highway. The finding that longer highways are more likely to be canceled is consistent with the observation that many of the cancellations have been related to the government having problems with securing the right of way.

Improving Government Capacity, Due Diligence, and Contract Design to Better Manage the Fiscal Risks of the Growing PPP Programs in South Asia

The fiscal risks from the current infrastructure PPP programs in South Asia are not negligible for some countries. Under a severely adverse scenario, the potential fiscal costs from early termination in 2020–21 amount to 3.3 percent to 4.3 percent of the government revenues in Bangladesh, India, Nepal, and Pakistan. The pipeline of PPP projects in South Asia is quite large, particularly in Bangladesh, which has the same number (30) of infrastructure projects in the pipeline as it has active projects. Such an expansion of the PPP program can lead to a significant increase in fiscal risks. Therefore, an important agenda in South Asia is improving the design and management of infrastructure PPPs to mitigate the corresponding fiscal risks, while ensuring timely implementation of financially responsible infrastructure projects to address the infrastructure deficit.

Five Overarching Lessons

The analysis identifies five overarching lessons from the global PPP data.

First and foremost, several factors that increase the risk of early termination of PPP projects are related to the financing risk of the project. Governments may alleviate some of the financial risk of PPPs by providing support (helping de-risk the projects) through capital grants, revenue subsidies, or in-kind transfers, which lead to reduced rates of early termination.

Second, the sector in which a PPP project operates, and the size of a project, in terms of its physical investment, matter in evaluating riskiness of a project. PPPs in the power and seaport sectors are less likely to experience early termination than PPPs in the other infrastructure sectors analyzed. Large physical investments lead to increased rates of early terminations.

Third, delegating PPP contracting and monitoring to state and local governments should be considered when it is institutionally and economically possible. PPPs show lower probability of early termination when they are contracted and monitored by state and local entities. The subnational governments could have better information to monitor and could be held more directly accountable for effective implementation of the project—but even here risk could arise (see chapter 4).

Fourth, PPPs tend to have reduced rates of early termination when the contract is executed in a country with stronger constraints on the power of the executive branch. These constraints could deliver the required discipline and decrease uncertainty during project implementation.

Fifth, macrofinancial shocks are an important cause of early termination of PPPs, highlighting the importance of macroeconomic management in enabling sustainable funding and financing of PPP projects.

Recommendations for Building Government Capacity and Undertaking Rigorous Due Diligence, Assessments, and Feasibility Studies

Government capacity to prepare, procure, and manage PPP projects must be built to ensure that the expected efficiency gains are indeed achieved and that the fiscal risks from contingent liabilities are contained and properly managed. Good practices for the preparation, procurement, and management of PPPs can help governments improve their capabilities to take advantage of PPPs at more acceptable levels of risks (World Bank 2019). An important good practice is to ascertain the fiscal implications of PPPs, including specifying their budgetary, accounting, and reporting treatment. The Ministry of Finance or central budget authority should approve the long-term financial implications of the project (World Bank 2019).

Given the complexity, magnitude, and inherently long-term nature of PPP projects, the procuring authority should exercise a good amount of due diligence and perform rigorous assessments to gauge the viability of infrastructure projects before deciding on a PPP procurement.

A sound PPP preparation starts with the identification of potential infrastructure projects that could be procured as PPPs. The results from the econometric analysis suggest that it is important to undertake feasibility studies to inform the structure of the PPP project, including assessing and deciding on the allocation of risks, and sounding out the market to gauge its appetite and capacity, which can reduce the probability of early termination.

Addressing Issues in Contract Design

In India, PPPs for national highways were more likely to terminate early if the contract put the private sponsor under larger financial commitments through higher premium payments to the government or lower capital grants or annuity payments from the government. The reason could be exposure to demand risk and a perverse incentive structure that encourages overly optimistic bids on payments to the government in order to win tenders on PPP contracts that will be financed with loans from state-owned banks with weak due diligence capacity.

Recommendations for Improving Contract Design

The success of project implementation will determine whether the project delivers the expected value for money and whether fiscal risks have been properly managed. Following established good practices, modification and renegotiation of the contract should be expressly regulated to lower the incentives to

use these changes opportunistically by either the private partner or the procuring authority.

Specific circumstances—force majeure, materially adverse government action, change in the law, refinancing—that may arise during the life of the contract should be also expressly regulated. Dispute resolution mechanisms should be in place allowing the parties to resolve differences in an efficient and satisfactory manner without adversely affecting the project (ADB et al. 2018).

Giving lenders step-in rights for cases when the private partner is at risk of default or if the PPP contract is under threat of termination for failure to meet service obligations is another good practice to avoid early termination and reduce the fiscal costs.

Having well-defined grounds for termination of the PPP contract and its associated consequences can also reduce fiscal costs from early termination (World Bank 2019).

Annex 1A. Methodology to Determine the Value at Risk of a Public-Private Partnership

The study employs the value-at-risk methodology. Accordingly, the fiscal risk from project i is valued as the maximum expected loss with 99 percent confidence:

$$EL_{i,99\%} = PD_{i,99\%} * EAD_i * LGD_i, \tag{1A.1}$$

where $PD_{i,99\%}$ is the probability of distress for project i such that there is 1 percent chance that the probability will exceed $PD_{i,99\%}$; EAD_i is the government's exposure to project i at the time of distress; and LGD_i is the government's loss given project i distress.

The $PD_{i,99\%}$, EAD_i, and LGD_i are obtained separately. The probability of distress of a public-private partnership (PPP) is predicted using a flexible parametric survival model of the realization of distress conditional on project-specific and country-specific institutional variables and macroeconomic shocks. The EAD_i is estimated based on the debt and equity invested in the project. The LGD_i is determined based on different practices by countries in case of termination of PPP contracts and the recovery rates of defaulted loans to infrastructure projects.

Econometric Model for Calculating the Probability of Distress

The probability of distress of a PPP at a specific point during its contract period is predicted by estimating a flexible parametric proportional hazards model (Royston and Parmar 2002; Royston and Lambert 2011).[28] The model is an extension of the parametric proportional hazards model with a Weibull baseline hazard function. The generalization allows for a non-monotonic baseline hazard function using restricted cubic splines. Accordingly, coefficients of the following equation are estimated to maximize the likelihood of the observed distribution of failure times:

$$\ln H\big(t|X_{it}\big) = \gamma_0 + \sum_{m=1}^{2} \gamma_m z_m \big(\ln t\big) + X_{i,proj}\beta_{proj}$$
$$+ X_{it,inst}\beta_{inst} + X_{it,macro}\beta_{macro},$$

$$(1A.2)$$

where $\ln H(t|X_{it})$ is the log cumulative hazard at time t for project i conditional on $X_{it} = (X_{i,proj}, X_{it,inst}, X_{it,macro})$. $X_{i,proj}$ is the vector of project-specific time-invariant covariates. $X_{it,inst}$ is the vector of country-specific, time-varying institutional covariates. $X_{it,macro}$ is the vector of country-specific, time-varying macroeconomic shocks. The terms under the summation operator represent the set of restricted cubic spline terms in log time scale, $z_m(\ln t)$. The time scale is chosen as the percentage of contract period elapsed. The restricted cubic spline functions are

$$z_1\big(\ln t\big) = \ln t$$
$$z_m\big(\ln t\big) = \big(\ln t - k_m\big)_+^3 - a_m \big(\ln t - k_{min}\big)_+^3$$
$$- \big(1 - a_m\big)\big(\ln t - k_{max}\big)_+^3 \quad \text{for } m > 1,$$

where k_m are the interior knots, which are picked at the centiles of the uncensored log

event-time distribution, and $a_m = (k_{max} - k_m)/(k_{max} - k_{min})$. Then, the likelihood function is

$$L\big(\gamma,\beta\big) = \prod_{j=1}^{N} \frac{S(t_j \mid X_j \beta,\gamma)}{S(t_{j0} \mid X_j \beta,\gamma)} \Big[h\big(t_j \mid X_j \beta,\gamma\big) \Big]^{d_j},$$

$$(1A.3)$$

where j denotes each observation used in the analysis. The number of observations in the estimation sample is the number of project years because the time-variant variables are all annual. The variable t_{j0} denotes the beginning of the period for a specific observation ending at time t_j, during which the covariates remain constant at X_j. The variable d_j equals 1 if the project goes into distress at time t_j, and $d_j = 0$ if the project survives time t_j.

To estimate the probability of distress at a specific interval (t_0,t), the survival function $S(\cdot)$ and the hazard function $h(\cdot)$ can be restated in terms of $\ln H(t/X_{it})$ in equation (1A.2) using the relations

$$S\big(t|X_{it}\big) = \exp\big\{-\exp\big[\ln H\big(t|X_{it}\big)\big]\big\}, \quad (1A.4)$$

$$h\big(t|X_{it}\big) = \frac{d}{dt}\exp\big[\ln H\big(t|X_{it}\big)\big], \quad (1A.5)$$

Then, after obtaining γ and β, the probability of distress for any period (t_0,t) for any project i can be recovered using the relationship between the survival and the cumulative hazard functions

$$\hat{S}\big(t_j \mid X_{it_j}\big) = \exp\big\{-\exp\big[\ln \hat{H}\big(t_j \mid X_{it_j}\big)\big]\big\},$$

$$(1A.6)$$

$$\hat{S}_i\big(t|t_0\big) = \prod_j \frac{\hat{S}\big(t_j \mid X_{it_j}\big)}{\hat{S}\big(t_{j0} \mid X_{it_j}\big)}. \quad (1A.7)$$

where j is any observation for project i such that $(t_{j0},t_j) \subseteq (t_0,t)$. Then, the probability of distress between (t_0,t) can be written as

$$\widehat{PD}_i = 1 - \hat{S}_i\big(t|t_0\big). \quad (1A.8)$$

The probability of distress at the 99th percentile is calculated using the standard errors obtained via the delta method:[29]

$$\widehat{PD}_{i,99\%} = \widehat{PD}_i + z_{1\%} \times s.e.\left(\widehat{PD}_i\right). \quad (1A.9)$$

Annex 1B. Definitions of Variables

The following variables were used in the study to identify systematic contractual, institutional, and macroeconomic factors that can help predict the probability that a PPP project will be terminated early.

TABLE 1B.1   Project-Level Variables

Variable	Measure	Source
Distress	1, if project is canceled;[a] 0, otherwise.	PPI database and authors' collection for Herrera Dappe, Melecky, and Turkgulu 2020
Contract period	Percentage of contract period elapsed until distress (as defined in the first row of the table); otherwise, until the end of 2018.	PPI database and authors' collection for Herrera Dappe, Melecky, and Turkgulu 2020
Type	*Greenfield* if the special purpose vehicle (SPV) builds and operates a new facility; *Brownfield* if the SPV takes over an existing asset and either rehabilitates or expands it.	PPI database
Sector	Electricity, natural gas, telecom, airports, railroads, toll roads, seaports, treatment plants, water utility.	PPI database
Direct government support	1, if capital, revenue, or in-kind subsidies exist; 0, otherwise.	PPI database
Indirect government support	1, if payment, debt, revenues, guarantee, etc. exist; 0, otherwise.	PPI database
Multilateral support	1, if a multilateral bank provides financial support; 0, otherwise.	PPI database and authors' collection for Herrera Dappe, Melecky, and Turkgulu 2020
Subnational government contract	1, if local or provincial/state government grants the contract; 0, otherwise.	PPI database and authors' collection for Herrera Dappe, Melecky, and Turkgulu 2020
Physical investment	Total investment in physical assets, in 2019 US$, billion.	PPI database and authors' collection for Herrera Dappe, Melecky, and Turkgulu 2020

Source: Herrera Dappe, Melecky, and Turkgulu 2020.
Note: The PPI database is the World Bank Private Participation in Infrastructure Project (PPI) database, Version 2019 H1, available at https://ppi.worldbank .org/en/ppidata. "Authors' collection" refers to the recoding of cases labeled as distressed in the data set as active or canceled based on information available through public sources, such as news articles.
a. A project is canceled if the private party has exited by selling or turning over its shares to the government or by ceasing operations.

TABLE 1B.2   Institutional Variables

Variable	Measure[a]	Source
Executive recruitment concept	Index of openness of executive recruitment, ranging from 1 (succession by birthright) to 8 (competitive election).	Polity IV Project
Executive constraints concept	Index of the degree of constraints on the executive, ranging from 1 (unlimited authority) to 7 (executive parity or subordination).	Polity IV Project
Political competition concept	Index of the degree of competition in politics, ranging from 1 (suppressed) to 10 (institutional electoral).	Polity IV Project

Note: "Executive" refers to the executive branch of government.
a. The values for the interruption, interregnum, and transition periods, during which the institutional variables take values outside of their regular ranges in Polity IV, were linearly interpolated. Specifically, when the political structure faces some sort of irregularity (interruption, interregnum, or transition), the database assigns the variable a value of −66, −77, or −88, depending on the type of irregularity. Interpolation implicitly assumes a continuous rather than an abrupt resolution to any sort of political irregularity.

TABLE 1B.3   **Macroeconomic Variables**

Variable	Measure	Source
Annual GDP per capita growth rate	Annual GDP per capita growth rate of the country, detrended and demeaned using the filter suggested by Hamilton (2018). Previous year's value, calculated using the "GDP per capita growth (annual %)" series from the WDI.	Herrera Dappe, Melecky, and Turkgulu 2020, based on Hamilton 2018; World Development Indicators (WDI)
Annual depreciation (detrended, previous year)	Depreciation rate of the local currency against the US dollar, detrended and demeaned using the filter suggested by Hamilton (2018). Previous year's value, calculated using the "DEC alternative conversion factor (LCU per US$)" series, from the WDI.	Herrera Dappe, Melecky, and Turkgulu 2020, based on Hamilton 2018; WDI
Banking crisis occurred (previous year)	1, if a systematic banking crisis occurred in the country during the previous year; 0, otherwise.	Laeven and Valencia 2018
Debt crisis occurred (previous year)	1, if a debt crisis occurred in the country during the previous year; 0, otherwise.	Laeven and Valencia 2018
Exchange rate crisis occurred (previous year)	1, if an exchange rate crisis occurred in the country during the previous year; 0, otherwise.	Laeven and Valencia 2018

Annex 1C. Distribution of South Asian Public-Private Partnership Projects by Sector

TABLE 1C.1   **Sectoral Distribution of Public-Private Partnership Projects with Financial Closure in South Asia, by Country**

Country		ICT	Energy	Transport	Water and sewerage	Total
Afghanistan	Projects	0	2	0	0	2
	US$, million	0	39	0	0	39
Bangladesh	Projects	5 (2)	31	8 (1)	1	45 (3)
	US$, million	76	5,372	1,097	333	6,877
Bhutan	Projects	1	1	0	0	2
	US$, million	0	240	0	0	240
India	Projects	7 (1)	414 (3)	543 (27)	20	984 (31)
	US$, million	1,624	162,375	117,595	1,337	282,932
Maldives	Projects	0	0	1 (1)	0	1 (1)
	US$, million	0	0	469	0	469
Nepal	Projects	2	34	1	1	38
	US$, million	12	2,491	378	0	2,880
Pakistan	Projects	0	73	8	0	81
	US$, million	0	28,159	3,005	0	31,164
Sri Lanka	Projects	1	75	3	0	79
	US$, million	81	2,244	1,062	0	3,387
Total	Projects	16 (3)	630 (3)	564 (29)	22	1,232 (35)
	US$, million	1,764	200,919	123,605	1,670	327,988

Source: Private Participation in Infrastructure database.
Note: The number of canceled projects appears in parentheses. Investment totals are in 2019 US$, million. ICT = information and communications technology; PPP = public-private partnerships.

Annex 1D. Imputing the Missing Values for Predictions

Physical Investment

The missing values for investments in physical infrastructure for small hydro projects in Nepal and Sri Lanka and for the wind and solar energy projects in India were imputed by estimating the amount of investment needed per megawatt for the same type of energy projects in the same country. Hence, the imputations are obtained from the following regression:

$$Physical\ Investment_i = \beta \times Capacity_i + u_i,$$

where i stands for project; β is the regression coefficient; and u_i is the residual.

- In the case of Sri Lankan small hydro projects, 41 observations were used to impute 3 missing values.
- In the case of Nepalese small hydro projects, 22 observations were used to impute 4 missing values.
- In the case of Indian wind projects, 91 observation were used to impute 4 missing values.
- In the case of Indian solar projects, 97 observations were used to impute 1 missing value.

Debt-to-Physical-Investment Ratio

To obtain the estimates for the missing financing variables—debt and equity—the debt-to-physical-investment ratio has been predicted using type, sector, country, and financial closure year dummies, using the following regression:

$$Debt\ to\ Physical\ Investment\ Ratio_i = \beta_0 + Type_i + Sector_i + Country_i + Financial\ Closure\ Year_i + u_i,$$

where i represents each project in South Asia. A total of 737 observations have been used to impute 344 missing values. The physical investment has been apportioned according to the predicted ratio between debt and equity.

Contract Period

Four kind of projects have been identified as missing contract period information: energy projects, airport projects, seaport projects, and toll road projects in India. The missing contract period data were imputed using the following regressions and were rounded to the nearest integer. The regression for energy projects in South Asia is

$$Period_i = \beta_0 + Type_i + Country_i + Financial\ Closure\ Year_i + u_i,$$

where i represents each energy project in South Asia. A total of 391 observations were used to impute 194 missing values.

The regression for airport projects in South Asia is

$$Period_i = \beta_0 + u_i,$$

where i represents each airport project in South Asia. This regression essentially finds the average contract length for airport projects without any predictors. The choice of the model is due to sample limitations. Eight observations were used to impute three missing values.

The regression for seaport projects in South Asia is

$$Period_i = \beta_0 + Type_i + Financial\ Closure\ Year_i + u_i,$$

where i represents each toll road project in India. A total of 53 observations were used to impute one missing value.

The regression for toll road projects in India is

$$Period_i = \beta_0 + Type_i + Financial\ Closure\ Year_i + Subnational_i + u_i,$$

where i represents each toll road project in India. The inclusion of the subnational contract indicator is due to the differences in the handling of contracts between the National Highways Authority of India and the state highways authorities. A total of 393 observations were used to impute 14 missing values.

Annex 1E. Model Selection

The model selection in the context of survival analysis is to choose the correct parametric model for the purposes of the study. This study estimates a nontraditional model—a flexible parametric model—rather than one of the usual out-of-the-box models using distributions such as the Weibull or the loglogistic models. The main reason is that the regular parametric models fail to fit the pattern of the baseline hazard function in this study. The baseline hazard is defined as the hazard profile of the project for which all the dummies are at their base cases, all shocks are set to zero, and all other continuous variables are set to their means.

To get an idea about the baseline hazard profile, a semi-parametric Cox model can be fit, and the baseline hazard can be extracted as a residual. Alternatively, the total contract period of the project can be partitioned based on the centiles of distress and—assuming that hazard is constant within each partition—a step function that would indicate the hazard profile over the contract period of a project. Figure 1E.1 shows the resulting baseline hazard profile using the two methods.

Figure 1E.1 shows that the baseline hazard must be increasing and then decreasing around 15 percent to 30 percent of the contract period. The overall shape of the baseline hazard function does not differ drastically compared to the non-parametric estimation of the overall hazard presented in the main chapter. However, observe that the baseline is scaled down to some extent. The parametric model chosen needs to be able to reasonably replicate the major characteristics of these curves.

Two of the common specifications for the baseline hazard are Weibull and loglogistic functions. These models are known to have proportional hazards properties and proportional odds properties, respectively. When the model is fit using Weibull and loglogistic hazard functions, the resulting estimates of the baseline hazard function are monotonically increasing, neither of which captures the unimodal concave aspect of the baseline hazard captured using the semi-parametric methods (see figure 1E.2). This result is potentially due to the fact that the sample overrepresents projects in the early stages of their contract periods, and the models, in their attempt to fit the data, underpenalize the lack of fit in the later stages.

Royston and Parmar (2002) provide generalizations of the parametric survival models using Weibull and loglogistic functions. These models partition the analysis period into multiple periods and, using restricted splines, make the relationship between the strict functional forms of Weibull and

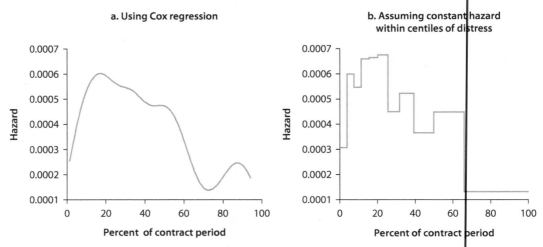

FIGURE 1E.1   **Baseline Hazard Profile Estimates Using Semi-parametric Methods**

a. Using Cox regression

b. Assuming constant hazard within centiles of distress

Source: Herrera Dappe, Melecky, and Turkgulu 2020.
Note: Using Gaussian kernel and optimal bandwith.

Source: Herrera Dappe, Melecky, and Turkgulu 2020.
Note: Using 11 interior knots.

loglogistic functions and the analysis period more flexible. The underlying distributions are no longer Weibull or loglogistic, but their proportionality properties are preserved. Hence, the flexible models are characterized by the proportionality property and the degree of freedom that they provide. Figure 1E.3 presents the baseline hazard functions using the flexible parametric methods with only a single interior knot, which means that two parameters are used in characterizing the baseline. Even introducing only one interior knot, the model captures the unimodal relationship implied by the semi-parametric methods in figure 1E.1.

More interior knots can be introduced to obtain a better fit using the flexible parametric approach. Observe that the relationship can still be improved. However, this quest may result in overfitting the sample. To this end, flexible parametric proportional hazards (PH) and proportional odds (PO) models with different degrees of freedom have been fit, and the Akaike information criterion (AIC) and the Bayesian information criterion (BIC) are used to select the appropriate model. Table 1E.1 shows the resulting AIC and BIC values. Observe that the PH(2) model yields the lowest AIC and BIC, so the analysis overall uses PH(2) model. The choice of the model does not have substantial qualitative or quantitative effects on the estimates.

FIGURE 1E.2   **Baseline Hazard Profile Estimates Using Parametric Methods**

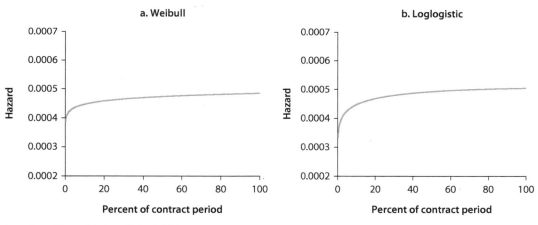

Source: Herrera Dappe, Melecky, and Turkgulu 2020.

FIGURE 1E.3   **Baseline Hazard Profile Estimates Using Flexible Parametric Methods**

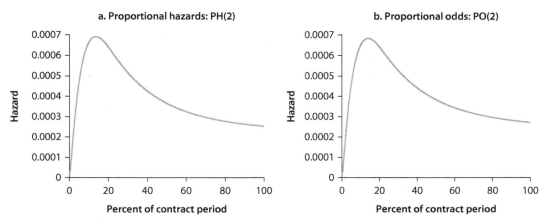

Source: Herrera Dappe, Melecky, and Turkgulu 2020.
Note: The analysis uses one interior knot.

TABLE 1E.1   **Akaike Information Criterion and Bayesian Information Criterion under Different Orders of Flexible Parametric Methods**

	PH(1)	PO(1)	PH(2)	PO(2)	PH(3)	PO(3)	PH(4)	PO(4)	PH(5)	PO(5)
AIC	1,504.0	1,510.7	**1,483.4**	1,492.6	1,485.3	1,494.5	1,489.8	1,497.1	1,490.6	1,499.8
BIC	1,578.8	1,585.6	**1,561.4**	1,570.6	1,566.3	1,575.5	1,580.2	1,584.4	1,584.1	1,593.3

Source: World Bank staff calculations.
Note: The number in parentheses refers to the model number. The bold PH(2) column marks the order at which AIC and BIC are minimized. AIC = Akaike information criterion; BIC = Bayesian information criterion; PH = proportional hazards; PO = proportional odds.

Annex 1F. Estimation Tables

TABLE 1F.1   **Estimated Fiscal Costs (at the 99th Percentile) from Early Termination of the Public-Private Partnership Portfolio in South Asia, 2020–24 (2019 US$, million)**

Country/ Scenario	Contract period	From the beginning of 2020 to the end of:					Number of projects
		2020	2021	2022	2023	2024	
Afghanistan							
Low	0.51	0.06	0.11	0.16	0.21	0.25	2
Medium	1.16	0.14	0.26	0.38	0.47	0.56	
High	1.42	0.17	0.32	0.46	0.58	0.69	
Bangladesh							
Low	379	49	92	130	162	191	30
Medium	643	79	151	214	268	316	
High	730	89	170	241	302	356	
Bhutan							
Low	4.11	0.35	0.69	1.01	1.32	1.62	1
Medium	5.32	0.45	0.89	1.31	1.71	2.10	
High	5.59	0.48	0.93	1.37	1.80	2.21	
India							
Low	9,663	853	1,656	2,409	3,110	3,766	848
Medium	16,371	1,444	2,803	4,076	5,263	6,371	
High	18,510	1,631	3,166	4,605	5,945	7,198	
Nepal							
Low	112	9	17	24	30	36	35
Medium	178	13	26	37	47	56	
High	197	15	29	41	52	62	
Pakistan							
Low	1,046	96	189	277	359	434	72
Medium	1,746	159	314	460	595	720	
High	1,959	178	352	515	667	806	
Sri Lanka							
Low	58	6	12	17	22	26	66
Medium	95	10	19	28	36	44	
High	107	11	22	32	41	49	

Source: Herrera Dappe, Melecky, and Turkgulu 2020.
Note: The 99th percentile refers to the confidence with which the calculated loss is not exceeded during a given period. PPPs = public-private partnerships.

TABLE 1F.2 Logit Regression Estimates of Likelihood of Cancellation of Indian National Highway Public-Private Partnerships

	(1)	(2)	(3)	(4)	(5)	(6)	(7)	(8)	(9)
Base case: Annuity									
Capital grant	0.68	0.58	1.16						
	(0.82)	(0.83)	(1.37)						
Premium	1.40*	1.18	1.95+						
	(0.812)	(0.84)	(1.20)						
NPV of payments to government				0.003**	0.002*	0.002*			
				(0.001)	(0.001)	(0.001)			
NPV of payments to government as share of project investment							0.74**	0.54+	0.92*
							(0.36)	(0.37)	(0.50)
Road length (log)		1.20**	2.219***		0.978*	1.93**		1.14**	2.10**
		(0.49)	(0.823)		(0.53)	(0.90)		(0.50)	(0.83)
Debt financing share of project investment			9.302*			8.98*			8.923*
			(5.271)			(4.62)			(4.73)
Constant	−2.20***	−7.68***	−20.54***	−1.42***	−5.93**	−17.62***	−1.31***	−6.65***	−18.39***
	(0.75)	(2.43)	(6.06)	(0.24)	(2.48)	(5.66)	(0.23)	(2.37)	(5.48)
Observations	123	123	109	123	123	109	123	123	109

Source: Herrera Dappe, Melecky, and Turkgulu 2020.
Note: To assess which contract features could be associated with cancellations, the following equation is estimated using the maximum likelihood method:

$$Canceled_i = f(\beta_0 + X_{i,proj}\beta_1 + u_i),$$
(1F.1)

where the dependent variable is the event of cancellation, $f(\cdot)$ is the logistic function, and $X_{i,proj}$ are project-specific variables. The 99th percentile refers to the confidence level with which the computed maximum loss is not exceeded during the reference period (such as one year or the duration of the project). NPV = net present value.
Standard errors in parentheses.
+ p < 0.15, * p < 0.1, ** p < 0.05, *** p < 0.01.

Notes

1. Fay and others (2019) estimate that infrastructure spending in South Asia was 4.5 percent of GDP in 2011.
2. In some cases, companies in developing countries are able to borrow at lower costs than the government. Such companies tend to have substantial export earnings and/or a close relationship with either a foreign firm or the home government (Durbin and Ng 2005; Grandes, Panigo, and Pasquini 2017).
3. For example, a government buying goods or services from the same supplier year after year is not an enduring and relational partnership and therefore not a PPP.
4. The incentive to adopt improvements requires that either the service quality can be specified by contract or the demand for the service depends on its quality. If quality is not contractible, PPPs may lead to innovations during the design stage that reduce both costs and quality. This might lead to the provision of some service with the least cost but not at socially optimal levels if the social benefits from the innovations are larger than the net savings incurred by the firm (Hart 2003; Martimort and Pouyet 2008).

5. The agency problem is a conflict of interest inherent in any relationship in which one party is expected to act in another's best interests.

6. Mobilizing private finance may also resolve a political problem hindering investment in infrastructure by the incumbent provider. For example, when fiscal rules prevent public financing of infrastructure, PPPs might still be politically and legally feasible by shifting liabilities off the central government's balance sheet and/or into the future (Budina, Polackova Brixi, and Irwin 2007). Another possibility is that when a different political faction can bar public financing of infrastructure within an incumbent's district, the incumbent can utilize private finance to skirt the political constraint.

7. Availability payments are periodic payments to the sponsor conditional on the availability of service at a prespecified level. Capacity payments are periodic payments from the government to the sponsor for upholding a certain level of capacity. Shadow tolls are payments per user to the sponsor from the government. Power purchasing agreements are contractual promises of prespecified levels of energy purchases by the government.

8. PPPs typically do not create direct implicit liabilities unless payments to the private party are expected to continue due to non-contractual or noncontingent reasons, such as continued political relationship even after the contract is over (Budina, Polackova Brixi, and Irwin 2007).

9. All dollar figures in the study are expressed in 2019 US dollars inflated using the US Consumer Price Index (CPI) series in the World Development Indicators.

10. The analysis used Version 2019 H1, available at https://ppi.worldbank.org/en/ppidata.

11. Financial closure refers to the securing of financing for the project by the sponsor.

12. The study uses Version 2019 H1, available at https://ppi.worldbank.org/en/ppidata.

13. Polity IV Project, Political Regime Characteristics and Transitions, 1800–2018, is available at http://www.systemicpeace.org/inscrdata.html.

14. The World Development Indicators are available at http://datatopics.worldbank.org/world-development-indicators/.

15. Data limitations preclude estimation using only the South Asian countries.

16. Merchant greenfield projects in the PPI data set are projects in which the private sponsor constructs and operates a new facility at its own risk in a liberalized market. A rental greenfield project in the PPI data set refers to projects in which the government agrees to rent the facility and the service from a private party as a temporary measure.

17. Equations (1A.4) and (1A.5) in annex 1A present the relationships among hazard, cumulative hazard, and cumulative survival probability presented in figures 1.5, 1.6, and 1.7.

18. In a greenfield project, a new facility or asset is built and operated for the period specified in the project contract. In a brownfield project, instead of building a new asset, the private entity takes over an existing asset and usually makes an improvement to it or expands it.

19. This figure of 1,056 active projects excludes the projects whose imputed or observed contract period has elapsed.

20. Only 209 of the 1,970 PPP projects included in the data set, which spans 1983 to 2017, are from emerging market economies and developing countries (Moody's Investors Service 2019).

21. Figure 1.6 depicts a decreasing hazard profile for projects past 20 percent of their contract periods.

22. Percentages are as of 2017, from World Revenue Longitudinal Data (WoRLD), available at http://data.imf.org/?sk=77413F1D-1525-450A-A23A-47AEED40FE78.

23. The analysis assumes that the *annual* government revenues during the 2020–24 period are the same as in 2019.

24. The statistics exclude two episodes in Ecuador because the adjusted currency conversion factor remained stable, even though the official rate of depreciation was 56.8 percent and 77.2 percent, in the banking crises of early 1980s and the late 1990s, respectively.

25. The scenario abstracts from the sequencing of different macro events because all events are assumed to occur in the same year.

26. In the chosen time frame, only two projects did not adhere to these two schemes. The first is a project that was awarded based on payment of a percentage of toll revenues.

The second is a hybrid annuity project that entitled the project company to both availability payments and a capital grant. The hybrid annuity model has become the preferred method more recently. Both projects were excluded from the analysis.

27. An annual discount rate of 8 percent has been assumed.

28. The model is estimated in the *Stata Journal* using the stpm2 routine, which has been authored by Lambert and Royston (2009).

29. The delta method provides a way to estimate standard errors for nonlinear predictions. The method is based on a central limit theorem that shows that the prediction is distributed with a standard normal distribution under certain conditions. The method calculates the standard errors using the variance-covariance matrix of the coefficient estimates.

References

ADB (Asian Development Bank). 2017. *Meeting Asia's Infrastructure Needs*. Manila: ADB.

ADB, DFID, JICA, and World Bank (Asian Development Bank, Department for International Development, Japan International Cooperation Agency, and the World Bank). 2018. *The WEB of Transport Corridors in South Asia*. Washington, DC: World Bank.

Budina, N., H. Polackova Brixi, and T. Irwin. 2007. "Public-Private Partnerships in the New EU Member States: Managing Fiscal Risks." Working Paper, World Bank, Washington, DC.

de Bettignies, J-E, and T. W. Ross. 2009. "Public–Private Partnerships and the Privatization of Financing: An Incomplete Contracts Approach." *International Journal of Industrial Organization* 27 (3): 358–68.

de Bettignies, J-E, and T. W. Ross. 2010. "The Economics of Public-Private Partnership: Some Theoretical Contributions." In *International Handbook on Public-Private Partnerships*, edited by Greame A. Hodge, Carsten Greve, and Anthony E. Boardman, 132–58. Cheltenham, United Kingdom: Edward Elgar.

de Vries, P. 2013. "Public Budget Norms and PPP: An Anomaly." In *The Routledge Companion to Public-Private Partnerships*, edited by Piet de Vries and Etienne B. Yehoue, 301–21. Oxon, United Kingdom: Routledge.

Durbin, E., and D. Ng. 2005. "The Sovereign Ceiling and Emerging Market Corporate Bond Spreads." *Journal of International Money and Finance* 24 (4): 631–49.

Engel, E., R. Fischer, and A. Galetovic. 2013. "The Basic Public Finance of Public-Private Partnerships." *Journal of the European Economic Association* 11 (1): 83–111.

EPEC (European PPP Expertise Centre). 2013. "Termination and Force Majeure Provisions in PPP Contracts: Review of Current European Practice and Guidance." EPEC, Luxembourg.

Fay, M., H. I. Lee, M. Mastruzzi, S. Han, and M. Cho. 2019. "Hitting the Trillion Mark: A Look at How Much Countries Are Spending on Infrastructure." Policy Research Working Paper 8730, World Bank, Washington, DC.

Grandes, M., D. T. Panigo, and R. A. Pasquini. 2017. "Corporate Credit Spreads and the Sovereign Ceiling in Latin America." *Emerging Markets Finance and Trade* 53 (5): 1217–40.

Grimsey, D., and M. K. Lewis. 2017. *Global Developments in Public Infrastructure Procurement: Evaluating Public-Private Partnerships and Other Procurement Options*. Cheltenham, United Kingdom: Edward Elgar.

Grout, P. A. 1997. "The Economics of the Private Finance Initiative." *Oxford Review of Economic Policy* 13 (4): 53–66.

Guasch, J. L. 2004. *Granting and Renegotiating Infrastructure Concessions: Doing It Right*. WBI Development Studies. Washington, DC: World Bank.

Hamilton, J. D. 2018. "Why You Should Never Use the Hodrick-Prescott Filter." *Review of Economics and Statistics* 100 (5): 831–43.

Hart, O. 2003. "Incomplete Contracts and Public Ownership: Remarks, and an Application to Public-Private Partnerships." *Economic Journal* 113 (486): C69–C76.

Heald, D., and G. Georgiou. 2010. "Accounting for PPPs in a Converging World." In *International Handbook of Public-Private Partnerships*, edited by Graeme A. Hodge, Carsten Greve, and Anthony E. Boardman, 237–61. Cheltenham, United Kingdom: Edward Elgar.

Herrera Dappe, M., M. Melecky, and B. Turkgulu. 2020. "PPP Distress and Fiscal Contingent Liabilities in South Asia." Background paper for *Hidden Debt*. World Bank, Washington, DC.

Iossa, E., and D. Martimort. 2012. "Risk Allocation and the Cost of Public-Private Partnerships." *RAND Journal of Economics* 43 (3): 442–74.

Iossa, E., and D. Martimort. 2015. "The Simple Microeconomics of Public-Private Partnerships." *Journal of Public Economic Theory* 17 (1): 4–48.

Irwin, T. C. 2007. *Government Guarantees: Allocating and Valuing Risk in Privately Financed Infrastructure Projects.* Directions in Development: Infrastructure. Washington, DC: World Bank.

ITF (International Transport Forum). 2018. *Private Investment in Transport Infrastructure: Dealing with Uncertainty in Contracts.* Paris: ITF.

Laeven, L., and F. Valencia. 2018. "Systematic Banking Crises Revisited." IMF Working Paper WP/18/206, International Monetary Fund, Washington, DC.

Lambert, P. C., and P. Royston. 2009. "Further Development of Flexible Parametric Models for Survival Analysis." *Stata Journal* 9 (2): 265–90.

Marin, P. 2009. *Public-Private Partnerships for Urban Water Utilities: A Review of Experiences in Developing Countries.* Washington, DC: World Bank.

Martimort, D., and J. Pouyet. 2008. "To Build or Not to Build: Normative and Positive Theories of Public–Private Partnerships." *International Journal of Industrial Organization* 26 (2): 393–411.

Moody's Investors Service. 2019. "Default and Recovery Rates for Project Finance Bank Loans, 1983–2017." Moody's Investors Service, New York.

Polackova, H. 1998. "Contingent Government Liabilities: A Hidden Risk for Stability." Policy Research Working Paper 1989, World Bank, Washington, DC.

Pratap, K. V., and R. Chakrabarti. 2017. *Public-Private Partnerships in Infrastructure: Managing the Challenges.* Singapore: Springer.

Reyes-Tagle, G., and K. Garbacik. 2016. "Policymakers' Decisions on Public-Private Partnership Use: The Role of Institutions and Fiscal Constraints." IDB Technical Note no. 1169, Inter-American Development Bank Washington, DC.

Royston, P., and P. C. Lambert. 2011. *Flexible Parametric Survival Analysis Using Stata: Beyond the Cox Model.* College Station, TX: Stata Press.

Royston, P., and M. K. B. Parmar. 2002. "Flexible Parametric Proportional-Hazards and Proportional-Odds Models for Censored Survival Data, with Application to Prognostic Modelling and Estimation of Treatment Effects." *Statistics in Medicine* 21 (15): 2175–97.

Rozenberg, J., and M. Fay, eds. 2019. *Beyond the Gap: How Countries Can Afford the Infrastructure They Need While Protecting the Planet.* Washington, DC: World Bank.

World Bank. 2019. *Guidance on PPP Contractual Provisions.* Washington, DC: World Bank.

Yehoue, E. B. 2013. "Financial and Sovereign Debt Crises and PPP Market Structure." In *The Routledge Companion to Public-Private Partnerships*, edited by Piet de Vries and Etienne B. Yehoue, 349–70. Oxon, United Kingdom: Routledge.

State-Owned Banks versus Private Banks in South Asia: Agency Tensions, Susceptibility to Distress, and the Fiscal and Economic Costs of Distress

2

The pros and cons of state banking are vigorously debated. State-owned commercial banks (SOCBs) can be established to help create markets and fulfill social goals and support fiscal policy (by raising additional revenues for public investment), but the operation of SOCBs has downsides because of possible inefficiencies, misuse, and financial distress. The upsides and downsides of SOCBs are increasingly being scrutinized by policy makers and the global community.

This chapter contributes to the debate by examining episodes of distress at SOCBs and private banks, the drivers of distress, bank adjustments in times of distress, and the costs of bank distress to the real economy in Bangladesh, India, Pakistan, and Sri Lanka. Distinguishing banks by ownership type is important because state commercial banking is prevalent in these countries, and in South Asia overall. The analysis identifies episodes of bank distress, explores several adjustment channels through which banks cope with distress, and examines the relative intensity with which state-owned and private banks in distress use these channels. The study examines how firms' links with SOCBs versus private banks affect their investment—focusing on small and medium enterprises (SMEs) and successful firms with high growth of sales.

South Asian economies rely on their banking system to help allocate resources for greater productivity and employment as well as financial inclusion for greater access to opportunities. These functions cannot be performed effectively when banks are distressed. Therefore, understanding the drivers of distress is important for devising and implementing effective policy remedies for SOCBs. The chapter therefore concludes with recommendations to strengthen SOCBs and the financial sector for the benefit of economies and societies overall.

The Upsides and Downsides of State-Owned Commercial Banks

By 2017, three countries stood out in the world because of the dominance of SOCBs in

Note: This chapter draws on the background research paper: Kibuuka, K., and M. Melecky. 2020. "State-Owned versus Private Banks in South Asia: Agency Tensions, Distress Factors, and Real Costs of Distress." Background paper for *Hidden Debt*. World Bank. Washington, DC.

their banking systems: Belarus, Iceland, and India. In each country, SOCBs held close to 70 percent of total banking system assets (Cull, Martinez Peria, and Verrier 2017).[1] Across South Asia, SOCBs hold a very high share of total banking system assets—about 40 percent, on average. However, the use of SOCBs is not confined to developing economies. In Germany, for instance, the share also hovers above 40 percent.

On the upside, using commercial and hybrid SOCBs can reflect state efforts to address market failures and create positive externalities (Atkinson and Stiglitz 1980; Stiglitz 1993; Cull, Martinez Peria, and Verrier 2017).[2] Specifically, the state could use the SOCBs to (1) promote competition, extend the reach of service delivery, and spur new markets in the financial sector (Cull, Martinez Peria, and Verrier 2017; Ferrari, Mare, and Skamnelos 2017; Mazzucato and Penna 2016); (2) help resolve coordination failures (de la Torre, Gozzi, and Schmukler 2007); and (3) play countercyclical and safe-haven roles in crises after markets have failed to internalize individual contributions to systemic risk (Micco and Panizza 2006; Bertay, Demirgüç-Kunt, and Huizinga 2015; Duprey 2015). The state may use SOCBs to create positive externalities by (1) financing projects with high nonmonetary social returns that have negative net present value (that is, their internal rate of return does not cross the private sector hurdle rate for investable projects) (Levy-Yeyati, Micco, and Panizza 2007), and (2) promoting strategically important industries, jumpstarting economic development, helping create new markets and national champions, and providing a source of revenue for social investments (Gerschenkron 1962; Ferrari, Mare, and Skamnelos 2017). For a global overview of development, hybrid, and commercial state-owned banks with an explicit social mandate and at least 30 percent ownership stake by the state, see de Luna-Martinez and Vicente (2012).

On the downside, using SOCBs involves risks of inefficiency and misallocation costs due to agency problems and political misuse (Cull, Martinez Peria, and Verrier 2017). The agency problem relates to the conflict of interest that bureaucrats/technocrats can have when tasked with managing government-owned banks. The conflict is between the government's interest in maximizing social welfare and the bureaucrats' or technocrats' interest in extracting benefits. This conflict gives rise to red tape, operational inefficiencies, and misallocation of resources (Banerjee 1997; Hart, Shleifer, and Vishny 1997). Politicians can misuse SOCBs to pursue their own interests, such as reelection and personal profit, by pushing to finance their supporters or those willing to pay the highest bribes. This misuse induces resource misallocation and economic inefficiency (Shleifer and Vishny 1994; Shleifer 1998). Politicians are more likely to favor government bank ownership when public accountability and judicial independence are low because they can extract more benefits with fewer personal consequences, Perotti and Vorage (2010) suggest.

The upsides and downsides of using SOCBs create tensions in practice. For instance, when SOCBs allocate credit inefficiently, their countercyclical role can be uncertain (Bertay, Demirgüç-Kunt, and Huizinga 2015; Coleman and Feler 2015). To address such tensions, several studies have reviewed and proposed some good practices to improve SOCB operations (Gutierrez et al. 2011; de la Torre, Gozzi, and Schmukler 2007).[3]

> Understanding the drivers of distress is important for devising and implementing effective policy remedies for state-owned commercial banks.

Data suggest that, in practice, SOCBs rarely have explicitly defined roles in terms of addressing market failures or creating positive externalities—at least in Europe and Central Asia (Ferrari, Mare, and Skamnelos 2017). If SOCBs have some social mandate, it may change over time: for instance, when the underlying market failure has been overcome or when policy makers reweigh competing social priorities. Unlike government-owned development financial institutions (DFIs),

SOCBs most often operate without an explicit social mandate—including in several South Asian countries such as India and Bangladesh. Thus, economists increasingly worry about the downside of SOCB operations. However, relatively little research has explored the downside behavior of SOCBs in distress and the costs of distress for central government and the economy. This chapter helps fill this gap.

Using bank-level and firm-level data for India and bank-level data for Bangladesh, Pakistan, and Sri Lanka, this chapter identifies episodes of distress at banks using a rule-of-thumb threshold for the interest rate coverage ratio (ICR), which indicates whether a bank has enough revenues to cover its interest expense. As a robustness check, the analysis also includes three additional indicators of financial performance and soundness. Highlighting the role of bank ownership, this examination takes into consideration the factors behind bank distress and bank adjustments in distress as well as the wider economic impact of ownership on investment in client firms. The latter analysis relies on bank–firm matched data from the Prowess database for India for the period 2009–18.

The methodology is described in annex 2A. Annex 2B presents regression results for the probability of distress for banks and their adjustments to distress.

The Omnipresence of State-Owned Commercial Banks in South Asia

The South Asia region has the highest share of SOCB assets in terms of total banking assets in the world, followed by the Europe and Central Asia region (see figure 2.1).[4] In South Asia, the share of SOCB assets is particularly high in India, Bhutan, and Sri Lanka when compared with the regional average. Despite a fair share of SOCB assets, Bangladesh and Pakistan fall below the regional average—but still above the average for the lower-middle-income country group.

In general in South Asia, SOCBs appear to be performing poorly when compared with privately owned commercial banks (PCBs) (figure 2.2). PCBs are better capitalized than SOCBs within the same country. The same goes for asset quality, profitability, and efficiency measures (figure 2.2). Across countries, Pakistan's SOCBs are, on average, performing better than SOCBs in Bangladesh

FIGURE 2.1   South Asia: Share of State-Owned Commercial Bank Assets in Total Banking Assets, 2016

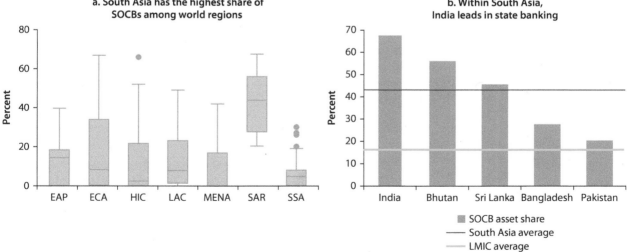

Source: World Bank Survey on Banking Supervision.
Note: EAP = East Asia and Pacific; ECA = Europe and Central Asia; HIC = high-income countries; LAC = Latin America and the Caribbean; LMIC = lower-middle-income countries; MENA = Middle East and North Africa; SAR = South Asia; SSA = Sub-Saharan Africa; SOCBs = state-owned commercial banks.

FIGURE 2.2 **Bangladesh, India, and Pakistan: State-Owned Commercial Banks' Underperformance Relative to Domestic and Foreign Private Banks, 2009–18 Average**

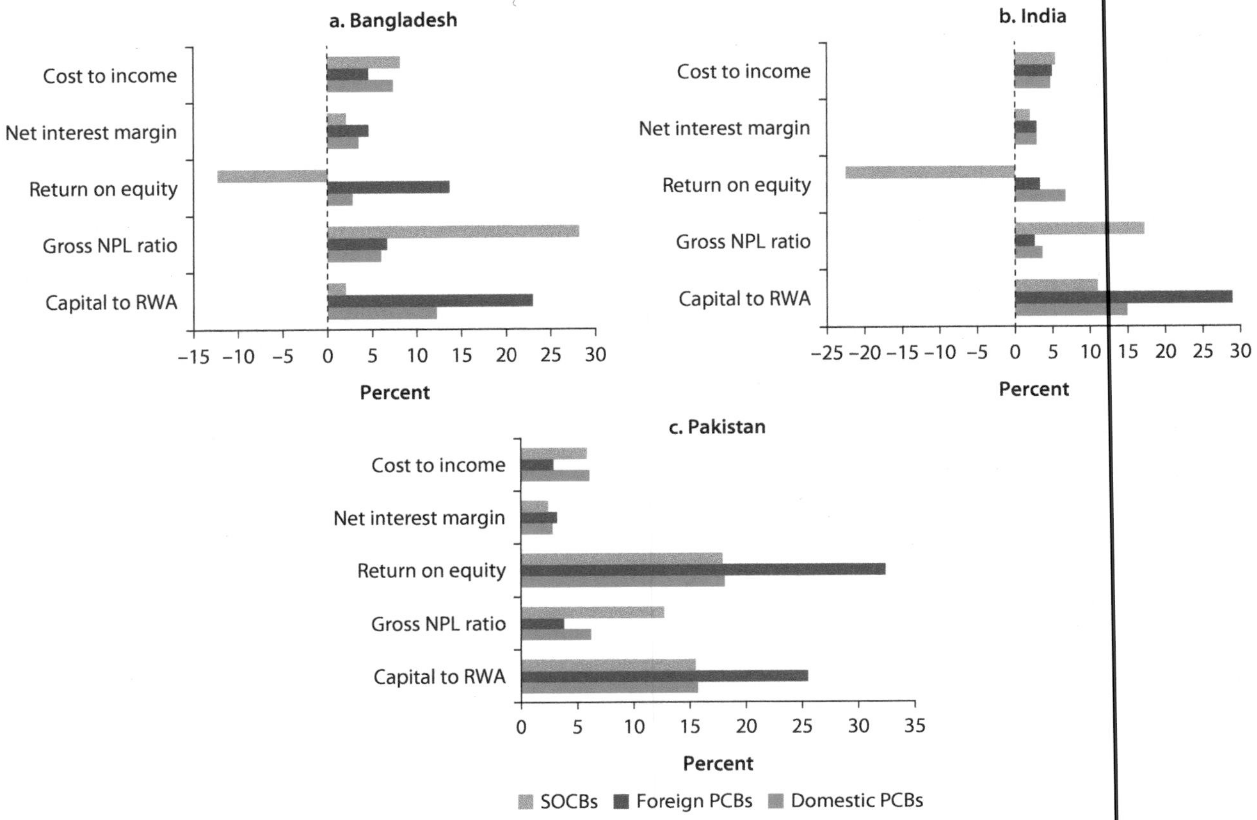

a. Bangladesh

b. India

c. Pakistan

■ SOCBs ■ Foreign PCBs ■ Domestic PCBs

Source: World Bank staff calculations using Fitch Connect data.
Note: Cost to income rescaled by dividing by 10. NPLs = nonperforming loans; PCBs = privately owned commercial banks; RWA = risk-weighted assets; SOCBs = state-owned commercial banks.

and India. The average capital adequacy ratio is well above the 10 percent national prudential threshold. Even though elevated at 12 percent, Pakistan's average nonperforming loan (NPL) ratio is the lowest compared with Bangladesh and India. SOCBs in Pakistan are, on average, the only profitable SOCBs in the comparison group. They have the lowest cost-to-income ratios, which are on par with more operationally efficient PCBs in South Asia.

Meanwhile, SOCBs in Bangladesh appear to have the weakest performance indicators: capital ratios below the 10 percent national prudential threshold and the Basel minimum; the highest NPL ratios (28 percent) among the South Asian peer group; the highest cost-to-income ratios and, as a result,

negative profitability. The performance of India's SOCBs is mixed: capital adequacy ratios are well above the 9 percent national prudential minimum and the Basel minimum, but NPL ratios hover at a worrying 17 percent. Despite the lowest cost-to-income ratio, profitability is strongly negative—particularly the return to equity.[5]

Bank Business Models by Ownership Type: The Example of India

As shown in the previous section, bank performance and operations vary greatly by type of ownership. To explore this further, this section focuses on India because more detailed bank data are readily available for it, and bank characteristics can be linked to firm-level investment data—a real outcome variable of interest for this chapter.

The banking system assets of India's scheduled commercial banks (SCBs) amounted to about 80 percent of GDP in 2018.[6] SOCBs (called public sector banks, PSBs, in India) dominate the banking sector in terms of assets, credit, and branches. PSBs hold 66 percent of total SCB assets, while domestically owned private banks (PVTBs) have about 28 percent; foreign commercial banks (FBs) hold about 6 percent; and small finance banks (SFBs) control a minimal 0.3 percent.[7] In terms of credit, PSBs control about 63 percent of total banking credit, PVTBs control about 29 percent, and other SCBs represent about 8 percent of total banking credit. By the end of 2018, PSBs operated 92,362 branches across India, three times more than the domestic and foreign private banks combined. The largest commercial bank by far is the State Bank of India (SBI), which controls 23 percent of total banking assets and 20 percent of total banking credit, and operates the largest branch network, with more than 23,382 branches and a dominant rural presence (figure 2.3).

Given their large branch network, PSBs can mobilize large amounts of retail deposits, which comprise the largest component of PSB funding (figure 2.4). Loan-to-deposit ratios are higher in other banks compared with PSBs, further reflecting their ability to mobilize greater amounts of deposits. Other banks must rely more on costlier modes of raising funds. For instance, SFBs rely largely on lines of credit to fund their lending activities (figure 2.4). Unlike other PSBs, SBI, as India's largest bank and a government corporation statutory body, can readily raise funds outside of India by borrowing from international global markets. Thus, total SBI borrowings (10 percent of total liabilities) are higher than the borrowings of other PSBs (7 percent of total liabilities). Meanwhile, leverage, as measured by the tier 1 capital-to-total-assets ratio, is above the prudential minimum of 4 percent for systemically important banks and 3.5 percent for other banks—stricter limits than the Basel minimum of 3 percent. Leverage is less than 6 percent for PSBs (at 5.6 percent for SBI and 5.1 for other PSBs) and above 10 percent for other banks, indicating that PSBs are more leveraged than other banks.

As noted, SOCBs do not tend to have explicit mandates to address market failures

FIGURE 2.3   India: Branch Networks and Total Credit, 2018

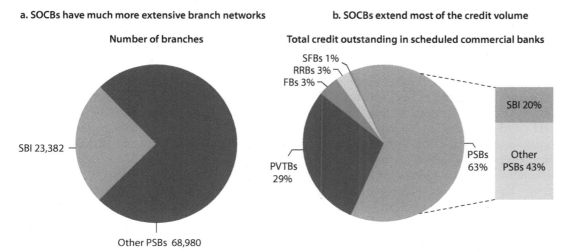

a. SOCBs have much more extensive branch networks

Number of branches

SBI 23,382

Other PSBs 68,980

b. SOCBs extend most of the credit volume

Total credit outstanding in scheduled commercial banks

SFBs 1%
RRBs 3%
FBs 3%
PVTBs 29%
PSBs 63%
SBI 20%
Other PSBs 43%

Source: Reserve Bank of India.
Note: FBs = foreign commercial banks; PSBs = public sector banks; PVTBs = domestically owned private banks; RRBs = regional rural banks; SBI = State Bank of India; SFBs = small finance banks; SOCBs = state-owned commercial banks.

or create positive externalities. Data on the sectoral allocation of credit and lending to typically underserved segments (such as small borrowers) and priority sectors (as identified by the Reserve Bank of India, RBI) show that PSBs do not focus on lending to these groups or sectors more than private banks.[8] In fact, most PSB credit goes to large borrowers and to the industry sector, a nonpriority sector. However, given their size, PSBs provide the largest absolute volume of lending to small borrowers. PSBs tend to lend much more to public sector entities compared with other banks, even though this lending comprises less than 10 percent of total loans (figure 2.4). Smaller banks—namely, SFBs and regional rural banks (RRBs)—do target priority sectors and small borrowers. More than 40 percent of their total credit is devoted to these segments.

Overall, banks earn most of their income from their lending activities. Foreign commercial banks tend to earn more through investments, as well as from fee-based and foreign exchange services. PSB business models tend to be more traditional, focusing on earning income through government securities and similar investments (30 percent of total income) and lending (more than 50 percent of total income). Unlike most PSBs, SBI earns almost 10 percent of its income from fee-based services—compared with an average of 3 percent earned by other PSBs. Because of its cheap source of borrowing, SBI has a higher net interest margin (2.4 percent) than other PSBs (2.0 percent). By contrast, net interest margin indicators for all other banks exceed 2.5 percent (reaching 6.7 percent for SFBs). Other efficiency indicators show that PSBs tend to be less efficient, devoting a higher share of their wage bill to intermediation costs (figure 2.4). This could imply overcompensation of the management or overemployment. The literature suggests the latter (Kumbhakar and Sarkar 2003).

In recent years, declining profitability has resulted in negative returns on capital and assets. Although some PSBs still have positive profit indicators—return on assets (ROA) and return on equity (ROE)—the general trend has been declining profitability. This is partially explained by lower levels of efficiency and rising costs and expenses (including staff costs and expenses), as well as rising nonperforming loans (figure 2.4).

In 2015, following the RBI's accelerated efforts to ensure that losses expected from distressed debt were adequately recognized and provisioned, an asset quality review was conducted. It revealed a higher level of NPLs than previously reported across the banking sector—most notably at the SOCBs. Many of these NPLs were attributed to infrastructure projects that had turned sour and accrued during a period when PSBs benefitted from regulatory forbearance. During 2019, NPLs remain the highest in PSBs in the Indian banking system—at about 10 percent in SBI and more than 17 percent in other PSBs—while the ratio is on average less than 4 percent for other banks. Since the discovery of high levels of NPLs, many banks have worked hard to write off and resolve outstanding problem assets. However, legal delays, inadequate infrastructure, and a large pipeline of insolvency cases have stretched out and will continue to lengthen resolution timelines. In response to these legal bottlenecks, the government in July 2019 increased the resolution time frame to 330 days, from the previously stipulated 270 days.

In addition to declining asset quality, capital positions have been weak within PSBs and have affected their lending capacity (figure 2.5). Even before the NPL finding, capital buffers were low, and the government developed a public-private recapitalization response—the Indradhanush plan—announced in August 2015. Given the limited private participation in this plan, government ownership in PSBs has increased because of the state capital injections to prop up these banks. However, following the NPL discovery, PSBs' capital positions deteriorated again as provisioning increased substantially with the need to adequately cover higher NPLs. Making matters worse, the introduction of Basel III starting in 2019 and the subsequent phase-in of implementation has led to higher prudential capital requirements. For the 2020

FIGURE 2.4   India: Selected Funding and Credit Indicators, 2018

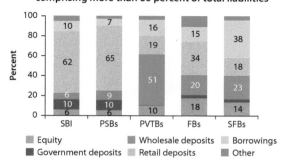

a. PSBs are mostly funded by retail deposits, comprising more than 60 percent of total liabilities

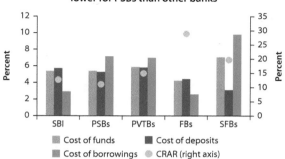

b. The cost of funding is generally lower for PSBs than other banks

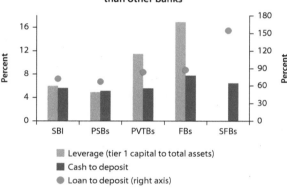

c. PSBs have lower leverage and funding ratios than other banks

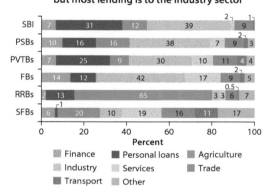

d. PSBs do not appear to have a sectoral mandate, but most lending is to the industry sector

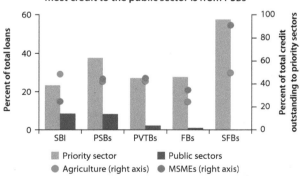

e. PSBs mostly lend to the nonpriority sector, but most credit to the public sector is from PSBs

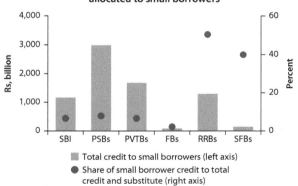

f. Less than 10 percent of total PSB credit is allocated to small borrowers

Source: Reserve Bank of India.
Note: CRAR = capital to risk-weighted assets ratio; FBs = foreign commercial banks; MSMEs = micro, small, and medium enterprises; PSBs = public sector banks; PVTBs = domestically owned private banks; RRBs = regional rural banks; Rs = Indian rupees; SBI = State Bank of India; SFBs = small finance banks.

FIGURE 2.5   India: Selected Business Model, Performance, and Soundness Indicators, 2018

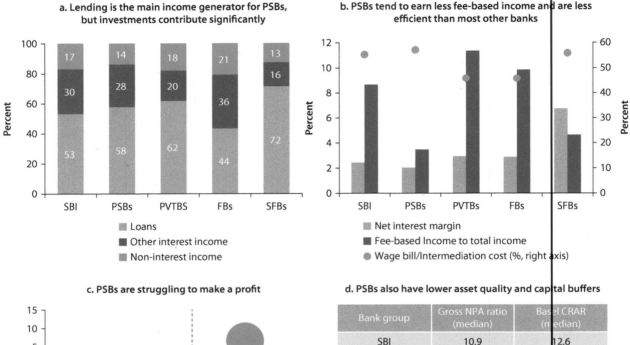

a. Lending is the main income generator for PSBs, but investments contribute significantly

b. PSBs tend to earn less fee-based income and are less efficient than most other banks

c. PSBs are struggling to make a profit

d. PSBs also have lower asset quality and capital buffers

Bank group	Gross NPA ratio (median)	Basel CRAR (median)
SBI	10.9	12.6
PSBs	17.2	11.0
PVTBs	3.6	14.9
FBs	2.6	28.9
SFBs	2.4	19.7

Source: Reserve Bank of India.
Note: CRAR = capital to risk-weighted assets ratio; FBs = foreign commercial banks; NPA = nonperforming assets; PSBs = public sector banks; PVTBs = domestically owned private banks; SBI = State Bank of India; SFBs = small finance banks.

financial year, the government budgeted for US$10 billion in PSB capital injections.

Data for Analysis of SOCBs in India and Other South Asian Countries

For further in-depth bank-level analysis in relation to firms, we used an Indian firm-level database called Prowess, which is managed by the Center for Monitoring the Indian Economy. The database consists of data reported by firms registered with the Registrar General of Companies. It is an unbalanced panel that covers the 1989 to 2018 period and contains detailed annual financial statement data as well as performance information on firms in India—both financial and nonfinancial. In addition, specifically for banks, Prowess provides an expanded set of financial soundness indicators. Prowess covers about

80 percent to 90 percent of SCBs in India, which account for most banking sector assets.

Using Prowess data, we constructed a balanced, bank-level panel including key financial soundness indicators and bank characteristics. As many of the key variables, particularly financial soundness indicators, were missing prior to 2009, the data set covers the 2009–18 period. For each year, there are 74 banks. However, not all banks have data for each of the key variables.[9] Table 2C.3, in annex 2C, presents the summary statistics of key variables in this data set for PSBs (panel a) and PVTBs (panel b).

For other South Asian countries, a detailed database that enables linking banks and firms is not readily available, to our knowledge. Therefore, we used the Fitch Connect database to analyze banks in the four biggest economies of South Asia: Bangladesh, India, Pakistan, and Sri Lanka. Together, they account for more than 90 percent of South Asia's GDP. We constructed a panel data set for each country covering the 2009–18 period and most banks in the system. The panel data set includes nearly 300 panel data

observations on SOCBs and nearly 700 observations on private banks. In the regression analyses, about 204 observations are used for Bangladesh, 243 for India, 153 for Pakistan, and 86 for Sri Lanka. In pooled regressions, about 686 were used for the four countries together. Figure 2.6 shows the pooled statistics for banks of South Asia's four main economies. It summarizes and contrasts the different business models and strategies of SOCB versus PCBs, using the mean across banks for the 2009–18 period divided by standard deviation. Detailed summary statistics and tests of differences between SOCB and PCB characteristics are reported pooled and by country in annex 2C.

The data suggest that private banks take more risks in lending than SOCBs: their ratio of risk-weighted assets to total assets is greater than those of SOCBs. Perhaps also for this reason, they keep greater liquidity buffers as self-insurance against greater risk. Private banks lend more from the deposits that they mobilize and employ nondeposit funding—including foreign savings. The greater interest margins and profitability of private

FIGURE 2.6 **South Asia's Four Main Economies: Business Models and Strategies of State-Owned Commercial Banks versus Privately Owned Commercial Banks, 2009–18**

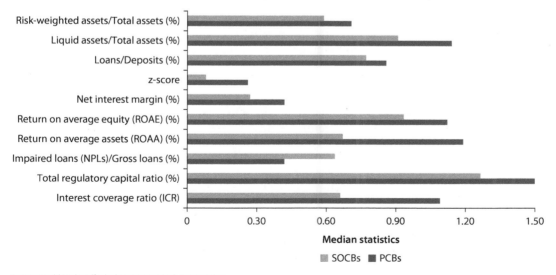

Sources: World Bank staff calculations using Fitch Connect data.
Note: Pooled data set for Bangladesh, India, Pakistan, and Sri Lanka. NPLs = nonperforming loans; PCBs = privately owned commercial banks; SOCBs = state-owned commercial banks.

banks may reflect returns commensurate with their greater risk taking, as well as their greater capacity to manage credit risk (lower median NPL ratios). Finally, the solvency standing (regulatory capital ratio) and two broader measures of distress based on balance sheet solvency (z-score) and cash flows (ICR) suggest greater resilience of private banks to risk.

Nevertheless, caution is warranted in interpreting aggregate median numbers for the region. The situation can vary considerably across countries and within countries across individual banks. For instance, risk taking is lower than the regional median for SOCBs in Pakistan and even more so for SOCBs in Sri Lanka, with median ratios of risk-weighted assets to total assets of 51 percent and 47 percent, respectively, compared with the regional median of 59 percent for SOCBs and 70 percent for private banks. In contrast, SOCBs in Bangladesh are the least profitable of the SOCBs in the region, based on the median statistics for the return on equity—3.6 percent for Bangladesh compared with 9.3 percent for the regional average (median). Indian SOCBs appear to sit comfortably around the median for the region on all considered SOCB characteristics except the ICR. Indian SOCBs, with a median ICR of 0.57, fall well below the regional median of 0.66. In none of the four major South Asian countries does the median ICR for SOCBs stand above 1. At the 75th percentile, the better performing SOCBs have ICRs well above 1 in Bangladesh, Pakistan, and Sri Lanka. However, India's better performing SOCBs still fail to cross the threshold—possibly indicating systemic distress in the sector from 2009 to 2018.

Recent literature argues that bank distress can arise because the firms and households that banks serve are in distress. For instance, uncertainty about economic policy can boost the default risk of both firms and households, which is then transmitted to banks (Ashraf and Shen 2019; Gopalakrishnan and Mohapatra 2019). The literature also highlights the possibility that government-owned banks may engage in adverse

selection of borrowers ("reverse cherry-picking"). For example, firms that maintain exclusive relationships with government-owned banks can enjoy privileged borrowing status with those banks: that is, the firms' sensitivity of investment to cash flows (their financing constraints) is lower. But such firms can be in worse financial condition relative to other firms—for instance, be more leveraged, invest less, be less profitable, and have worse growth prospects (Srinivasan and Thampy 2017). Such adverse selection of borrowers can increase the default risk of government-owned banks because they lend to weaker firms on average.

For this reason, we also controlled for characteristics of client firms by linking banks to firms. For each bank, we constructed a client firm portfolio and calculated average characteristics of this portfolio, such as average firm size (total assets); leverage (debt-to-equity ratio); investment orientation (investments to assets); and profitability (return on assets). Because of data availability constraints, we controlled for client firm characteristics only for Indian banks. The main characteristics of the client firms of PVTBs and SOCBs are summarized in figure 2.7. Detailed summary statistics, along with statistical tests of difference in average characteristics, are reported in table 2C.6, in annex 2C. The statistics suggest that client firms of SOCBs could be much less profitable, more leveraged, and perhaps bigger—reflecting the findings of the recent literature. However, these median characteristics of banks' client firms mask significant variations. Therefore, the statistical test of difference between client firm characteristics of SOCBs and private banks shows that only leverage differs. That is, client firms of SOCBs are significantly more leveraged.

Understanding Bank Distress and Its Main Factors

Conceptually, our econometric framework builds on the value at risk (VaR) methodology. It examines two types of losses. The first is the *financial loss* that could be passed on

FIGURE 2.7   **India: Characteristics of the Average Client Firms of Scheduled Commercial Banks, 2009–18**

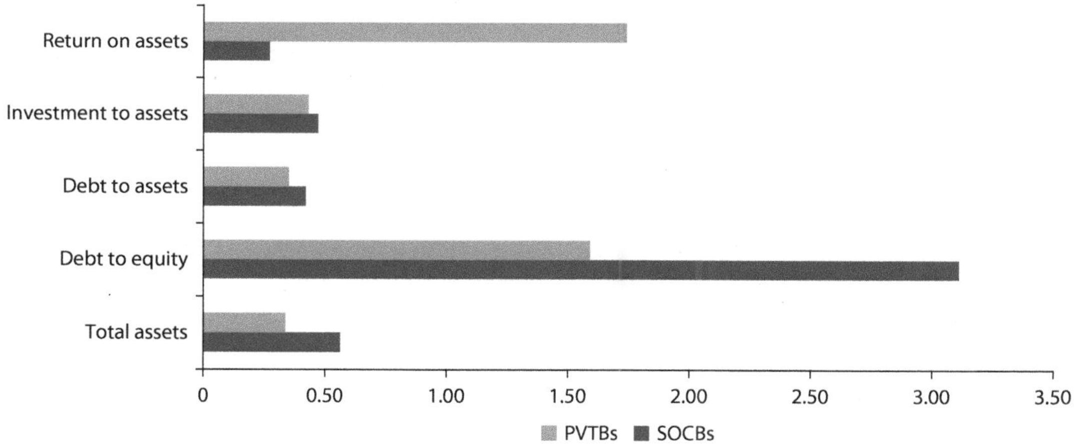

Sources: World Bank staff calculations using Prowess data.
Note: All numbers are in percent except for total assets, which are in Rs, 100 billion. PVTBs = domestically owned private banks; SOCBs = state-owned commercial banks.

to the central government in part or entirely, depending on the budget constraints SOCBs face—that is, softer versus harder budget constraints. Gauging this loss involves estimating the probability of SOCB distress (PD) and financial loss given SOCB distress (loss given distress, LGD). The second type is the *economic loss* from SOCB distress due to forced adjustments by distressed SOCBs, such as in the form of changes in capital, debt, lending, or investments, which in turn can affect firms, consumers, and the government. Here, the focus is on the loss of private firms' investment due to the frequent distress of SOCBs: that is, unrealized investments compared with the counterfactual of private firms being able to make investments through financing from banks not in distress regardless of whether those banks are private or state owned.

Identifying Distress Using Financial Soundness Indicators

We define a *distress event* as the breach of a threshold. In principle, the threshold could be determined by an economic relationship or a practical rule of thumb. The threshold value together with an actual value of an indicator variable then help identify a distress event.

A bank is considered to be in distress when it does not have enough revenues to cover its interest due: that is, when its ICR drops below 1. As robustness checks, we used three other indicators: ROA dropping below zero percent; the bank capital to risk-weighted assets ratio (CRAR) measured against a threshold related to the amount of capital above the minimum prudential requirement that banks want to keep;[10] and the bank's z-score, a popular solvency indicator in the literature (Laeven and Levine 2009; Ashraf and Shen 2019). The average annual probability of distress for a given group of banks—such as private banks or SOCBs—could be estimated as the average probability of distress using historical data on identified distress events (see equation (2A.1), in annex 2A, for details).

For the big picture of the analyzed data, figure 2.8 plots the ICRs for banks in India (panel a) using Prowess data—disaggregating new and old private banks—and in Bangladesh, Pakistan, and Sri Lanka (panels b, c, and d) using Fitch Connect data.[11]

One can observe that in India, the ICR of new private banks is comfortably above 1 most of the time for most of the individual banks—even though some outliers fall below 1. The situation is progressively worse

FIGURE 2.8   **India, Bangladesh, Pakistan, and Sri Lanka: Interest Coverage Ratio by Bank Type, 2009–18**

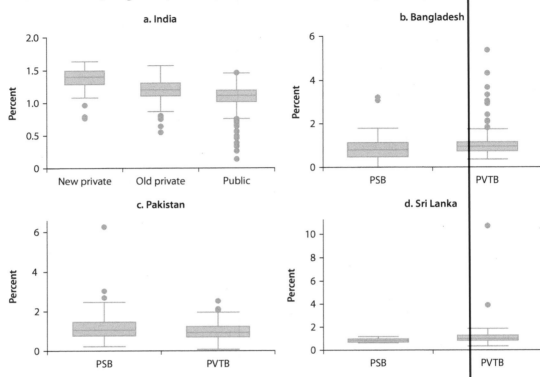

Sources: For panel a, World Bank staff calculations using Prowess data; for panels b, c, and d, World Bank calculations using Fitch Connect data.
Note: There are 400 observations for India, 237 for Bangladesh, 141 for Pakistan, and 98 for Sri Lanka. In panel a, New private bank, Old private bank, and Public are defined as in Mishra, Prabhala, and Rajan (2019). PSBs = public sector banks; PVTBs = domestically owned private banks.

for old private banks and the SOCBs (or public banks). Not only do outliers occur more frequently, skewing the distribution more toward zero, but the 25th percentile of the distribution (the lower T arm of the candle graph) reaches way below 1—showing that these distress events repeat frequently.

In Bangladesh, Pakistan, and Sri Lanka, private banks do not differ significantly from the SOCBs, and their situation could be equally concerning. Figure 2.8 shows that half the time, half the banks—regardless of whether private or public—would be considered in a state of distress: that is, have an ICR below 1. Given how much these economies rely on their banking system to help with resource allocation for greater productivity and jobs, as well as financial inclusion for greater access to opportunities, it is unlikely that these functions can be performed effectively by banks in distress. Understanding

the drivers of distress is important for developing and implementing effective remedies.

Examining the Distress Factors

To assess the difference in the probability of distress between private banks and SOCBs and whether certain bank characteristics could drive bank vulnerability to distress, we ran a logit regression of the probability of distress on bank characteristics including size, age, and ownership type. We also included characteristics indicating the bank funding and business model (such as the loan-to-deposit ratio, net foreign exchange exposure, and ratio of risk-weighted assets to total assets) and macrofinancial shocks (commodity price shocks, portfolio capital flows). Equation (2A.2), in annex 2A, provides mode details of this regression estimation.

In running the logit regression, we were most interested in uncovering whether SOCBs are on average more prone to distress than privately owned banks—controlling for factors such as size, funding models, and average bank specific effects. The nondistressed private banks serve as the control group in this difference-in-difference estimation. In addition, we singled out foreign banks and old private banks; the latter are thought to be the closest control group for SOCBs because they existed during the nationalization period (from 1969 to 1980) when majority state ownership was established in the existing SOCBs (Mishra, Prabhala, and Rajan 2019).

Broader public governance issues could drive the inherent weaknesses in PSBs. However, in a vicious cycle, weak banks with poor governance structures that have suffered reoccurring episodes of distress have been the main recipients of government capital injections—which have in turn increased the share of government ownership. In addition, once these banks receive additional capital, they are expected to increase lending mainly to support priority sectors or government programs that are not always viable, which further increases their risk of distress. Therefore, the results could simply reflect the recurring higher probability of weak banks being regularly in distress, of receiving recurring government support, of increasing their directed lending, and of lacking decisive intervention to resolve their underlying problems. *If additional capital injections are not coupled with meaningful reforms, then these SOCBs may continue to exhibit recurring or even intensifying distresses.*

This government bailout dynamic introduces a possible selection bias that can result in overestimates of the coefficient on the SOCB/PSB dummy. To address this issue, we simply retained the classification of PSBs, old and new PVTBs, and foreign banks used at the beginning of the sample and kept it fixed. Future research could allow for the ownership type to change over time and adjust for the described issue using selection bias correction (or an instrumental variable approach).

Overall Results, with a Focus on India

Our baseline logit regression focused on the likelihood of bank distress and in particular on distress of SOCBs compared with other types of banks (table 2B.1, in annex 2B). The results suggest that, on average, SOCBs in India (PSBs) are significantly more likely to experience distress compared with PVTBs.

Interestingly, the result is not driven by SBI because this bank is not significantly more or less prone to distress, as shown in column 2 of table 2B.1. New private banks and foreign banks are not significantly different from old private banks—although the lower probability of distress for foreign banks could be borderline significant. Given that SBI is the largest bank in India, its failure or perception of its failing would significantly shake confidence in the system. As such, this bank is very likely to receive rapid state attention in the event of any signs of distress. Indeed, a high propensity for extraordinary state support underpins this bank's credit rating by Fitch, among others.[12] The coefficient on the SBI dummy is positive, suggesting that, on average, SBI could be more prone to distress compared with old PVTBs; however, the result is not statistically significant. This finding is likely driven by the overall weakening of financial soundness indicators, particularly in recent years, with the nonperforming assets ratio breaching the 10 percent threshold and the ROA turning negative in 2018. Importantly, the likelihood of distress increases with the share of government ownership, as shown in table 2B.1, column 3.[13] We estimated that SOCBs with a government share of at least 50 percent but less than 70 percent could be less prone to distress than SOCBs in which government has more than 70 percent share of ownership.

These findings suggest that SOCBs could be more fragile by design (Calomiris and Haber 2014). That is, the overall governance surrounding SOCBs potentially exposes them to more or greater shocks, such as from directed lending, directed support of government programs, political interference in management, forced overemployment, or unqualified employment (Cole 2009; Ashraf, Arshad, and Yan 2018; Richmond et al. 2019).[14]

The estimations also indicate that smaller banks are relatively more prone to distress than their larger counterparts. This is not surprising given the characteristics and more concentrated business models of smaller banks. Notably, smaller banks rely more on borrowings to fund their activities; can be more exposed to riskier segments of the market (such as priority sectors and small borrowers); and have limited diversification to help pool shocks. SOCBs are larger, on average, and can therefore manage concentrated risk better.

The results further suggest that banks with a greater loan-to-deposit ratio are more prone to distress. The ratio could also be a proxy for the bank's funding structure and risk: that is, how much of its loan book is funded by own deposits relative to other sources of funding. Higher loan-to-deposit ratios can thus indicate less diverse sources of funding, which can increase the likelihood of distress. In particular, banks with loan-to-deposit ratios above 100 percent are more exposed to liquidity shocks—for instance, because of their borrowing exposures to the money market and private market credit lines. This finding dovetails with that of the International Monetary Fund's *Global Financial Stability Report* (IMF 2013) that higher loan-to-deposit ratios (greater reliance on wholesale funding) are, across the board, linked to higher levels of distress in banks in advanced and emerging economies. The result with respect to loan-to-deposit ratios is relatively more important for private sector banks because SOCBs in India have a loan-to-deposit ratio significantly below 100 percent, on average. In India, the correct interpretation could involve lower capacity to intermediate deposits. That is, banks that are not able to intermediate the volume of deposits they mobilize are less efficient and more vulnerable to distress.

The age of a bank and its foreign currency exposure do not appear to significantly affect the likelihood of distress. The estimated negative coefficient on foreign currency exposure may coincide with the low levels of foreign currency lending within the domestic banking system and firm access to foreign currency via other forms of financing, such as international capital markets. Therefore, a bank that has access to sizeable foreign currency liabilities would need to be sound and capable of competing with international financiers.

Although SOCBs are significantly different from private banks in terms of several bank characteristics, as shown in table 2B.3, in annex 2B, inclusion of these characteristics does not diminish the significance of the SOCB dummy in explaining greater probability of distress at SOCBs. However, inclusion of one characteristic does remove that significance: the nonperforming loan ratio. This finding suggests that credit risk management and culture are key to the more frequent distress at SOCBs. It coincides with the finding of Mishra, Prabhala, and Rajan (2019), who studied the pace of adoption of credit scoring technology and found that while new private banks adopt scoring quickly for all borrowers, SOCBs (PSBs) adopt scoring quickly for new borrowers but not for existing borrowers. They conjecture that organizational culture, possibly from formative experiences in sheltered markets, explains the patterns of adoption of credit scoring technology. In addition, our finding does not rule out broader governance issues and political economy influence in forming the structures and decisions underpinning credit risk management in SOCBs.

Our results are robust to using the bank z-score as the measure of distance to distress and rerunning the regression with ordinary least squares (OLS; see table 2B.2). Here, the significant effect of the degree of government shareholding survives the inclusion of the NPL ratio in the regression. In addition, the SBI effect becomes significant and survives the inclusion of the NPL ratio in the regression. This additional finding keeps open the question of the effect of broader governance issues beyond credit risk management. These issues could include problems with staffing and career management of executives, soft budget constraints, cronyism, and political links.

Broadening the Analysis to Include
Bangladesh, Pakistan, and Sri Lanka

We now broaden the analysis to cover the main economies of South Asia, in addition to India—Bangladesh, Pakistan, and Sri Lanka—although we have less data available. To analyze the distress at SOCBs relative to private banks in these countries, we ran similar logit regressions using the distress events identified by ICR falling below 1 as the dependent variables. Here, we could only control for bank characteristics because the Fitch Connect database does not allow the mapping of banks to their clients (as the Prowess data set does for India). Also, some of the bank characteristics that we control for could be slightly different. Table 2B.3, in annex 2B, reports the estimation results for each country (columns 1–4) and for all countries pooled (South Asia regional estimation) (column 5).

On the pooled basis that could be representative of the South Asia region, the probability of distress is higher for SOCBs than private banks—even if controlling for several bank characteristics on which SOCBs differ from private banks (see panel c of table 2C.1, in annex 2C). However, this pooled estimation masks some country differences. In Sri Lanka, the probability of SOCB distress is higher than that of private banks and significant—as in India. By contrast, such a high probability cannot be confirmed in Bangladesh and Pakistan, where state ownership does not seem to play a role in explaining the probability of distress. This result could be due to several controls that pick up main differences between SOCBs and private banks in terms of bank characteristics, or it could simply be that SOCBs in Bangladesh and Pakistan are less different from private banks. (Compare the absolute value of the *t* statistic for the differences between SOCBs and private banks in panel c of tables 2C.2, 2C.3, and 2C.4. They are much higher for India than for Bangladesh and Pakistan.) Still, at least for India and Sri Lanka, the issues with broader governance and political economy seem valid.

From the estimates on the control variables, we observe that bank size continues to diminish the probability of distress across the region. Here, apart from greater business diversification, we can also conjecture that more intensive supervision of larger and systematically important banks helps diminish the probability of distress at larger banks. The earlier observation for India that banks that can intermediate less of the volume of mobilized deposits are more vulnerable to distress is also valid for Bangladesh and Pakistan. It is not valid, however, for Sri Lanka, where the median loan-to-deposit ratio is about 100 percent—significantly higher than in the other three countries—and whose coefficient is estimated to be positive and borderline significant. With at least 50 percent of banks in the Sri Lankan system running loan-to-deposit ratios above 100 percent, the indicator plays a more traditional role. It reflects the exposure to liquidity risk. The higher the exposure, the greater the probability of distress (that is, of ICR falling below 1). The ratio of liquid assets to total assets has a similar interpretation for all countries: greater liquidity buffers lower the probability of distress. Greater risk taking—reflected in a higher ratio of risk-weighted assets to total assets—is a sign of resilience among South Asian banks ("Pooled" column, table 2B.3) perhaps indicating relatively lower lending to SOEs, especially those in Bangladesh and to some extent India. Risk taking does not seem to be a trait of resilient banks in Sri Lanka, however.

Understanding How Banks Adjust in Distress

Next, we examine the adjustments that banks make in episodes of distress to shed light on the possible fiscal and economic losses that arise as distressed banks—particularly SOCBs—adjust their capital, lending, debt, and investment. That is, assuming that some budgetary constraint exists for banks, and perhaps softer constraints for SOCBs, we assess how SOCBs adjust relative to private banks. We define the loss given distress (LGD) as the monetary loss due to all forced adjustments that the PSB in distress must perform to survive, restructure, or close. The LGD for

SOCBs is estimated relative to the control group of similar private banks for our difference-in-differences estimation.

The LGD can be estimated based on the monetary value of all the adjustments that happen when a distress occurs. For SOCBs, we focus on the following five categories of adjustments:

1. Percent change in capital
2. Percent change in provisioning
3. Percent change in debt
4. Percent change in lending
5. Percent change in fixed assets (including sale of fixed assets).

To estimate the adjustment size for each of these five categories for distressed SOCBs relative to private banks, we regress each variable in categories 1–5 on the distress dummy, the interaction of the distress dummy with the SOCB dummy, and control variables—including bank and time fixed effects (see appendix 3A for a detailed description of the estimation methodology).

Overall Results, with a Focus on India

Our estimation results, summarized in figure 2.9, suggest that compared with distressed PVTBs (the control group), distressed SOCBs tend to adjust to distress by increasing capital relatively more than distressed PVTBs (see tables 2B.4 and 2B.5, in annex 2B, for detailed results). This finding could reflect the government's efforts to promptly recapitalize at least systemically important public banks—most notably, India's SBI. It can also reflect the softer budget constraints that SOCBs as a group enjoy compared with private banks. These softer budget constraints can then increase moral hazard among SOCBs and distort their incentives to properly manage credit and other risk taking, as well as act in a timely manner to restore their performance when it declines.

To a lesser extent, during the initial year of distress, SOCBs tend to increase fixed assets (invest)—or at least do not drop their plans to accumulate fixed assets. This result could be linked to the government capital injections that often come with the conditionality to continue supporting priority lending sectors and government programs and stimulate economic growth. If SOCBs are unable to stimulate growth through lending—for instance, because breaching prudential requirements can trigger regulations that prohibit increasing the lending portfolio—the SOCBs can use their investments to help stimulate growth and meet government conditions of recapitalization.

FIGURE 2.9   Differences in How State-Owned Commercial Banks and Domestically Owned Private Banks Adjust in Times of Distress

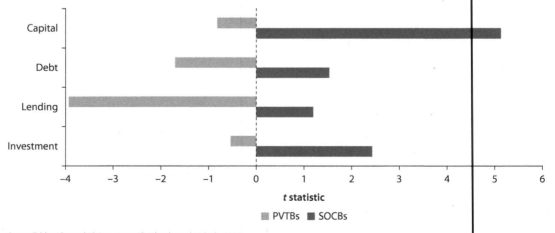

Source: Tables 2B.4 and 2B.5, in annex 2B; Kibuuka and Melecky 2020.
Note: The bars depict the *t* statistics of the estimated adjustment coefficients. PVTBs = domestically owned private banks; SOCBs = state-owned commercial banks.

Moreover, our estimation results show that distressed PVTBs tend to reduce lending significantly in the initial year of distress. Compared with distressed PVTBs, distressed SOCBs do not decrease their lending significantly in the initial year of distress. PVTBs do not appear to use other adjustment channels significantly. It may be more difficult and expensive for them to raise additional equity or borrow in times of distress; the estimation results for debt somewhat support this conjecture. Namely, PVTBs can somewhat reduce their debt financing during periods of distress compared with SOCBs, whose borrowing can be relatively less affected or even increase in periods of distress relative to PVTBs. Note, however, the possible offsetting results for distressed SOCBs' debt across the contemporaneous and lagged PSB dummy (table 2B.4, panel b, column 2). With the disciplining pressure of difficult access to additional debt in times of distress in mind, PVTBs could be keeping larger buffers to draw on and serve as a cushion during episodes of distress—which could mitigate the likelihood of distress in the first place. (For instance, the capital adequacy ratio and net interest margins of PVTBs are higher than those of SOCBs; see table 2C.1, in annex 2C.) Also for this reason, PVTBs' preferred adjustment channel can be to reduce lending to clients—both by a prior strategic choice and necessity in times of distress.

Our estimation results are robust to alternative threshold measures of distress (table 2B.5): namely, the ROA turning negative and the CRAR falling below 11 percent.[15] During the initial year of distress, distressed SOCBs tend to increase capital when the ICR falls below 1, or profitability turns negative, or when the ROA turns negative. When CRAR falls below 11 percent, distressed SOCBs may also increase total capital, but this estimation result is not statistically significant. This may be the case because when CRAR levels reach around 11 percent, they still exceed prudential requirements of 9 percent; thus, SOCBs may opt to adjust in other ways than increasing capital.

Distressed private banks tend to increase provisions during the initial year of distress as well as the subsequent period as profitability turns negative. In contrast, distressed SOCBs do not seem to significantly increase these buffers during similar distress events because they appear to rely on capital infusions to address these issues. This difference in adjustment channels in the face of similar distress events could reflect the difference in governance in these banks—private banks rely on their own resources, while SOCBs rely on government resources to address the distress issue. The robustness checks broadly concur with the baseline results—although they are not as statistically significant (CRAR) or their timing is slightly different (ROA).

Regarding debt dynamics, distressed PVTBs reduce their debt borrowing in times of distress, while distressed SOCBs enjoy softer borrowing conditions than distressed PVTBs. The difference between SOCBs' and PVTBs' debt borrowings in times of distress could also relate to the prevailing type of debt instruments the banks use. SOCBs tend to borrow from public institutions and agencies such as the RBI, while PVTBs tend to access and are more exposed to foreign capital markets and their stricter covenants, and thus discipline.

Other significant results indicate that private banks reduce lending during the initial year of distress when their CRAR falls below 11 percent. Because these banks tend to maintain higher CRARs, they may prioritize building capital buffers over increasing lending when these ratios fall below 11 percent. In addition, because their income sources are more diversified relative to SOCBs, private banks can reduce lending without significantly affecting their income.

We now turn to fixed assets and investment dynamics during times of distress. Perhaps because PVTBs find it difficult to adjust investment plans in the near term, distressed PVTBs with a CRAR below 11 percent or negative profitability (ROA) tend to reduce investment in fixed assets only in the year following distress—compared with distressed SOCBs, which can sustain investment. The differences in adjustment by PVTBs and SOCBs when faced with a CRAR below 11 percent or negative profitability (ROA) further illustrate PVTBs' focus on self-reliance compared with

SOCBs, which enjoy softer budget constraints and backing by government capital to support their operations and survival. *The self-reliance of private banks versus potential moral hazard of SOCBs can severely undermine market discipline and the efficient functioning of financial markets.*

In sum, sound SOCBs may help sustain lending to firms throughout the cycle and in the face of financial shocks. However, weaker SOCBs could fall into distress more often than private banks and reduce lending in times of distress compared with sound SOCBs. However, if private banks get into distress—including because of common macro shocks—they reduce lending much more than distressed SOCBs and even more so than sound SOCBs. Significantly reducing lending is the adjustment private banks select in times of their less frequent distress. SOCBs have softer budget constraints regarding both equity injections and additional debt borrowings. Compared with private banks, the softer budget constraint and conditions of government recapitalization (to help stimulate growth) could encourage SOCBs to sustain their investments (fixed asset accumulation) even when distressed. However, the soft budget constraints inflict substantial fiscal costs and erode discipline and competition in the financial market.

Broadening the Analysis to Include Bangladesh, Pakistan, and Sri Lanka

Can the adjustment patterns estimated for Indian banks be generalized to the three other main South Asian economies? To address this question, we ran the same estimations on a pool of data obtained from Fitch Connect for Bangladesh, India, Pakistan, and Sri Lanka. The timing of the data and the estimation variables were adjusted to better correspond with the fiscal year timing of the Prowess database for India. The estimation results are reported in table 2B.6, in annex 2B.

Our estimation results show that entering a period of distress, the capitalization of both SOCBs and private banks is declining. Unlike the Prowess data estimate, the Fitch Connect data estimates suggest that both private banks

and SOCBs get recapitalized. The results by country reveal that the private bank recapitalization happens in Bangladesh, India, and Sri Lanka, but less so in Pakistan. SOCBs are also promptly recapitalized, most significantly in Bangladesh, less so in Pakistan, and least so in Sri Lanka. Although the recapitalization appears statistically more significant for private banks, it is almost three times larger for publics banks, on average. The same hypothesis and result for India of SOCBs having softer budget constraints than private banks are thus broadly confirmed for other main South Asian economies. Provisions are released by private banks after the distress event, while SOCBs do not release accumulated provisions—which could further confirm their greater reliance on new capital injections.

Lending by private banks declines significantly after the distress event, while SOCBs continue to increase lending. Again, the conditions of SOCB recapitalization may often require them to continue to stimulate the economy—and if not breaching prudential rules, increase their lending. This pattern is most significant in Bangladesh and less so in India and Pakistan. In Sri Lanka, SOCBs curtail lending after distress—even more so than private banks. This could relate back to low recapitalization of SOCBs in Sri Lanka and to their harder budget constraints relative to other SOCBs in the region. This result highlights the trade-off between increasing fiscal discipline through harder budget constraints and having SOCBs absorb risks and continue lending even when big shocks hit.

After episodes of distress, investments increase at SOCBs, while they decrease mildly at private banks. This finding could again reflect the conditions of recapitalization that require SOCBs to stimulate the economy. If such stimulation is not possible through increased lending because of prudential constraints, increasing fixed investments is another way to implement such stimulus. These results are consistent with the Prowess estimation for India. This pattern is also strongly evident in Bangladesh. By contrast, this investment stimulus of SOCBs in distress and after recapitalization is absent in Pakistan and Sri Lanka.

In Bangladesh, Pakistan, and Sri Lanka, debt financing of private banks is unaffected or decreases slightly right before and during episodes of distress. After the period of distress, SOCBs also appear to decrease debt financing. This finding contrasts with the estimates for India, which showed increasing debt financing of SOCBs in distress and confirmed the hypothesis of soft budget constraints. This disparity may in part arise because the Prowess and Fitch Connect data are not entirely compatible in their definition of categories and dating, as mentioned.

Analyzing the Effect of Firms' Banking with SOCBs Compared with Private Banks

SOCB distress can have vital economic impacts on firm financing and private investments. For instance, if SOCBs are more prone to distress than private banks, and in distress, predominantly adjust by reducing longer-term lending to SMEs, small private firms doing business primarily with SOCBs will suffer a greater loss of access to financing or unrealized investments over time. In contrast, if SOCBs are as equally prone to distress as private banks and, thanks to softer budget constraints, can issue debt or get equity injection and continue lending even in distress, private firms doing business primarily with SOCBs will experience a smaller loss of access to financing and unrealized investments over time. We try to shed some light on these matters next.

Estimating the Effect of Banking with SOCBs on Investment by Client Firms

As a first step in our analysis, we linked firms to banks in the Prowess data set. This linking of firms with banks is possible only for India. With these links established, we could merge our panel bank-level data set for India with the firm-level data set for India constructed in Melecky and Sharma (2020). As a result, we built a firm-level panel with key firm characteristics, such as total firm assets, firm age, and sector, as well as key indicators of banks, notably bank ownership type.

While our analysis relates banks to all firms, it focuses on successful firms with higher sales growth and SMEs to understand whether SOCBs can help reallocate capital to more productive firms and whether they can effectively work with more opaque SMEs as well as with large corporations. Namely, do successful firms with high sales growth get enough credit from both private and state banks to invest and realize their potential? Controlling for their size and age, do SMEs get adequate access to finance from both private and state banks to invest and grow? And do successful SMEs with growing sales get adequate lending support from SOCBs—compared with support from private banks—to grow and create productive jobs?

Our regression analysis controlled for firm-specific effects and common shocks using firm-level fixed effects and year dummies. It focused on one key outcome measure relating to firms: their ability to sustain investments, measured as (log-log) change in fixed assets. Because firms use multiple banks, we used two types of dummy variables in our estimations. The first dummy captured whether any of the banks to which the firm is linked is an SOCB (yes = 1, otherwise 0). The second dummy captured whether a majority of the linked banks are SOCBs (yes = 1, otherwise 0). We report the estimation results in table 2B.7 using the former type of classification (dummy variable) because the results from the two dummies are not materially different.

Our estimation results suggest that, on average, larger and older firms invest (grow their fixed assets) more than smaller or younger firms. Also, firms invest and then gradually deplete (depreciate) investments before investing again—hence, the negative correlation with the lagged investment value. Importantly, more successful firms with a higher growth of sales invest more. As for the links with SOCBs versus private banks, the story of firm investment needs to be unpacked in two stages.

First, firms that move from banking with a private bank to banking with a SOCB invest less on average—controlling for firm characteristics and past investments (table 2B.7, column 2). Even when switching to SOCBs, firms with higher growth of sales invest more than other firms that switch to SOCBs. However, firms with high growth of sales still invest less when switching to SOCBs rather than when banking with private banks.

Second, the big story emerges in the relation of SMEs to SOCBs. When we control for SMEs,[16] the results show a stark contrast between SMEs and larger firms. Namely, larger firms that switch to banking with SOCBs invest more on average; this suggests that the earlier negative estimate was driven by SMEs. Larger firms with higher growth of sales invest more than other larger firms that switch to SOCBs—even more so than average firms that switch to a private bank (0.0342 +

0.0124 = 0.0466). However, SMEs that switch to SOCBs invest significantly less than other firms (table 2B.7, column 4). The estimate is economically more significant than the effect of size, age, or sales growth. Moreover, successful SMEs with high sales growth are held back even more by switching to SOCBs in trying to realize their investment potential (see column 5 of table 2B.7, the triple interaction with PSB × Sales growth × SME). This could suggest that SOCBs are particularly challenged by screening SME creditworthiness and potential for investment. Future research could focus on whether this result could be due to SOCBs not lending enough to SMEs overall or the willingness of SOCBs to lend to SMEs only for working capital needs, on average. The result reflects the anecdotal evidence about SOCB lending practices and credit underwriting.

Anecdotal evidence suggests that SOCBs focus more on meeting the lending quotas for

---

BOX 2.1   Main Findings of the Overall Analysis

State-owned banks, smaller banks, and banks with a higher intermediation ratio of loans to deposits—but still less than 100 percent—are more prone to distress. The higher average vulnerability of state-owned commercial banks (SOCBs) to distress may increase with the share of state ownership, or at least it does in India.

SOCBs adjust in distress differently than private banks because of their soft budget constraints. Weaker SOCBs enter distress more often than private banks, and when distressed, they reduce lending more than healthy state banks. Although private banks enter distress less frequently, when they do, they reduce lending much more than state banks in distress—and therefore, much more than healthy SOCBs.

In terms of financing, SOCBs enjoy softer budget constraints, readily obtaining state equity and debt support. The softer budget constraints, as well as conditions of government recapitalization, enable SOCBs to sustain lending to clients and their own investments in times of distress.

However, the soft budget constraints impose substantial fiscal costs and erode market discipline. This raises the question of whether this costly insurance and risk-absorbing function of SOCBs pays off in terms of wider economic benefits, such as sustained firm investment.

The type of bank ownership (public versus private) affects the investment of client firms, with important effects on the economy. Namely, larger firms that switch to banking with SOCBs as opposed to banking mainly with private banks invest more than other firms. This is especially true for larger firms with a higher growth of sales. The opposite is true for SMEs. SMEs that switch to SOCBs invest significantly less than other firms—especially successful SMEs with high sales growth. This finding may be explained in part by the weak risk management culture at state commercial banks—including their low capability to appraise SMEs' creditworthiness and screen individual SME investment projects for viability (Mishra, Prabhala, and Rajan 2019).

the volume of extended credit than they focus on the quality of project screening and underwriting. These quotas are more easily met by serving larger firms—including state-owned enterprises implicitly backed by a government guarantee—than opaque and risker SMEs. While this anecdotal evidence may also apply to some private banks, private banks have stronger credit screening capabilities and can be more successful in reaching the higher return-risk frontier that crediting SMEs offers. SOCBs are simply not as good at managing risks—especially on the credit side (Mishra, Prabhala, and Rajan 2019).

Main findings for the overall analysis are summarized in box 2.1.

Policy Recommendations

SOCBs have a large footprint in South Asia, especially in India. Their unique ability to reach out and mobilize deposits is not matched by their ability to provide credit efficiently to the economy. However, state ownership in banks can help shield local populations and microenterprises from shocks by, for example, providing contingent credit after natural disasters such as droughts, floods, and hurricanes (World Bank 2020). Historically, this positive role of state ownership has come at the cost of more frequent distresses at weaker state-owned banks and substantial—and increasing—fiscal outlays

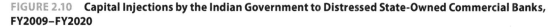

Proposed reforms call for better defining SOCB's social mandates, matching costly social mandates with earmarked subsidies, moving to harder budget constraints, and considering a role for wholesale funding in providing credit to the economy.

on bank recapitalization. Figure 2.10 shows how capital injections to distressed SOCBs have soared recently in India.

The effort to consolidate state-owned banking in India is a welcome step—especially for smaller state banks with weak governance and the ability to efficiently intermediate mobilized deposits. Yet, even with substantial consolidation, further reforms of SOCBs may be needed. One question is whether state-owned banks should remain retail lenders or whether they should intermediate the deposits they mobilize through wholesale funding of private banks, as well as adequately regulated and supervised nonbank credit institutions that could reach SMEs more efficiently and spur productive local investment.

Another question is how to define the missing mandates for the many SOCBs to correctly set incentives, increase transparency, and enhance financial accountability. One proposal is to divide state commercial banks into purely commercial state banks that maximize profit and SOCBs with a single or

FIGURE 2.10 **Capital Injections by the Indian Government to Distressed State-Owned Commercial Banks, FY2009–FY2020**

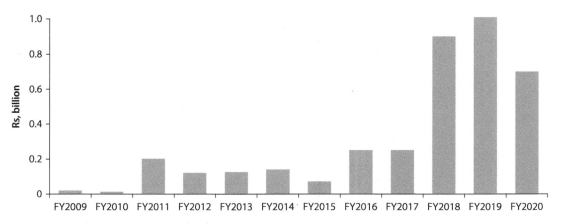

Source: Tables 2B.4 and 2B.5, in annex 2B; World Bank staff computations.
Note: The bars depict the *t* statistics of the estimated adjustment coefficients.

limited number of well-defined social objectives. On behalf of the central government, the state bank ownership unit should carefully monitor the performance of both types of banks through specific key performance indicators (KPIs), track closely the extra costs of fulfilling any social mandate, and enforce steps to strengthen transparency and accountability.

1. *Purely commercial state banks*. Like their private sector counterparts, purely commercial state banks would focus on profitability—perhaps with greater emphasis on sustainability and a longer profit-maximizing horizon.[17] The main mandate would be to raise revenue for government spending that could focus on socially beneficial areas, such as human capital development. The KPIs for these banks would be similar to those of private banks, but could cover and be monitored over longer horizons to ensure greater sustainability. These banks would have relatively hard budget constraints and be forced to adjust if they got into distress, as private banks do. Management of these banks, including the board of directors, would be accountable by losing autonomy quickly in the event of undue distress or mismanagement—first to the state agency in charge of state bank ownership and later to the agencies charged with temporary administration and resolution. Purely commercial state banks, as well as all other state-owned banks, must be properly supervised to ensure a level playing field with private banks—including the treatment of lending to nonbank financial institutions, both private and state-owned.

2. *SOCBs with a social mandate(s)*. These banks would have a broader mandate than raising state revenue/maximizing profit, such as advancing financial inclusion in rural areas. Accordingly, their incentive structure and management would differ. The KPIs would encompass a combination of profitability and impact measures—contributing to a long-term development objective of the government as featured in national financial development strategies. Time horizon(s) for performance/impact evaluation would correspond to these objectives and strategies. Over prespecified horizons, impact would be audited using a monitoring and evaluation framework established for this purpose.

This second type of state bank warrants some special considerations.

1. *Subsidies and Incentives*. The social mandate could impose higher-than-market *operational costs* (for example, to build new infrastructure to reach new customers in rural areas) and higher-than-market *expected losses* from loans (cost of credit) and other financial services (for example, due to lower financial literacy, capabilities, and greater riskiness of the newly reached customers). Therefore, the required subsidies (compensation) to cover the higher-than-market operational and credit costs would need to be explicitly and thoroughly assessed, estimated, and provided on an annual basis in the central government budget and included in the medium-term fiscal expenditure framework. The required level of subsidy would need to be monitored and adjusted once data on operational costs and *expected* losses from fulfilling the social mandate have regularly been collected and analyzed. Once the subsidies (regular fiscal provisions) for higher-than-market operational costs and credit costs are in place, state banks could operate under a relatively hard budget constraint.

2. *Governance and supervision*. Management of these banks, including the board of directors, would be accountable for sustainable financial performance and evaluated/audited impact by losing its autonomy in a prompt corrective action scheme involving replacement of directors and management by the government

agency performing the ownership function for state banks; temporary administration by the supervisor (such as the central bank) to financially stabilize troubled banks; or the unwinding and closure of the bank if its performance (on returns and impact) proves unsustainable. Again, such state-owned banks must be properly and independently supervised to ensure they remain sound and help create rather than distort the banking market.

3. *Accounting for unexpected losses.* If the social mandate involves taking idiosyncratic risks that could be well diversified, no policy treatment of unexpected losses would be required, in theory. However, higher-than-market *unexpected losses* (surprise variation of expected losses during some credit cycles/downturns) can arise because of bank social mandates. Unexpected losses at state-owned banks may occur only occasionally—in one or a few years during the credit cycle that can typically last five to seven years—and not necessarily during every credit cycle. These higher-than-market unexpected losses would require subsidies (fiscal reserves) if assessed to be systematically attributable to the bank's social mandate—as opposed to, for example, corruption, fraud, or faulty governance. The unexpected losses could be assessed as systematic if they stemmed from the inherently larger exposure to, for instance, concentration or foreign exchange risks that come with the social mandate. The larger-than-market exposures to these risks are triggered occasionally by economy-wide shocks—such as local currency depreciation or supply-chain disruption—outside of the bank's control.

More specifically, some SOCBs are mandated to go beyond exposures to systemic risk with which the market is comfortable because their activities involve some inherent concentration risk and higher unexpected losses. The latter can arise because of the banks' mandated focus on regions (such as focusing on extending credit to a few lagging regions); or an asset class (such as lending to opaque and risky micro, small, and medium enterprises [MSMEs] or promoting access to housing finance to the bottom 40 percent of the population); or an industry (such as cofinancing in infrastructure public-private partnerships [PPPs]) (see chapter 1). These banks would have to hold more and diverse assets to pool across several types of concentration risks and diversify them to the extent possible. However, some national residual concentration risk can remain. The government would have to reinsure the residual concentration risk using fiscal reserves and create fiscal space for contingent debt. To relieve the fiscal space of the reinsurance claims and costs, state commercial banks with plausibly higher-than-market unexpected losses could seek reinsurance individually or as a group in the international markets or with international financial institutions that can pool the residual national concentration risk and, to a large extent, diversify it away through global distribution.

For infrastructure financing, for example, more efficient financing models than SOCBs could exist. A major study by the Asian Development Bank, UK Department for International Development, Japan International Cooperation Agency, and World Bank (ADB, DFID, JICA, and World Bank 2018; see also spotlight ES.1) provides an extensive discussion of the financing options for infrastructure projects through public, corporate, and project finance (and their hybrids) depending on the project characteristics. Here, probably the most efficient option is project bond financing through local currency markets, with its ability to distribute the concentration and foreign currency risks of large commercially viable projects, as well as mobilize financing with long maturity. This option requires as one precondition the development of a deep and liquid government bond market in local currency—still something lacking in South Asia.

In contrast, for state commercial banks with social mandates such as financial inclusion of MSMEs, lagging regions, or vulnerable segments of the population, only limited alternative models could be available—including working with various (local) nonbank credit institutions and microfinance organizations to reach the underserved, as well as specialized private banks (such as banks focused on SMEs). But these alternatives are not likely to diversify the concentration and correlation risks very efficiently. The efforts to fulfill such social mandates require a multi-pronged approach through payments, deposits, credit, contingency credit (for instance, after disasters; World Bank 2020), and even insurance—but perhaps most importantly through trust, relationships, and local expertise to meet goals and set KPIs.[18] Delivering financial education locally together with financial services could be one way to build local trust, relationships, and expertise.

Special considerations for countercyclical lending. SOCBs are often praised for providing countercyclical lending, which can be a useful direct tool to support macrofinancial stabilization—especially in downturns. This objective of mitigating the downturns of credit cycles also requires state commercial banks to assume losses (expected and unexpected) higher than the market. Because state commercial banks are more likely to be distressed than private banks—and this likelihood increases with the share of state ownership—they will need to be recapitalized for lending in downturns when nonperforming loans for all banks rise systematically.

This recapitalization absorbs substantial fiscal resources (also captured in figure 2.10) that, in fiscally constrained countries, can crowd out other socially beneficial fiscal expenditures, such as on health care, education, or infrastructure—unless reserves are created beforehand. Because the recapitalization requirements could be large, the alternative social costs of using state-owned banks for macrofinancial stabilization could also be large. Moreover, because SOCBs tend to omit productive SMEs from their lending—and the omission is likely to be worse during downturns, when uncertainty increases—these alternative social costs are topped up with the cost of lost productivity growth in the medium to long term.

Management, performance, and fiscal backing. The KPIs for the management and board of banks with risk-absorbing mandates would have to create and manage the tension between taking enough risk and managing it sustainably from the perspectives of effective pooling, reinsurance, and fiscal contingent liabilities. In principle, the activities financed by these banks should generate enough revenue—through risk-adjusted returns and/or future tax returns—not to jeopardize fiscal sustainability. If the generation of such direct and indirect monetary returns is not possible but the banks can still generate meaningful socioeconomic (non-monetary) benefits in the medium to long term,[19] the central government may create reserves to cover the unexpected cost of this essentially "social assistance" and, for instance, made the fiscal council responsible for authorizing its release to banks. Similar arrangements can be applied to banks performing macrofinancial stabilization, a function that may not generate sufficient direct or indirect monetary returns but may trigger implicit contingent liabilities for the central government. The skill mix of the board of directors will need to reflect the tensions that must be professionally managed and the knowledge base, experience, and independence that such management requires.

In closing, SOCBs have a role to play in South Asian markets, but it is unclear whether the wider economic benefits can outweigh the large fiscal costs (often triggered in the form of fiscal contingent liabilities). The successes of SOCBs have included faster inclusion of the population in the use of digital payments and bank deposits, provision of fintech/bigtech platforms,[20] and bringing financial education to rural areas. The shortfalls involve costly recapitalizations because of weak governance, operational inefficiencies, credit misallocation, and lack of risk management that can trigger large contingent liabilities.

The macrofinancial benefits can involve some stabilization of the credit cycle through countercyclical lending. But this benefit comes at a large cost of greater capital misallocation to less productive firms and large fiscal costs of recapitalization that is needed to backstop lending in downturns and that can crowd out other important public expenditures, such as on health care and education. The proposed reforms are urgently needed for SOCBs in South Asia and beyond to clearly generate net socioeconomic benefits.

Annex 2A. Methodology for Determining Bank Distress

Identifying Distress Using Financial Soundness Indicators

We define a distress event as the breach of a quantitative threshold. In principle, the threshold could be determined by an economic relationship (identity), predicted/expected value, or even a practical rule of thumb. The threshold value $\bar{I}$, together with an actual value of an indicator I, then help determine distance to distress and generate a dummy variable, $D_{i,n,t}$, identifying observed distress.

We identify distress at Indian public sector banks (PSBs) using selected indicators of financial soundness. The main indicator of distress is if the interest coverage ratio (ICR) drops below 1. As robustness checks, we use the return on assets (ROA) dropping below zero; the bank capital adequacy ratio (CAR) against a threshold related to the minimum prudential requirement banks want to keep; and non-zero emergency liquidity assistance (ELA) provided by the central bank to a commercial bank. For ELA, we are missing data because it is difficult to distinguish between regular and emergency liquidity transactions as reported in the banks' public financial accounts.

The average annual probability of distress (PD) can be estimated as the average probability of distress using historical data on identified distress events:

$$PD_i = \frac{1}{T*N}\Sigma_{n=1}^N \Sigma_{t=1}^T D_{i,n,t} = \left\{1 \mid I_{i,n,t} \geq \bar{I}_i; 0\right\}, \quad (2A.1)$$

where $D_{i,n,t}$ is the distress 0/1 dummy variable and i = [private sector banks; public sector banks].

Examining the Distress Factors

To assess whether certain bank characteristics could drive bank vulnerability to distress, we run a logit regression for $D_{n,t}$ on bank characteristics (size; age; bank type, whether public sector or private); funding model of the bank (the loan-to-deposit ratio, net foreign exchange exposure); and macrofinancial shocks (commodity price shocks, portfolio capital flows). All are included in the vector of control variables, $X_{i,n,t}$, together with year fixed effects:

$$\frac{p(D_{i,n,t})}{1-p(D_{i,n,t})} = \alpha X_{i,n,t} + \varepsilon_{i,n,t}. \quad (2A.2)$$

We avoid including the indicators, $I_{n,t}$ or their transformations that are used to identify distress: that is, $D_{i,n,t}$. Including those would result in estimating a tautological relationship. By adding year fixed effects, we capture common time factors and any other relevant macroeconomic shocks. This approach also reduces the need to cluster errors.

By running the logit regression, we are most interested in uncovering whether state-owned commercial banks (SOCBs) are on average more prone to distress than privately owned banks—conditional on other factors, such as size, funding models, and governance indicators. Here, domestically owned private banks (PVTBs) serve as the control group.

Adjustments in Distress and Loss Given Distress

Let us define the loss given distress (LGD) as the monetary loss due to all forced adjustments that the PSB in distress must perform to survive, restructure, or close. Therefore, compared with the traditional expected loss formula, our LGD is equal to the loss given distress multiplied by the exposure in distress. The LGD is estimated relative to the control group of similar private banks.

The LGD can be estimated based on the monetary value of all the adjustments that happen when a distress event occurs ($D_{n,t} = 1$). For PSBs, we focus on the following adjustment, $ADJ|D_{n,t} = 1$, through five categories of adjustment j:

1. Percent change in capital
2. Percent change in provisioning
3. Percent change in debt
4. Percent change in lending
5. Percent change in fixed assets (including sale of fixed assets).

The LGD for an individual PSB can be estimated as follows:

$$LGD_{(i,n,t)} = \sum_{(j=1)}^{J} w_j ADJ_{i,j,n,t} \mid D_{i,n,t} = 1, \quad (2A.3)$$

where $ADJ_{i,j,n,t}$ is the monetary loss due to adjustment j of bank n of type i in distress at time t. Setting $w_j = 1$ assumes that all adjustments in distress are equally important.

To estimate the adjustment size for each category j for distressed SOCBs relative to private banks, we run the following regression:

$$ADJ_{j,n,t} = \theta^{PSB}[PSB_n * D_{n,t-l}] + \theta D_{n,t-l} + FE_n + CE_t + \epsilon_{n,t}, \quad (2A.4)$$

where θ^{PSB} is the parameter of interest. FE_n are bank fixed effects. CE_t are common time effects. We interact the distress dummy with the PSB dummy to estimate the difference in adjustment between distressed PSBs and PVTBs. The lag l takes values 0 and 1.

Estimating the Impact of SOCB Distress on Investments by Private Firms

Our outcome variables of interest are the economic impacts of SOCB distress on firm financing and private investment. The impact of SOCB distress can vary by the type of dominant adjustment that SOCBs undertake in distress—and the size of the adjustment.

We utilize a reduced-form framework for SOCB distress relative to private bank distress. We run the following regression:

$$FIN_{n,t} = \beta_i D_{i,n,t} + \gamma X_{n,t} + \epsilon_{n,t}, \quad (2A.5)$$

where $FIN_{n,t}$ is firm lending (log-log growth in debt) and investment (log-log growth in fixed assets), respectively; and X are controls, including sector, year, and firm fixed effects. β_i is our coefficient of interest, which is expected to be negative. That is, a firm linked to a bank that experiences distress will have greater problems in undertaking investment, other things remaining equal. If $|\beta_{SOCB}| > |\beta_{private}|$, distresses of SOCBs are more harmful than distresses of private banks. For instance, compared with private banks, SOCBs could be adjusting in times of distress mostly by reducing lending, while serving firms that do not have other banking options (links to private banks). If $|\beta_{SOB}| \cong |\beta_{Private}|$ and β is significantly negative overall, distresses of private and public banks are equally harmful. Note that here SOCBs could be still more problematic if they experience distress more frequently than private banks. If $|\beta_{SOB}| < |\beta_{Private}|$, distress of SOCBs could be less harmful: for example, because SOCBs can sustain lending and avoid closing branches even if in distress—including due to the soft budget constraints they could enjoy. Then, especially during systematic stresses—such as during economic recessions, near-financial crisis, or financial crisis episodes—SOCB presence in the banking system could support the resilience of lending through the cycle and private investments. But the cost of this resilient lending could be borne by higher taxes or more government debt.

The results of the regressions are presented in annexes 2B and 2C.

Annex 2B. Regression Tables: Probability of Distress for South Asian Banks and Adjustments to Distress, 2009–18

TABLE 2B.1 **Probability of Distress for Indian Banks: Baseline Regression Results, 2009–18**

	(1)	(2)	(3)	(4)	(5)	(6)
PSB – Dummy	0.111***	0.110***		0.00659	0.00645	
	(3.44)	(3.43)		(0.65)	(0.64)	
New PVTB – Dummy	−0.0481	−0.0521		−0.00990	−0.00954	
	(−0.99)	(−1.03)		(−0.89)	(−0.86)	
Foreign – Dummy	−0.0645	−0.0632		−0.0326	−0.0324	
	(−1.46)	(−1.42)		(−1.43)	(−1.42)	
SBI – Dummy		0.0762			0.0100	
		(1.29)			(0.72)	
Govt shareholding ≥50% and <70%			0.116***			0.0162
			(3.88)			(0.92)
Govt shareholding >70%			0.134***			0.0121
			(3.95)			(0.80)
Bank size (log total assets)	−0.0288**	−0.0275**	−0.0241***	−0.00982	−0.00984	−0.00924
	(−2.88)	(−2.63)	(−3.32)	(−1.40)	(−1.39)	(−1.45)
Age (years)	−0.000663	−0.000691	−0.000420	−0.000139	−0.000136	−0.0000945
	(−1.93)	(−1.94)	(−1.44)	(−1.01)	(−0.99)	(−0.72)
Loan to deposit ratio (log)	−0.125**	−0.126**	−0.133**	−0.00535	−0.00523	−0.00902
	(−2.77)	(−2.73)	(−2.80)	(−0.59)	(−0.58)	(−0.70)
FX liabilities to total liabilities (log)	0.00992	0.0101	0.00546	0.00481	0.00475	0.000718
	(1.54)	(1.57)	(0.81)	(1.37)	(1.36)	(0.32)
NPL ratio (log)				0.0256	0.0254	0.0368*
				(1.95)	(1.92)	(2.39)
Firm characteristics						
Average total assets (log)	−0.00139	−0.00270	−0.00683	0.00176	0.00184	−0.000503
	(−0.12)	(−0.23)	(−0.59)	(0.52)	(0.53)	(−0.13)
Average debt to equity (log)	−0.00719	−0.00715	−0.00107	−0.00385	−0.00376	−0.00289
	(−0.60)	(−0.59)	(−0.10)	(−0.97)	(−0.95)	(−0.70)
Average investment to assets (log)	0.0196	0.0183	0.0226	−0.0111	−0.0110	−0.00717
	(0.83)	(0.79)	(0.88)	(−1.05)	(−1.05)	(−0.64)
Average return on assets	0.00187	0.00184	0.00125	0.000704	0.000701	0.000435
	(1.59)	(1.58)	(1.39)	(1.32)	(1.32)	(1.19)
Observations	503	503	503	480	480	480
R-squared	0.349	0.349	0.335	0.601	0.601	0.570
Year time dummies	Yes	Yes	Yes	Yes	Yes	Yes

Source: Kibuuka and Melecky 2020.
Note: The estimations are performed on Prowess data. Bank ICR < 1; logit regressions with robust standard errors (marginal effects at the means). *t* statistics in parentheses. FX = foreign exchange; Govt = government; ICR = interest coverage ratio; NPL = nonperforming loans; PSB = public sector bank; PVTB = domestically owned private bank; SBI = State Bank of India.
* p < 0.05, ** p < 0.01, *** p < 0.001.

TABLE 2B.2   Probability of Distress for Indian Banks: Robustness Test Using z-Score, 2009–18

	(1)	(2)	(3)	(4)	(5)	(6)
PSB – Dummy	1.224**	0.729	1.236**	0.722		
	(2.89)	(1.48)	(2.90)	(1.47)		
New PVTB – Dummy	−1.651*	−1.645**	−1.512*	−1.417*		
	(−2.36)	(−2.65)	(−2.08)	(−2.16)		
Foreign – Dummy	−6.964***	−6.534***	−6.933***	−6.568***		
	(−8.45)	(−8.59)	(−8.40)	(−8.57)		
SBI – Dummy			2.442**	2.342**		
			(2.94)	(3.09)		
Govt shareholding ≥50% and <70%					2.636***	2.623***
					(5.44)	(4.92)
Govt shareholding >70%					2.009***	1.148*
					(4.93)	(2.07)
Bank size (log total assets)	0.170	0.0858	0.141	0.0122	0.865***	0.630***
	(1.00)	(0.55)	(0.79)	(0.07)	(5.07)	(4.46)
Age (years)	0.00583	−0.00171	0.00704	0.000101	0.0151*	−0.00181
	(0.79)	(−0.28)	(0.94)	(0.02)	(2.14)	(−0.29)
Loan to deposit ratio (log)	−1.290	−2.226	−1.281	−2.213	−1.869**	−3.526
	(−1.84)	(−1.30)	(−1.83)	(−1.29)	(−2.82)	(−1.84)
FX liabilities to total liabilities (log)	0.218	0.0940	0.206	0.0963	−0.731***	−0.737***
	(1.16)	(0.64)	(1.10)	(0.66)	(−5.25)	(−6.10)
NPL ratio (log)		0.878***		0.889***		0.860***
		(5.07)		(5.15)		(4.47)
Firm characteristics						
Average total assets (log)		0.672		0.741*		0.216
		(1.87)		(2.02)		(0.51)
Average debt to equity (log)		−0.476*		−0.457		0.0478
		(−2.01)		(−1.93)		(0.19)
Average investment to assets (log)		0.324		0.282		2.044*
		(0.39)		(0.34)		(2.02)
Average return on assets		−0.00195		−0.00233		−0.0135
		(−0.44)		(−0.52)		(−1.34)
Observations	538	468	538	468	538	468
R-squared	0.392	0.607	0.393	0.609	0.317	0.523
Year time dummies	Yes	Yes	Yes	Yes	Yes	Yes

Sources: Kibuuka and Melecky 2020; Fitch Connect database.
Note: t statistics in parentheses. FX = foreign exchange; Govt = government; NPL = nonperforming loans; PSB = public sector bank; PVTB = domestically owned private bank; SBI = State Bank of India.
* p < 0.05, ** p < 0.01, *** p < 0.00.

TABLE 2B.3 **Probability of Distress for South Asian Banks, 2009–18**

	(1) Bangladesh	(2) India	(3) Pakistan	(4) Sri Lanka	(5) Pooled
PSB – Dummy	0.104	0.428**	−0.0979	0.669	0.425***
	(0.48)	(3.14)	(−0.68)	(1.82)	(5.25)
Bank size (log total assets)	−0.0766	−0.0736**	−0.244***	0.337***	−0.0762***
	(−1.44)	(−2.60)	(−3.76)	(3.42)	(−3.35)
Loan to deposit ratio (log)	−1.390***	−0.225*	−0.209*	0.540	−0.371***
	(−4.09)	(−2.18)	(−2.04)	(1.44)	(−3.71)
NPL ratio (log)	0.0491	−0.0229	0.0930	0.421***	0.0766**
	(0.98)	(−1.01)	(1.54)	(3.44)	(2.64)
Liquid assets to total assets ratio (log)	−0.445***	−0.105**	−0.287**	−0.259	−0.278***
	(−3.85)	(−2.73)	(−3.19)	(−1.79)	(−6.49)
RWA to total assets (log)	−0.319	−0.0751	−0.0262	0.314	−0.331*
	(−1.71)	(−0.93)	(−0.10)	(0.62)	(−2.21)
Observations	204	243	153	86	686
R-squared	0.235	0.579	0.286	0.549	0.283
Year time dummies	Yes	Yes	Yes	Yes	No
Country time dummies	No	No	No	No	Yes

Sources: Kibuuka and Melecky 2020; Fitch Connect database.
Note: Bank ICR < 1; logit regressions with robust standard errors (marginal effects at the means). t statistics in parentheses. ICR = interest coverage ratio; NPL = nonperforming loans; PSB = public sector bank; RWA = risk-weighted assets.
* $p < 0.05$, ** $p < 0.01$, *** $p < 0.001$.

TABLE 2B.4 **Baseline Regressions: Adjustments Given Distress, 2009–18**

a. Adjustment to Capital, Provisions, and Lending during Bank Distress

	Total capital		Provisions		Lending	
	(1)	(2)	(1)	(2)	(1)	(2)
Distress: ICR < 1	−0.0210	−0.0290	−0.0486	−0.0783	−0.0661	−0.123***
	(−0.64)	(−0.82)	(−0.26)	(−0.40)	(−1.03)	(−3.93)
Distress: ICR < 1 – Lagged		0.0427		0.105		0.00796
		(0.72)		(0.53)		(0.21)
Distress × PSB	0.255***	0.251***	0.206	0.330	−0.0175	0.0446
	(4.77)	(5.13)	(0.90)	(1.40)	(−0.27)	(1.19)
Distress × PSB – Lagged		−0.00198		−0.443		−0.0345
		(−0.02)		(−1.95)		(−0.83)
Constant	0.0648*	0.0645*	−0.199	−0.199	0.197***	0.199***
	(2.36)	(2.36)	(−1.76)	(−1.78)	(6.91)	(7.11)
Observations	643	642	616	616	662	661
R-squared	0.0384	0.0394	0.0628	0.0647	0.133	0.138
Year time dummies	Yes	Yes	Yes	Yes	Yes	Yes
Bank fixed effects	Yes	Yes	Yes	Yes	Yes	Yes
Sample	All banks	All banks	All banks	All banks	All banks	All banks

(continues next page)

TABLE 2B.4 Baseline Regressions: Adjustments Given Distress, 2009–18 (continued)

b. Adjustment to Fixed Assets and Debt during Bank Distress

	Fixed assets		Debt	
	(1)	(2)	(1)	(2)
Distress: ICR < 1	−0.0236	−0.0215	−0.231	−0.247
	(−0.57)	(−0.54)	(−1.92)	(−1.70)
Distress: ICR < 1 – Lagged		−0.0435		0.0492
		(−1.14)		(0.24)
Distress × PSB	0.0929	0.119*	0.182	0.256
	(1.91)	(2.43)	(1.30)	(1.53)
Distress × PSB – Lagged		−0.0547		−0.255
		(−1.14)		(−1.11)
Constant	0.133***	0.135***	0.470***	0.470***
	(4.90)	(4.94)	(4.64)	(4.63)
Observations	662	661	604	604
R-squared	0.0204	0.0327	0.114	0.120
Year time dummies	Yes	Yes	Yes	Yes
Bank fixed effects	Yes	Yes	Yes	Yes
Sample	All banks	All banks	All banks	All banks

Source: Kibuuka and Melecky 2020.
Note: The estimations are performed on Prowess data. *t* statistics in parentheses. ICR = interest coverage ratio; PSB = public sector bank.
* p < 0.05, ** p < 0.01, *** p < 0.001.

TABLE 2B.5 Adjustments in Distress Compared with Private Banks Using Alternative Indicators of Distress, 2009–18

a. OLS Regressions with Robust Standard Errors

	Capital		Provisions		Debt	
	ROA < 0	CRAR < 11%	ROA < 0	CRAR < 11%	ROA < 0	CRAR < 11%
Distress	0.0233	−0.110	0.340*	−0.213	−0.159	−0.105
	(1.15)	(−1.34)	(2.31)	(−0.97)	(−0.86)	(−0.35)
Distress lagged	−0.00977	0.0465	−0.454*	0.0539	−0.315	0.0676
	(−0.55)	(1.30)	(−2.33)	(0.32)	(−1.65)	(0.18)
Distress × PSB	0.173***	0.111	−0.0693	0.149	0.117	0.144
	(4.94)	(1.05)	(−0.40)	(0.68)	(0.60)	(0.47)
Distress × PSB – Lagged	0.0387	−0.0674	0.0878	−0.0233	0.109	−0.110
	(0.47)	(−1.17)	(0.42)	(−0.12)	(0.50)	(−0.29)
Constant	0.0456	0.0644*	−0.184	0.0119	0.458***	0.359***
	(1.87)	(2.54)	(−1.92)	(0.19)	(4.74)	(3.76)
Observations	633	499	613	496	590	472
R-squared	0.0344	0.0293	0.0835	0.0396	0.121	0.134
Year time dummies	Yes	Yes	Yes	Yes	Yes	Yes
Bank fixed effects	Yes	Yes	Yes	Yes	Yes	Yes
Sample	All banks	All banks	All banks	All banks	All banks	All banks

(continues next page)

TABLE 2B.5   **Adjustments in Distress Compared with Private Banks Using Alternative Indicators of Distress, 2009–18** (continued)

b. OLS Regressions with Robust Standard Errors

	Lending		Fixed assets	
	ROA < 0	**CRAR < 11%**	**ROA < 0**	**CRAR < 11%**
Distress	0.117	−0.0924*	0.0499	−0.0354
	(0.51)	(−2.24)	(0.79)	(−0.93)
Distress lagged	−0.228	−0.0782	−0.0790*	−0.117*
	(−1.70)	(−1.17)	(−2.64)	(−2.50)
Distress × PSB	−0.142	0.0657	0.0271	0.106
	(−0.75)	(1.39)	(0.36)	(1.98)
Distress × PSB − Lagged	0.195	0.0540	0.0159	0.136*
	(1.23)	(0.78)	(0.41)	(2.06)
Constant	0.176***	0.190***	0.117***	0.0747***
	(6.43)	(5.09)	(4.66)	(5.05)
Observations	652	510	652	510
R-squared	0.0952	0.144	0.0487	0.0476
Year time dummies	Yes	Yes	Yes	Yes
Bank fixed effects	Yes	Yes	Yes	Yes
Sample	All banks	All banks	All banks	All banks

Source: Kibuuka and Melecky 2020.
Note: The estimations are performed on Prowess data. *t* statistics in parentheses. CRAR = capital to risk-weighted assets ratio; OLS = ordinary least squares; PSB = public sector bank; ROA = return on assets.
* p < 0.05, ** p < 0.01, *** p < 0.001.

TABLE 2B.6   **Bank Adjustments in Distress across Bangladesh, India, Pakistan, and Sri Lanka, 2009–18**

Dependent variable: Total capital	Capital	Provisions	Lending	Investment	Debt
Distress: ICR < 1	−0.0631	0.0466	0.0481	0.0437	−0.182
	(−1.78)	(0.62)	(1.15)	(1.07)	(−0.78)
Distress × PSB	−0.0147	0.0159	−0.0488	−0.0659	−0.272
	(−0.18)	(0.10)	(−0.92)	(−0.88)	(−0.37)
Distress: ICR < 1 − (*t*+1) Lag	0.0648*	−0.234*	−0.179	−0.0747	0.00983
	(2.32)	(−2.35)	(−1.93)	(−1.43)	(0.06)
Distress × PSB − (*t*+1) Lag	0.224	0.251	0.171	0.140*	−0.917
	(1.54)	(0.68)	(1.80)	(2.35)	(−1.54)
Observations	829	775	828	817	553
R-squared	0.331	0.430	0.535	0.371	0.349

Sources: Kibuuka and Melecky 2020; Fitch Connect database.
Note: Pooled estimation for Bangladesh, India, Pakistan, and Sri Lanka. *t* statistics in parentheses. Regression includes year dummies/country-year dummies and fixed effects. ICR = interest coverage ratio; PSB = public sector bank.
* p < 0.05, ** p < 0.01, *** p < 0.001.

TABLE 2B.7 **Effect of Borrowing from State-Owned Commercial Banks on Investment by Client Firms, 2009–18**

	(1)	(2)	(3)	(4)	(5)
Growth rate of gross fixed assets ($t-1$)	−0.190***	−0.191***	−0.191***	−0.199***	−0.201***
	(−18.41)	(−18.52)	(−18.51)	(−19.37)	(−19.57)
Firm size (log total assets)	0.114***	0.116***	0.116***	0.103***	0.103***
	(10.86)	(10.82)	(10.82)	(9.84)	(9.83)
Age (years)	0.218***	0.218***	0.216**	0.218***	0.221***
	(3.30)	(3.30)	(3.28)	(3.32)	(3.36)
Growth rate of sales	0.0355***	0.0358***	0.0275**	0.0259**	0.0260**
	(7.48)	(7.50)	(3.12)	(2.93)	(2.95)
PSB		−0.0272*	−0.0280*	0.0342*	0.0329*
		(−1.97)	(−2.04)	(2.32)	(2.24)
PSB × Sales growth			0.0110	0.0124	0.0346**
			(1.04)	(1.18)	(2.98)
PSB × SME				−0.210***	−0.207***
				(−10.33)	(−10.22)
PSB × Sales growth × SME					−0.0491***
					(−4.52)
Firm fixed effects	Yes	Yes	Yes	Yes	Yes
Sector-year fixed effects	Yes	Yes	Yes	Yes	Yes
Firm ownership	Private	Private	Private	Private	Private
Observations	26,488	26,142	26,142	26,142	26,142
R-squared	0.384	0.386	0.386	0.395	0.397

Source: Kibuuka and Melecky 2020.
Note: The estimations are performed on Prowess data. OLS regression with industry-time fixed effects and firm fixed effects. Standard errors clusters at the firm level, where PSB = 1 if at least one of the banks is a PSB, and 0 otherwise; SME = 1 if the firm is a SME based on India Chamber of Commerce definitions. *t* statistics in parentheses. OLS = ordinary least squares; PSB = public sector bank; SME = small and medium enterprise.
*p < 0.05, ** p < 0.01, *** p < 0.001.

Annex 2C. Regression Tables for South Asian Scheduled Commercial Banks: Country Results, 2009–18

TABLE 2C.1   Pooled Data Set for South Asia: Summary Statistics for Scheduled Commercial Banks, 2009–18

a. Public sector banks	Number of observations	Mean	Standard deviation	25th percentile	50th percentile	75th percentile
Interest coverage ratio (ICR)	291	1.06	1.59	0.50	0.66	0.87
Total regulatory capital ratio (%)	280	15.95	13.67	11.02	12.65	14.55
Impaired loans (NPLs)/Gross loans (%)	256	10.51	11.30	2.56	6.36	15.13
Return on average assets (ROAA) (%)	276	0.57	1.42	0.22	0.67	1.12
Return on average equity (ROAE) (%)	276	5.87	18.05	3.47	9.34	15.43
Net interest margin (%)	276	3.2	1.7	2.2	2.7	3.6
z-score	292	−16.08	17.52	−19.84	−7.98	−5.91
Loans/Deposits (%)	297	116.81	170.66	69.15	77.06	87.50
Liquid assets/Total assets (%)	297	12.24	11.77	5.86	9.09	14.76
Risk-weighted assets/Total assets (%)	243	56.21	18.72	47.80	58.86	64.33
Gross loans (US$, million)	297	24,911.45	47,320.07	1,640.85	10,127.01	27,884.60
Total assets (US$, million)	297	40,315.98	76,324.62	3,328.45	17,489.58	44,920.93

b. Private banks	Number of observations	Mean	Standard deviation	25th percentile	50th percentile	75th percentile
Interest coverage ratio (ICR)	690	5.27	43.08	0.78	1.09	1.89
Total regulatory capital ratio (%)	691	25.20	31.67	12.52	14.99	21.55
Impaired loans (NPLs)/Gross loans (%)	622	6.44	10.09	1.77	4.19	7.18
Return on average assets (ROAA) (%)	649	1.30	1.41	0.75	1.19	1.83
Return on average equity (ROAE) (%)	649	11.49	15.81	6.23	11.21	16.39
Net interest margin (%)	648	4.4	1.8	3.4	4.2	5.1
z-score	694	−41.91	70.70	−41.46	−26.11	−15.64
Loans/Deposits (%)	732	468.23	4,578.58	72.19	85.85	101.14
Liquid assets/Total assets (%)	741	16.21	15.58	6.85	11.40	18.88
Risk-weighted assets/Total assets (%)	591	69.79	19.62	56.60	70.71	81.92
Gross loans (US$, million)	734	2,949.55	8,488.22	269.28	1,170.45	2,270.54
Total assets (US$, million)	741	5,388.02	13,907.40	475.59	1,882.30	3,976.16

c. T-tests on means	Mean difference	t statistic
Interest coverage ratio (ICR)	4.207*	(2.56)
Total regulatory capital ratio (%)	9.242***	(6.35)
Impaired loans (NPLs)/Gross loans (%)	−4.069***	(−5.00)
Return on average assets (ROAA) (%)	0.724***	(7.10)
Return on average equity (ROAE) (%)	5.626***	(4.50)
Net interest margin (%)	1.159***	(9.26)
z-score	−25.83***	(−8.99)
Loans/Deposits (%)	351.4*	(2.07)
Liquid assets/Total assets (%)	3.972***	(4.46)
Risk-weighted assets/Total assets (%)	13.58***	(9.39)
Gross loans (US$, million)	−21,961.9***	(−7.95)
Total assets (US$, million)	−34,928.0***	(−7.83)

Source: Kibuuka and Melecky 2020.
Note: The estimations are performed on Prowess data. NPLs = nonperforming loans.
*p < 0.05, ** p < 0.01, *** p < 0.001.

TABLE 2C.2 **Bangladesh: Summary Statistics for Scheduled Commercial Banks, 2009–18**

a. Public sector banks	Number of observations	Mean	Standard deviation	25th percentile	50th percentile	75th percentile
Interest coverage ratio (ICR)	40	0.91	0.66	0.48	0.79	1.13
Total regulatory capital ratio (%)	35	9.03	12.39	7.27	10.10	10.63
Impaired loans (NPLs)/Gross loans (%)	41	27.30	14.67	16.73	24.94	35.09
Return on average assets (ROAA) (%)	38	−0.19	2.17	−0.38	0.29	1.10
Return on average equity (ROAE) (%)	38	−5.87	32.36	−9.81	3.63	9.54
Net interest margin (%)	38	2.4	1.3	1.6	2.4	3.3
z-score	40	−13.55	18.93	−15.95	−4.24	−3.10
Loans/Deposits (%)	44	70.16	23.33	60.67	65.26	76.26
Liquid assets/Total assets (%)	44	18.72	7.21	13.76	19.54	23.14
Risk-weighted assets/Total assets (%)	35	62.08	25.86	49.12	59.21	74.34
Gross loans (US$, million)	44	2,762.27	1,710.47	1,507.15	2,605.55	4,305.73
Total assets (US$, million)	44	5,484.82	3,905.07	2,140.28	4,616.16	8,236.91

b. Private banks	Number of observations	Mean	Standard deviation	25th percentile	50th percentile	75th percentile
Interest coverage ratio (ICR)	241	2.98	18.40	0.76	1.02	1.47
Total regulatory capital ratio (%)	233	21.85	26.02	11.42	12.71	18.59
Impaired loans (NPLs)/Gross loans (%)	234	6.20	11.08	2.51	4.30	5.73
Return on average assets (ROAA) (%)	227	1.44	1.54	0.79	1.10	1.81
Return on average equity (ROAE) (%)	227	15.22	20.75	8.53	11.63	16.45
Net interest margin (%)	227	4.5	1.9	3.5	4.3	5.2
z-score	245	−37.20	62.65	−37.61	−21.70	−15.54
Loans/Deposits (%)	262	261.88	874.96	79.37	86.55	98.98
Liquid assets/Total assets (%)	266	17.66	14.42	9.81	13.67	20.79
Risk-weighted assets/Total assets (%)	225	79.61	16.59	70.80	80.25	90.10
Gross loans (US$, million)	262	1,165.11	823.29	370.38	1,131.70	1,735.05
Total assets (US$, million)	266	1,684.12	1,168.89	512.35	1,664.22	2,589.33

c. T-tests on means	Mean difference	t statistic
Interest coverage ratio (ICR)	2.071	(1.74)
Total regulatory capital ratio (%)	12.82***	(4.75)
Impaired loans (NPLs)/Gross loans (%)	−21.10***	(−8.78)
Return on average assets (ROAA) (%)	1.632***	(4.44)
Return on average equity (ROAE) (%)	21.09***	(3.89)
Net interest margin (%)	2.044***	(8.24)
z-score	−23.65***	(−4.73)
Loans/Deposits (%)	191.7***	(3.54)
Liquid assets/Total assets (%)	−1.066	(−0.76)
Risk-weighted assets/Total assets (%)	17.53***	(3.89)
Gross loans (US$, million)	−1,597.2***	(−6.08)
Total assets (US$, million)	−3,800.7***	(−6.41)

Sources: Kibuuka and Melecky 2020; Fitch Connect database.
Note: NPLs = nonperforming loans.
*p < 0.05, ** p < 0.01, *** p < 0.001.

TABLE 2C.3   India: Summary Statistics for Scheduled Commercial Banks, 2009–18

a. Public sector banks	Number of observations	Mean	Standard deviation	25th percentile	50th percentile	75th percentile
Interest coverage ratio (ICR)	160	0.59	0.15	0.47	0.57	0.69
Total regulatory capital ratio (%)	159	12.14	1.36	11.08	12.23	13.08
Impaired loans (NPLs)/Gross loans (%)	159	6.43	5.94	2.21	4.10	9.65
Return on average assets (ROAA) (%)	159	0.33	0.85	0.16	0.54	0.87
Return on average equity (ROAE) (%)	159	5.82	15.05	3.17	9.41	15.55
Net interest margin (%)	159	2.5	0.5	2.2	2.5	2.8
z-score	160	−7.80	3.23	−8.29	−6.76	−5.80
Loans/Deposits (%)	160	78.24	8.31	73.06	77.63	83.04
Liquid assets/Total assets (%)	160	6.92	4.02	4.08	6.87	9.27
Risk-weighted assets/Total assets (%)	126	60.46	9.91	56.70	60.53	64.33
Gross loans (US$, million)	160	44,352.38	57,786.25	19,694.49	25,694.77	47,855.01
Total assets (US$, million)	160	71,209.07	93,511.33	31,785.23	42,153.50	75,204.03

b. Private banks	Number of observations	Mean	Standard deviation	25th percentile	50th percentile	75th percentile
Interest coverage ratio (ICR)	186	12.91	79.91	0.71	1.17	2.05
Total regulatory capital ratio (%)	181	31.95	49.19	13.71	15.38	19.09
Impaired loans (NPLs)/Gross loans (%)	163	4.36	11.23	0.98	1.80	4.62
Return on average assets (ROAA) (%)	176	1.12	1.09	0.70	1.24	1.74
Return on average equity (ROAE) (%)	176	8.23	9.34	3.58	9.61	14.16
Net interest margin (%)	175	4.0	1.5	3.0	3.8	4.8
z-score	186	−45.35	58.66	−45.04	−32.13	−17.85
Loans/Deposits (%)	185	1,325.66	9,009.76	71.39	84.67	102.42
Liquid assets/Total assets (%)	189	13.42	15.93	5.13	8.05	14.92
Risk-weighted assets/Total assets (%)	138	71.81	20.46	60.75	71.04	79.96
Gross loans (US$, million)	187	7,887.81	15,693.37	640.14	2,320.22	7,039.58
Total assets (US$, million)	189	14,164.31	25,061.59	1,166.56	4,663.29	19,520.47

c. T-tests on means	Mean difference	t statistic
Interest coverage ratio (ICR)	12.32*	(2.10)
Total regulatory capital ratio (%)	19.80***	(5.41)
Impaired loans (NPLs)/Gross loans (%)	−2.074*	(−2.08)
Return on average assets (ROAA) (%)	0.787***	(7.41)
Return on average equity (ROAE) (%)	2.412	(1.74)
Net interest margin (%)	1.493***	(12.10)
z-score	−37.56***	(−8.72)
Loans/Deposits (%)	1,247.4	(1.88)
Liquid assets/Total assets (%)	6.501***	(5.41)
Risk-weighted assets/Total assets (%)	11.36***	(5.81)
Gross loans (US$, million)	−36,464.6***	(−7.74)
Total assets (US$, million)	−57,044.8***	(−7.49)

Source: Kibuuka and Melecky 2020.
Note: The estimations are performed on Prowess data. NPLs = nonperforming loans.
*p < 0.05, ** p < 0.01, *** p < 0.001.

TABLE 2C.4   Pakistan: Summary Statistics for Scheduled Commercial Banks, 2009–18

a. Public sector banks	Number of observations	Mean	Standard deviation	25th percentile	50th percentile	75th percentile
Interest coverage ratio (ICR)	37	1.33	1.04	0.77	1.06	1.47
Total regulatory capital ratio (%)	38	23.52	11.56	16.07	21.95	25.72
Impaired loans (NPLs)/Gross loans (%)	37	12.77	8.70	7.07	12.48	16.46
Return on average assets (ROAA) (%)	32	0.93	1.15	0.65	1.06	1.27
Return on average equity (ROAE) (%)	32	7.40	9.89	4.37	9.45	11.80
Net interest margin (%)	32	4.2	1.9	3.1	3.7	4.3
z-score	37	−35.25	25.54	−57.62	−29.91	−11.93
Loans/Deposits (%)	38	169.00	266.74	54.83	61.85	72.40
Liquid assets/Total assets (%)	38	11.95	6.06	8.10	11.36	13.87
Risk-weighted assets/Total assets (%)	38	51.40	18.66	39.15	43.50	59.68
Gross loans (US$, million)	38	1,941.80	2,475.47	343.99	973.91	2,386.87
Total assets (US$, million)	38	4,212.10	5,809.75	1,023.58	1,555.32	4,503.73

b. Private banks	Number of observations	Mean	Standard deviation	25th percentile	50th percentile	75th percentile
Interest coverage ratio (ICR)	123	1.20	0.78	0.72	0.98	1.40
Total regulatory capital ratio (%)	135	17.91	11.21	12.52	14.90	19.27
Impaired loans (NPLs)/Gross loans (%)	130	11.70	7.98	6.50	10.66	14.26
Return on average assets (ROAA) (%)	119	0.76	1.43	0.46	0.93	1.41
Return on average equity (ROAE) (%)	119	8.63	17.39	4.62	13.22	17.63
Net interest margin (%)	119	3.7	1.1	2.9	3.6	4.3
z-score	119	−21.56	13.95	−33.25	−20.18	−8.90
Loans/Deposits (%)	135	62.58	22.14	47.43	58.65	74.96
Liquid assets/Total assets (%)	135	12.82	14.22	6.33	8.85	13.13
Risk-weighted assets/Total assets (%)	135	52.17	12.71	43.82	50.70	60.10
Gross loans (US$, million)	135	1,922.54	1,812.03	639.35	1,491.07	2,659.02
Total assets (US$, million)	135	4,965.81	5,132.63	1,288.33	3,548.30	6,952.84

c. T-tests on means	Mean difference	t statistic
Interest coverage ratio (ICR)	−0.131	(−0.71)
Total regulatory capital ratio (%)	−5.615*	(−2.66)
Impaired loans (NPLs)/Gross loans (%)	−1.071	(−0.67)
Return on average assets (ROAA) (%)	−0.177	(−0.73)
Return on average equity (ROAE) (%)	1.229	(0.52)
Net interest margin (%)	−0.544	(−1.58)
z-score	13.70**	(3.12)
Loans/Deposits (%)	−106.4*	(−2.46)
Liquid assets/Total assets (%)	0.869	(0.55)
Risk-weighted assets/Total assets (%)	0.767	(0.24)
Gross loans (US$, million)	−19.25	(−0.04)
Total assets (US$, million)	753.7	(0.72)

Sources: Kibuuka and Melecky 2020; Fitch Connect database.
Note: NPLs = nonperforming loans.
*p < 0.05, **p < 0.01, ***p < 0.001.

TABLE 2C.5   **Sri Lanka: Summary Statistics for Scheduled Commercial Banks, 2009–18**

a. Public sector banks	Number of observations	Mean	Standard deviation	25th percentile	50th percentile	75th percentile
Interest coverage ratio (ICR)	54	2.38	3.18	0.66	0.86	1.52
Total regulatory capital ratio (%)	48	27.64	24.84	12.91	14.95	24.86
Impaired loans (NPLs)/Gross loans (%)	19	4.03	5.18	0.00	1.80	7.33
Return on average assets (ROAA) (%)	47	1.76	1.65	0.86	1.18	2.08
Return on average equity (ROAE) (%)	47	14.47	8.48	6.38	12.66	21.62
Net interest margin (%)	47	5.6	2.1	3.9	5.1	6.9
z-score	55	−29.13	17.20	−33.78	−26.18	−15.37
Loans/Deposits (%)	55	230.31	298.39	92.59	99.88	123.30
Liquid assets/Total assets (%)	55	22.74	20.37	9.09	16.11	28.59
Risk-weighted assets/Total assets (%)	44	43.52	24.32	24.29	47.13	60.81
Gross loans (US$, million)	55	1,945.31	2,688.73	128.11	424.57	5,076.80
Total assets (US$, million)	55	3,254.59	4,111.84	163.58	524.81	6,657.75

b. Private banks	Number of observations	Mean	Standard deviation	25th percentile	50th percentile	75th percentile
Interest coverage ratio (ICR)	140	2.62	2.63	0.97	1.32	3.49
Total regulatory capital ratio (%)	142	29.00	21.06	15.25	19.66	36.80
Impaired loans (NPLs)/Gross loans (%)	95	3.42	2.82	1.29	2.72	5.14
Return on average assets (ROAA) (%)	127	1.79	1.35	1.16	1.66	2.38
Return on average equity (ROAE) (%)	127	12.02	7.79	7.50	11.84	17.19
Net interest margin (%)	127	5.5	1.8	4.3	5.2	6.1
z-score	144	−62.28	109.98	−69.03	−37.11	−20.36
Loans/Deposits (%)	150	136.27	118.01	87.12	98.75	136.53
Liquid assets/Total assets (%)	151	20.20	17.06	7.13	14.25	28.71
Risk-weighted assets/Total assets (%)	93	68.63	15.56	61.34	67.71	77.58
Gross loans (US$, million)	150	834.30	1,096.94	69.29	330.63	1,242.97
Total assets (US$, million)	151	1,305.37	1,649.87	174.91	496.50	2,072.62

c. T-tests on means	Mean difference	t statistic
Interest coverage ratio (ICR)	0.237	(0.49)
Total regulatory capital ratio (%)	1.368	(0.34)
Impaired loans (NPLs)/Gross loans (%)	−0.604	(−0.49)
Return on average assets (ROAA) (%)	0.0305	(0.11)
Return on average equity (ROAE) (%)	−2.445	(−1.73)
Net interest margin (%)	−0.156	(−0.45)
z-score	−33.15***	(−3.51)
Loans/Deposits (%)	−94.04*	(−2.27)
Liquid assets/Total assets (%)	−2.534	(−0.82)
Risk-weighted assets/Total assets (%)	25.11***	(6.27)
Gross loans (US$, million)	−1,111.0**	(−2.98)
Total assets (US$, million)	−1,949.2**	(−3.42)

Sources: Kibuuka and Melecky 2020; Fitch Connect database.
Note: NPLs = nonperforming loans.
*p < 0.05, ** p < 0.01, *** p < 0.001.

TABLE 2C.6   India: Average Characteristics of the Client Firms of Commercial Banks, 2009–18

a. Public sector banks	Number of observations	Mean	Standard deviation	25th percentile	50th percentile	75th percentile
Total assets (Rs, billion)	190	57.95	22.72	41.50	56.28	69.87
Debt to equity	190	5.11	8.00	2.40	3.11	4.54
Debt to assets	190	0.43	0.05	0.40	0.42	0.46
Investment to assets	190	0.48	0.07	0.43	0.47	0.52
Return on assets	190	−0.13	5.11	−0.99	0.27	1.36
b. Private banks	Number of observations	Mean	Standard deviation	25th percentile	50th percentile	75th percentile
Total assets (Rs, billion)	387	54.67	71.33	17.64	33.65	60.51
Debt to equity	377	2.83	8.35	0.96	1.59	2.44
Investment to assets	387	0.50	0.29	0.38	0.43	0.55
Return on assets	387	0.29	12.79	0.06	1.74	3.30
c. T-tests on means	Mean difference	t statistic				
Total assets (Rs, billion)	−3.28	(−0.82)				
Debt to equity	−2.280**	(−3.16)				
Investment to assets	0.0173	(1.12)				
Return on assets	0.423	(0.56)				

Source: Kibuuka and Melecky 2020.
Note: The estimations are performed on Prowess data. Rs = Indian rupees.
* $p < 0.05$, ** $p < 0.01$, *** $p < 0.001$.

Notes

1. Based on data from the Bank Regulation and Supervision Survey, World Bank.
2. Some SOCBs operate as commercial banks while still implementing government programs, typically funded directly from the budget, so some call them hybrid commercial banks (Ferrari, Mare, and Skamnelos 2017).
3. While most of the prominent guidelines on corporate governance issued by the Organisation for Economic Co-operation and Development (OECD) could be extended to SOCBs, these guidelines are not really tailored to the risk-managing business of hybrid commercial banks. See https://www.oecd.org/corporate/guidelines-corporate-governance-soes.htm.
4. The report uses the World Bank Country and Lending Groups classifications to group countries by region and income groups.
5. This chapter does not include analogous statistics for specialized development banks in Bangladesh and Pakistan because they are not typical SOCBs. Although they may conduct retail operations, their financing is much less market based, and lending operations are typically confined to narrower mandates. The latter include supporting agricultural activity in subregions, helping modernize agriculture and boosting productivity, and the supporting small businesses and the setting up of industries. The specialized banks in both countries are inefficient and unprofitable and have large pools of NPLs on their books. Only a much better capital position distinguishes Pakistan's specialized banks from their counterparts in Bangladesh.
6. A scheduled bank, in India, refers to a bank that is listed in the 2nd Schedule of the Reserve Bank of India Act, 1934.
7. Small finance banks are a type of niche bank in India. Banks with a small finance bank license can provide the basic banking services of accepting deposits and extending lending.
8. Priority sector lending is imposed by the RBI on commercial banks to provide a specified portion of bank lending to a few specific sectors, such as agriculture (notably farm credit, as well as agriculture infrastructure and ancillary services); micro, small, and medium enterprises; export credit; education; housing; social infrastructure (such as hospitals, schools, and water and sanitation systems);

renewable energy; and weaker sectors (such as small and marginal farmers, beneficiaries of government-sponsored schemes, minority communities, people with disabilities, and the like). Priority sector lending also includes credit lines provided to nonbank financial institutions for on-lending to priority sectors.

9. While most banks have data on the key variables, resulting in about 700 observations in each regression, data on foreign exposures and dividends have a number of missing variables, resulting in regressions with about 300 and 500 observations, respectively.

10. In India, for instance, SOCBs are instructed to keep their CRAR above 11 percent.

11. Old private banks are those that existed when nationalization led to creating the current SOCBs. New private banks have been established more recently. See Mishra, Prabhala, and Rajan (2019) for details on the old and new private banks.

12. See the Fitch Rating Action dated April 30, 2020.

13. This finding dovetails with that of Sarkar and Sensarma (2010) that even partial privatization can help significantly improve the financial performance of SOCBs in India.

14. For instance, Ashraf, Arshad, and Yan (2018) find that political pressure on state-owned banks is prevalent only in those countries with weak political institutions. Strong political institutions in the form of effective constraints on policy change decisions by incumbent government administrations and greater democratic accountability are helpful in eliminating political pressure on state-owned banks in developing countries. Also, Richmond and others (2019) report one consistent feature across state-owned firms in both the financial sector and real sector: overemployment relative to their private sector counterparts.

15. SOCBs have been instructed by the Indian government to maintain capital above 11 percent, even though the regulatory minimum is 9 percent. We opt for this higher threshold because it shows greater sensitivity and richer adjustments than the threshold of 9 percent. Anecdotal evidence suggests that banks typically "dress up" their regulatory reporting between on-site supervision visits. By the time they report a CRAR of 9 percent or less on audited statements and to off-site supervision, they actually are significantly below 9 percent and have attempted to adjust way before that time.

16. The chapter uses the government of India's definition for SMEs: annual turnover of no more than Rs 2.5 billion, or US$33.5 billion.

17. Even here, it could be argued that any profit-maximizing horizons longer than the market would assume could benefit the banking system in terms of stability and thus generate social benefits.

18. See, for example, the G20 Principles for Financial Inclusion (https://www.afi-global.org/sites/default/files/afi%20g20%20principles.pdf); the International Labour Organization's Rural Policy Brief on "Empowering Rural Communities through Financial Inclusion" (https://www.ilo.org/wcmsp5/groups/public/---ed_emp/documents/publication/wcms_159004.pdf); and Barajas et al. (2020).

19. This could include new jobs, connectivity to markets, broadening social networks, and other aspects of social inclusion for which a clear monetary value is difficult to assign.

20. An example is the integrated digital banking platform YONO offered by the State Bank of India (https://www.sbiyono.sbi/wps/portal/login).

References

ADB, DFID, JICA, and World Bank (Asian Development Bank, United Kingdom Department for International Development, Japan International Cooperation Agency, and World Bank). 2018. *The WEB of Transport Corridors in South Asia*. Washington, DC: World Bank.

Ashraf B. N., S. Arshad, and L. Yan. 2018. "Do Better Political Institutions Help in Reducing Political Pressure on State-Owned Banks? Evidence from Developing Countries." *Journal of Risk and Financial Management* 11 (3): 1–18.

Ashraf, B. N., and Y. Shen. 2019. "Economic Policy Uncertainty and Banks' Loan Pricing." *Journal of Financial Stability* 44: 100695.

Atkinson, A. B., and J. E. Stiglitz. 1980. *Lectures on Public Economics*. London: McGraw Hill.

Banerjee, A. V. 1997. "A Theory of Misgovernance." *Quarterly Journal of Economics* 112 (4): 1289–332.

Barajas, A., T. Beck, M. Belhaj, and S. Ben Naceur. 2020. "Financial Inclusion: What Have We Learned So Far? What Do We Have to Learn?"

IMF Working Paper WP/20/157, International Monetary Fund, Washington, DC.

Bertay, A. C., A. Demirgüç-Kunt, and H. Huizinga. 2015. "Bank Ownership and Credit over the Business Cycle: Is Lending by State Banks Less Procyclical?" *Journal of Banking & Finance* 50: 326–39.

Calomiris, C. W., and S. H. Haber. 2014. *Fragile by Design: The Political Origins of Banking Crises and Scarce Credit*. Princeton, NJ: Princeton University Press.

Cole, S. 2009. "Fixing Market Failures or Fixing Elections? Agricultural Credit in India." *American Economic Journal: Applied Economics* 1(1): 219–50.

Coleman, N., and L. Feler. 2015. "Bank Ownership, Lending, and Local Economic Performance during the 2008–2009 Financial Crisis." *Journal of Monetary Economics* 71: 50–66.

Cull, R., M. S. Martinez Peria, and J. Verrier. 2017. "Bank Ownership: Trends and Implications." IMF Working Paper no. 17/60, International Monetary Fund, Washington, DC.

de la Torre, A., J. C. Gozzi, and S. L. Schmukler. 2007. "Stock Market Development under Globalization: Whither the Gains from Reforms?" *Journal of Banking and Finance* 31 (6): 1731–54.

de Luna-Martinez, J., and C. L. Vicente. 2012. "Global Survey of Development Banks." Policy Research Working Paper 5969, World Bank, Washington, DC.

Duprey, T. 2015. "Do Publicly Owned Banks Lend against the Wind?" *International Journal of Central Banking* 11 (2): 65–112.

Ferrari, A., D. S. Mare, and I. Skamnelos. 2017. "State Ownership of Financial Institutions in Europe and Central Asia." Policy Research Working Paper WPS 8288, World Bank, Washington, DC.

Gerschenkron, A. 1962. *Economic Backwardness in Historical Perspective: A Book of Essays*. Cambridge, MA: Harvard University Press.

Gopalakrishnan, B., and S. Mohapatra. 2019. "Insolvency Regimes and Firms' Default Risk under Economic Uncertainty and Shocks." MPRA Paper 96283, Munich Personal RePEc Archive, University Library of Munich, Germany.

Gutierrez, E., H. P. Rudolf, T. Homa, and E. B. Beneit. 2011. "Development Banks: Role and Mechanisms to Increase Their Efficiency."

Policy Research Working Paper 5729, World Bank, Washington, DC.

Hart, O. D., A. Shleifer, and R. Vishny. 1997. "The Proper Scope of Government: Theory and Application to Prisons." *Quarterly Journal of Economics* 112: 1127–62.

IMF (International Monetary Fund). 2013. "Changes in Bank Funding Patterns and Financial Stability." Chapter 3 in *Global Financial Stability Report: Transition Challenges to Stability*. Washington, DC: IMF.

Kibuuka, K., and M. Melecky. 2020. "State-Owned versus Private Banks in South Asia: Agency Tensions, Distress Factors, and Real Costs of Distress." Background paper for *Hidden Debt*. World Bank, Washington, DC.

Kumbhakar, S., and S. Sarkar. 2003. "Deregulation, Ownership, and Productivity Growth in the Banking Industry: Evidence from India." *Journal of Money, Credit and Banking* 35: 403–24.

Laeven, L., and R. Levine. 2009. "Bank Governance, Regulation and Risk Taking." *Journal of Financial Economics* 93 (2): 259–75.

Levy-Yeyati, E., A. Micco, and U. Panizza. 2007. "A Reappraisal of State-Owned Banks." *Economia* 7 (2): 209–59.

Mazzucato, M., and C. C. R. Penna. 2016. "Beyond Market Failures: The Market Creating and Shaping Roles of State Investment Banks." *Journal of Economic Policy Reform* 19 (4): 305–26.

Melecky, M., and S. Sharma. 2020. "Hidden Liabilities from State-Owned Enterprises in South Asia." Background paper for *Hidden Debt*, World Bank, Washington, DC. Unpublished.

Micco, A., and U. Panizza. 2006. "Bank Ownership and Lending Behavior." *Economics Letters* 93 (2, November): 248–54.

Mishra, P., N. Prabhala, and R. G. Rajan. 2019. "The Relationship Dilemma: Organizational Culture and the Adoption of Credit Scoring Technology in Indian Banking." Johns Hopkins Carey Business School Research Paper no. 19-03, Johns Hopkins University, Baltimore.

Perotti, E., and M. Vorage. 2010. "Bank Ownership and Financial Stability." Tinbergen Institute Discussion Paper TI 2010-022/2, Tinbergen Institute, Amsterdam.

Richmond, C. J., D. Benedek, E. Cabezon, B. Cegar, P. A. Dohlman, M. Hassine, B. Jajko, P. Kopyrski, M. Markevych, J. A. Miniane,

F. J. Parodi, G. Pula, J. Roaf, M. Song, M. Sviderskaya, R. Turk Ariss, and S. Weber. 2019. "Reassessing the Role of State-Owned Enterprises in Central, Eastern and Southeastern Europe." IMF Departmental Paper 19/11, European Department, International Monetary Fund, Washington, DC.

Sarkar, S., and R. Sensarma. 2010. "Partial Privatization and Bank Performance: Evidence from India." *Journal of Financial Economic Policy* 2 (4): 276–306.

Shleifer, A. 1998. "State versus Private Ownership." *Journal of Economic Perspectives* 12: 133–50.

Shleifer, A., and R. W. Vishny. 1994. "Politicians and Firms." *Quarterly Journal of Economics* 109 (4): 995–1025.

Srinivasan, A., and A. Thampy. 2017. "The Effect of Relationships with Government-Owned Banks on Cash Flow Constraints: Evidence from India." *Journal of Corporate Finance* 46 (C): 361–73.

Stiglitz, J. E. 1993. "The Role of the State in Financial Markets. *World Bank Economic Review* 7 (suppl. 1): 19–52.

World Bank. 2020. *South Asia Economic Focus, Spring 2020: The Cursed Blessing of Public Banks*. Washington, DC: World Bank.

South Asia's State-Owned Enterprises: Surprise Liabilities versus Positive Externalities 3

State-owned enterprises (SOEs) in South Asia offer many important benefits. They provide public goods and help address market failures related to risky, long-term investments and natural monopolies. However, because their operations and liabilities are backed by government guarantees, they also expose governments to large financial risks and potential (contingent) liabilities. Using firm-level panel data from India, this chapter assesses whether SOEs are more prone to financial distress than comparable private firms—and thus impose unforeseen liabilities and expenditure needs on the governments. It further studies whether SOEs' financial distress relates to the persistent underperformance and indebtedness of some SOEs or to the greater risks that SOEs confront compared to private firms. Drilling deeper, the chapter tests alternative hypotheses for the underperformance of SOEs, including weak corporate governance and soft budget constraints in the form of both debt and equity bailouts. To illustrate some

possible positives of SOE operations, the chapter searches for evidence that SOEs could provide strategic direction in their industries when they undertake riskier long-term investments, such as into research and development (R&D). In other words, can SOE investments in R&D crowd in additional R&D investment of private firms in the same industry?

The Importance of Paying More Attention to the Hidden Liabilities of SOEs in South Asia

Nonfinancial state-owned enterprises (SOEs) have a large footprint in South Asia. Total SOE revenues amount to nearly 8 percent of GDP in Sri Lanka, 12 percent in Pakistan, and 19 percent in India (see table 3A.1).[1] These shares are significant by international standards, although some other countries—particularly formerly socialist countries of Eastern Europe and East Asia—have much larger SOE sectors. The total number of SOEs

Note: This chapter draws on the background research paper: Melecky, M., S. Sharma, and D. Yang. 2020. "State-Owned Enterprises: The Distresses, Adjustments, and Fiscal Contingent Liabilities in South Asia." Background paper for *Hidden Debt*. World Bank, Washington, DC.

exceeds 200 in Pakistan, 400 in Sri Lanka, and 1,300 in India. Although present in nearly all sectors of the economy, they concentrate in the energy, transport, utilities, and trading sectors.

Rationales for government involvement in SOEs. One major rationale for government ownership of firms in South Asia, as in other parts of the world, is the need to address market failures related to natural monopolies. Network industries in energy and transportation have high fixed costs, often leading to their monopolization. In such cases, an unregulated private sector cannot be relied upon to produce goods and services efficiently and affordably. Public sector ownership could improve welfare if the government's capacity to regulate the private sector is limited (Stigler 1971; Peltzman 1976; Dal Bo 2006). This could be why South Asian SOEs are concentrated in network sectors such as energy, transport, and communication, where the potential for such market failures is high.

Another major rationale for public ownership is that long-term and risky investments in innovation are underfunded by private investors because failures in financial markets limit funding (Hall and Lerner 2010). In Europe, SOEs tend to invest more in R&D than private firms, particularly in sustainable technologies with low commercial returns (Bortolotti, Fotak, and Wolfe 2019). Some SOEs in South Asia are undertaking such investments. For example, the Solar Energy Corporation of India has been a pioneer in the commercialization of solar power—an investment with high risk and potential positive spillovers.[2] Our analysis of firm-level data from India indicates that SOEs on average spend more on R&D than private firms do—and account for a disproportionate share of total R&D spending in several industries. Moreover, the R&D activities of SOEs in South Asia have positive spillovers on the performance of private firms, regression analysis suggests.

Relatedly, SOEs can complement the private sector by helping solve coordination problems. An example is a case of a strong complementarity between new technologies and specialized skills in an industry, with the

> Many individual SOEs are persistent loss-makers and financially unsustainable. While the performance of SOEs should not be judged solely on commercial terms, these large and persistent SOE losses often culminate in costly government bailouts.

risk that coordination failures between private firms and skills providers could block the supply of needed skills.[3] The public sector could play a role in breaking the deadlock. Not surprisingly, many SOEs in South Asia have been early leaders in technical fields. For example, RITES India, the engineering arm of the Indian Railways Corporation, today provides infrastructure consulting services in India and abroad.[4]

South Asian SOEs also serve broader developmental or public interest objectives. The economic rationale for public ownership is less compelling in these situations. A case in point is the mobilization of SOEs to improve the connectivity of remote or underserved areas. For example, India's flagship BharatNet Program, which aims to extend the reach of the telecom network to remote and rural villages and is one of the largest rural connectivity projects of its kind, in the world, is implemented in part by a state-owned enterprise, BBNL (Bharat Broadband Network Limited) (BBNL 2019). Pakistan Railways subsidizes select routes to provide mobility and connectivity to far-flung areas (Government of Pakistan 2016).

How important are financial risks of SOEs to governments? Although SOEs can contribute to development objectives, they are a source of financial risk to South Asian governments. Moreover, not all the risk is justified for achieving the development objectives through state ownership. Owning firms exposes government budgets and debt position to a host of external, macroeconomic, and sector-specific shocks that depend on the industry profile of the SOE sector. To an extent, this risk is an unavoidable side effect of public ownership of firms. However, South Asia's SOE sectors regularly generate big losses. For example, the SOE sectors of

Pakistan and Sri Lanka generated net losses in two out of the three years between 2015 and 2017, and India's state public sector enterprises (SPSEs), the SOEs owned by subnational governments, lost an amount equal to 0.5 percent of GDP in 2017.

For example, in 2014 the Sri Lankan government had to inject SL Rs 123 billion (approximately 1.2 percent of GDP) from the budget into SOEs.[5] In the same year, the Indian government approved a total assistance package of Rs 411 billion (approximately 0.3 percent of GDP) to revive 46 "sick" federal government–owned SOEs (Government of India 2014).

Many individual SOEs are persistent loss-makers and financially unsustainable, often culminating in costly government bailouts.

Analyzing fiscal contingent liabilities from government ownership of SOEs. The main part of this chapter analyzes the fiscal contingent liabilities from government ownership of firms (SOEs) in South Asia. The analysis relies mainly on a detailed firm-level panel data set for India that has good coverage of firms that are majority privately owned as well the SOEs majority owned by the federal government (central public sector enterprises, or CPSEs). It is the only such data set available for the South Asian countries. This firm-level analysis is supplemented with more aggregate data from reports published by South Asian governments.

This analysis begins by assessing the incidence of SOE distress. A firm is defined to be in distress when its earnings are not enough to cover its interest payments. The interest coverage ratio (ICR) is used to capture this relationship. The firm-level data from India show that Indian CPSEs are generally more likely to be in distress than comparable private firms. This is not because CPSEs are concentrated in particular sectors where profit margins are lower, nor because they are engaged in inherently more risky activities. Yet CPSE distress tends to last longer, often exceeding one year. While data limitations preclude a similar analysis for other countries, this study finds that persistent

loss-making SOEs—prone to distress—are present throughout the region.

Next, this study assesses the magnitude of the contingent liabilities arising from SOE operations for the government fiscal stance (budget and debt positions). This requires information on the government's financial commitments in case of SOE distress and the conditions under which they are triggered. Such information is not easily available. Even explicit government commitments, such as guarantees on SOE debt, are not always well documented. The data available suggest that explicit commitments are sizable. For example, SOE loans amounting to 1 percent of GDP were under government guarantee in Pakistan in 2017. The implicit government commitment to cover SOE debt is even harder to quantify due to data limitations.[6] This study presents approximate upper-bound estimates by assessing the total liabilities of SOEs in high likelihood of needing bailout funding. The upper-bound estimate is large. For example, the total liability of all chronically distressed Indian national-level CPSEs has ranged, since 2008, between 3 percent and 5 percent of national GDP. This figure excludes subnational SOES, the SPSEs, which are in a much worse shape. Pakistan's numbers are even more concerning. In the past five years, the total liabilities of loss-making SOEs in Pakistan has hovered around 12 percent of GDP.

The proximate cause of these contingent liabilities is the persistent financial underperformance of SOEs. The Indian panel data set shows that on average, CPSEs earn significantly less revenue per unit labor and per unit capital than private firms. They also have significantly higher debt-to-asset ratios than other firms. These findings are largely in line with the existing evidence base.[7]

Explaining the underperformance of SOEs. Why do SOEs underperform? One school of thought ascribes underperformance to an internal "agency problem" (Ehrlich et al. 1994): It is more difficult to align the incentives of managers and owners in the public sector because pay scales are more compressed, job security is higher, and employee monitoring is less rigorous compared with the private sector. Interestingly, South Asian governments have been "corporatizing" SOEs to professionalize their management and make it easier to monitor their performance by strengthening their corporate governance. For example, the Indian government issued corporate governance guidelines for CPSEs in 2010 and now rates CPSEs on compliance with the guidelines (Government of India 2010).[8] We find that although there is a positive cross-sectional correlation between CPSEs' corporate governance ratings and their commercial performance, improvements in these ratings over time are not significantly associated with improved performance. Therefore, insufficient evidence exists to conclude that corporatization has a causal impact on SOE performance.

Another, perhaps related, hypothesis is that SOEs underperform private firms because they operate in a more constrained or distorted environment.[9] For example, they could be under pressure to hire excess workers (Shleifer and Vishny 1994). Indeed, our analysis of SOE performance measures suggests that CPSEs, on average, overemploy labor and capital. Similarly, Baird et al. (2019) exploit a natural experiment in India to show that excessive hiring by SOEs has caused a high level of labor misallocation in the manufacturing sector.

SOE pricing decisions are also constrained. For example, Indian SOEs in industries such as petroleum, electricity distribution, gas, and fertilizers have had to charge below-cost prices to subsidize consumers and farmers (Khanna 2012). In 2016, the electricity tariff for agricultural use was about 31 percent of the cost of supply, while the tariff for the residential sector was 77 percent of the average cost of supply (Zhang 2019). Likewise, Pakistan Railways subsidizes select routes to provide mobility and connectivity to far-flung areas (Government of Pakistan 2016).

Another potential external factor is the much-studied soft budget constraint of SOEs—the perception that SOEs have the implicit and unconditional support of the government (Kornai 1986). For example, SOEs might have access to softer loans with lower interest rates and looser conditions, as suggested by their persistently higher debt ratios. We find that, compared with private firms, there is a stronger positive association between accumulated losses and the debt-asset ratio among SOEs. This suggests that SOEs are more prone to covering losses through additional loans. Given that direct government loans are only a fraction of total SOE debt, SOEs must have preferential access to bank loans. This opens a question about the nexus between state-owned enterprises and state-owned banks, and more broadly, the preference of even private banks for lending to SOEs compared with similar privately owned companies.

Exploring the soft budget constraint hypothesis. We explore the soft budget constraint hypothesis further by comparing how CPSEs and private firms in India adjust their assets and liabilities when in financial distress or when experiencing a revenue shock. The growth of fixed assets declines significantly for private firms when they are in distress, but this relationship is significantly weaker among CPSEs. Similarly, the growth of debt and equity capital declines significantly for private firms when they experience a negative shock, but does not for CPSEs. Correspondingly, the growth rate of debt increases more for private firms when they experience a positive shock than for CPSEs.

The lower sensitivity of SOE assets, debt, and equity to shocks is consistent with the hypothesis that SOEs enjoy greater access to soft funding because governments implicitly guarantee to bail them out. Banks can afford to discount shocks when assessing SOE creditworthiness if they believe there is an implicit government guarantee on SOE debt. In China, implicit government guarantees on SOEs are found to have reduced the sensitivity of SOE credit costs to risk (Allen et al. 2017) and to make SOE debt more attractive to financial markets (Jin, Wang, and Zhang 2018). Credit rating agencies explicitly include the likelihood of government support and bailout when assessing the credit risks of SOEs.[10] Similarly, the lower sensitivity of equity investment in SOEs to shocks could be due to the belief among private investors that their equity is implicitly insured. Similar issues arise in the context of public-private partnerships (see chapter 1).

Although this soft budget constraint is not the only potential cause of SOE underperformance, it is likely to have been pivotal to the growth of unnecessary contingent liabilities from SOEs. Not only does it cause SOEs to underperform by reducing market pressures on SOE managers (Jensen 1986; Maskin and Xu 2001), but it also enables debt to build up in loss-making SOEs. The constrained environment of SOEs could also temper the effectiveness of internal SOE reforms. For example, Berkowitz, Ma, and Nishioka (2017) argue that the apparent efficiency gains from SOE corporatization in China were in fact due to a contemporaneous tightening of their operating environment. Bartel and Harrison (2005) show that the effectiveness of partial SOE privatization in Malaysia depended on external factors such as access to soft loans.

Policy lessons and implications. The most immediate policy lesson of our analysis is that the contingent liabilities from SOEs are nontransparent, and policy makers in South Asia are not paying enough attention to them. Given the limitations of publicly available data, it is difficult to quantify even SOEs' total liabilities or debt, much less their explicit and implicit government commitments. *Governments must better assess and monitor the fiscal risks from SOEs, incorporate them into their fiscal planning and debt management, and make funding provisions so that SOE distress and rescue, when justified, does not entail serious disruptions to critical public spending.*

The deeper policy question is how to mitigate unnecessary contingent liabilities stemming from SOE operations. *The evidence presented in this chapter leads us to recommend a combination of internal reforms at the SOE level and external reforms in the operating and broader controlling environment.* These reforms are discussed in the final part of the chapter.

Describing the Opaque and Complex SOE Sector in South Asia Using Data

Analyses Must Cope with a Lack of Data about South Asian SOEs

This chapter relies mainly on publicly available official reports and statistical tables to present stylized facts about the SOE sector in various South Asian countries, such as its size, performance, and liabilities.

- *India.* The main official data source for Indian CPSEs are annual reports on CPSEs published by the Department of Public Enterprises. Data on SOEs owned by the state governments of India (state public sector enterprises, SPSEs) are less easily available. Our main data sources were state-level SOE audit reports published by the Comptroller and Auditor General of India (CAGI).
- *Pakistan.* Data on Pakistani SOEs are from the annual *Federal Footprint: SOEs Annual Report,* published by the Ministry of Finance.
- *Sri Lanka.* Sri Lankan data are from the annual SOE *Performance Report,* published by the Department of Public Enterprises, and from the *Annual Report of the Ministry of Finance.* These data were supplemented by a publicly available database compiled from various government reports by the independent think tank Advocata Institute.
- *Bangladesh.* Bangladesh does not produce annual SOE reports. Our data for Bangladesh are based on the statistical tables published in the annual *Bangladesh Economic Review,* produced by the Ministry of Finance.
- *Bhutan.* Data on Bhutanese SOEs are from the *State Enterprises Annual Report,* published by the Ministry of Finance.

Annex 3A lists these data sources and the country-specific definition/categorization of SOEs used in this report.

The data available in these official reports are generally at an aggregate level. India, Pakistan, and Sri Lanka have been publishing SOE-level revenue and balance sheet data in recent years. However, data for only a limited set of variables are available. For example, it is not always possible to measure value added and profits or to obtain SOE-level information on government support. India publishes firm-level data on CPSEs, but not SPSEs. This gap is worrying because much of the debt and accumulated losses reside in SPSEs.

Given the limited availability of official firm-level data, our firm-level analysis for South Asia relies on an Indian firm-level database called Prowess, which is maintained by the Center for Monitoring the Indian Economy (CMIE). Prowess contains detailed information on the balance sheet and performance of Indian firms, including a large share of India's CPSEs. It is based on data reported by firms registered with the Registrar General of Companies. While Prowess is not fully representative of the formal manufacturing sector in India, it has good coverage of medium and large firms. On average over the years, Prowess has covered 80 percent to 90 percent of the Indian CPSE sector by number and more than 95 percent of it by total revenue. It is a panel data set, unlike the repeated cross-sectional Annual Survey of Industries. This enables us to track CPSEs over time and look at their debt dynamics.

Prowess data consist of an unbalanced panel covering the period 1989–2018 with an uneven (growing) number of firms over time. To ensure that the sample used in the regression analysis stays constant across different regressions with different outcome variables, we excluded observations that are missing values for any of the key variables needed for our analysis. The average sample size of this data set is about 12,000 firms per year.[11] We further cleaned the data set by replacing the values of outliers (those exceeding the 98th percentile) with the value for the 98th percentile. Table 3B.1, in annex 3B, presents summary statistics of key variables in Prowess for 2016. CPSEs constitute about 1 percent of the Prowess sample.

The SOE Sector in South Asia Is Large and Complex

South Asia has a sizable nonfinancial state-owned enterprise sector. Sri Lanka has 400 nonfinancial SOEs, with the total revenue of the 42 largest "strategically important" nonfinancial SOEs equal to 8 percent of the GDP (figure 3.1).[12] Pakistan has more than 200 such firms, and their revenue amounts to 12 percent of GDP. India has 331 SOEs that

are under the federal government (CPSEs) and more than 1,000 SOEs under state governments (SPSEs). Together, they generate revenue equal to 19 percent of GDP. In Bhutan, most strikingly, SOE revenues equal 38 percent of GDP.[13]

Although economically significant, South Asia's SOE sector is not a global outlier in terms of size. Many formerly socialist countries still have a larger SOE sector than most South Asian countries do. For example, despite a major privatization drive in the previous two decades, China still had more than 150,000 SOEs in 2019; their total value added comprised about 20 percent of national output (Harrison et al. 2019). SOEs also have a major presence in much of Central, Eastern, and Southern Europe, accounting for more than 15 percent of value added in Belarus, Poland, and Russia. This region has a total of 51,000 SOEs; Russia alone has more than 30,000 (Richmond et al. 2019).

South Asian SOEs are concentrated in energy, utilities, transport, and telecommunications. This concentration is most stark in the case of Pakistan, where the energy and transport sectors together account for 95 percent of SOE revenues (figure 3.2). For Sri Lanka, this share is 84 percent. While a precise breakdown of SOE revenue or investment by sector is not available for Bangladesh and Indian SPSEs, they too confirm to this pattern. In Bangladesh, the government has a monopoly on water and sewage services and dominates the energy sector through the Bangladesh Oil, Gas, and Mineral Corporation (PETROBANGLA), Bangladesh Power Development Board (PDB), and Bangladesh Petroleum Corporation (BPC) (World Bank 2019a). Two-thirds of the investment of Indian SPSEs is concentrated in electricity generation and distribution, with the rest spread unevenly in manufacturing, finance, and infrastructure.

SOEs are also present in manufacturing, services, and other sectors, such as the procurement and distribution of agricultural commodities. Indian CPSEs are particularly diverse; the manufacturing and services sector account for 62 percent and 20 percent of their

FIGURE 3.1   Total Number and Average Revenue of South Asian State-Owned Enterprises, 2017

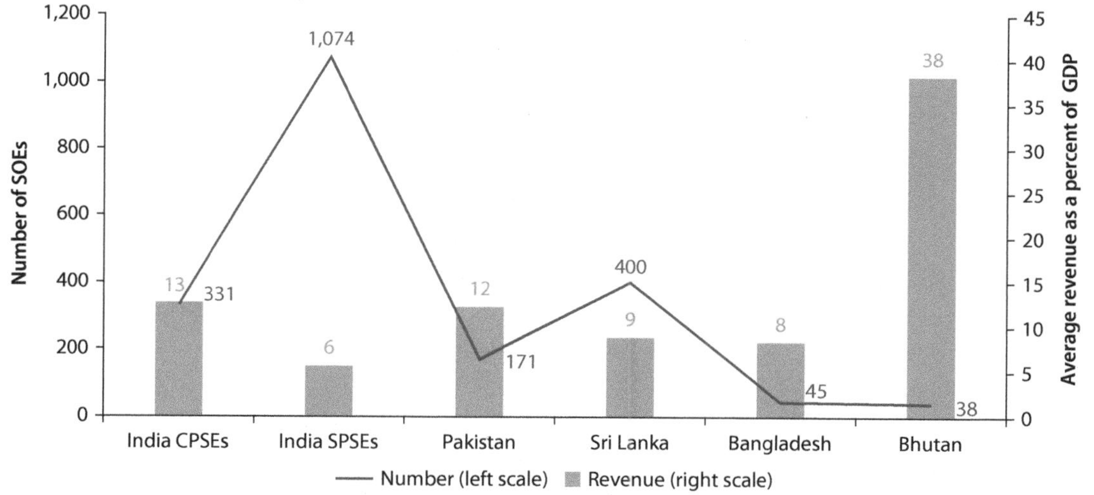

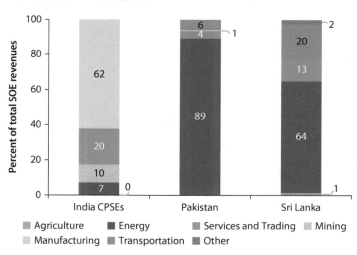

Source: World Bank staff compilations based on data from government reports, various years (see details in annex 3A).
Note: The total number of SOEs is as of 2017. Revenue is expressed as a percentage of GDP. Data are averaged over 2015–17 to smooth out annual fluctuations, except for Indian SPSEs and Sri Lanka, where data are available only for 2017. CPSEs = central public sector enterprises; SOEs = state-owned enterprises; SPSEs = state public sector enterprises.

total revenue, respectively. CPSEs are also present in mining, energy, and transport sectors. Bangladesh and Sri Lanka SOEs have a significant presence in the manufacturing, services, energy, and transportation sectors. In Bangladesh, for example, while many industrial SOEs have been privatized, the state still retains ownership of manufacturing companies such as the Bangladesh Jute Mills Corporation, Bangladesh Steel & Engineering Corporation, and Bangladesh Textile Mills Corporation (BTMC).

The SOE sector is often an aggregate loss-maker. The limited data on the commercial performance of the SOE sector suggests that the total profitability of the sector varies across countries and over time, with loss-making years not uncommon (figure 3.3). In recent years, India's CPSE sector and Bangladesh's SOE sector have consistently generated net profits. Pakistan's SOE sector generated a net profit in 2014 and 2015, but a net loss in the next two years. Pakistan's SOE sector also shows a tendency toward rapidly declining profitability in recent years, with its net income dropping at an annual rate of 57 percent on average from 2014 to 2017.

FIGURE 3.2   State-Owned Enterprise Revenue by Sector in India, Pakistan, and Sri Lanka, 2016–17

Source: World Bank staff compilations based on data from government reports, various years (see details in annex 3A).
Note: CPSEs = central public sector enterprises; SOE = state-owned enterprise.

Sri Lanka's SOE sector generated losses in 2015 and 2017. Indian SPSEs operated at a total loss in 2017. The losses can be large: Pakistan's SOE sector and India's SPSE sector each lost about 0.6 percent of GDP in 2017.

FIGURE 3.3   **Net Profit/Loss of South Asian State-Owned Enterprises, 2014–17**

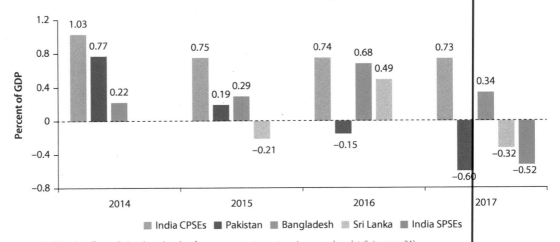

Source: World Bank staff compilations based on data from government reports, various years (see details in annex 3A).
Note: Net profit/loss for Bhutan was around 11 percent on average over 2014–17. CPSEs = central public sector enterprises; SOEs = state-owned enterprises; SPSEs = state public sector enterprises.

Although the fraction of SOEs making a loss is sizable, a few large SOEs in specific sectors often account for a large share of the total loss. The share of SOEs that reported a loss in 2017 ranged from 24 percent to 35 percent across South Asian countries (figure 3.4). However, in every country studied, the top 10 loss-making SOEs accounted for more than 80 percent of the total SOE sector loss. The big loss-making SOEs were heavily concentrated in energy, utilities, transportation, and telecommunications.

The persistence of chronic loss-makers among South Asian SOEs is also notable. We do not have the data to track SOE-level profits over time, except in the case of Pakistan and India for CPSEs. In both countries, of the CPSEs that generated a loss in any one of the five years preceding 2018, more than half had generated losses in three of those five years. About 20 percent had generated losses in all five years (figure 3.5).

South Asian SOEs receive significant financial inflows from their governments in the form of equity injections, grants, and loans. Comprehensive data on government financial outlays on SOEs are not easily available. We often had to combine snippets of data from various sources to get a fuller picture. We are still not sure whether we have the full picture: for example, there are no figures on capital injection in Pakistan's SOE reports, and we are not sure whether this is truly because the government has not injected any capital into SOEs in recent years.

FIGURE 3.4   **Share of State-Owned Enterprises That Reported a Loss in India, Pakistan, Sri Lanka, and Bangladesh, 2017**

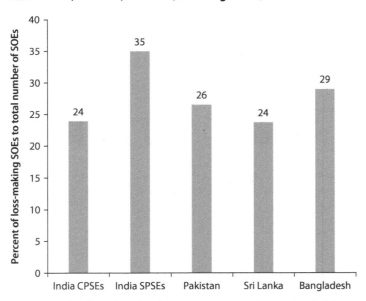

Source: World Bank staff compilations based on government reports, various years (see details in annex 3A).
Note: Data are for 2017. CPSEs = central public sector enterprises; SOEs = state-owned enterprises; SPSEs = state public sector enterprises.

Similarly, we could not obtain figures for government loans to Sri Lankan SOEs. Yet, the available data suggest that government outlays are substantial. For example, on average during 2015–17, Pakistani SOEs received government loans and grants amounting to 0.9 percent and 0.8 percent of GDP, respectively (figure 3.6). Indian SOEs received grants and subsidies amounting to 0.7 percent of GDP.

> In every country studied, the top 10 loss-making SOEs accounted for more than 80 percent of the total losses in the SOE sector.

Analyzing the Roots and Extent of Hidden Liabilities in South Asian SOEs

This section studies the risk of distress in SOEs using regression analysis, by contrasting public and private ownership of firms while controlling for important firm characteristics. It then assesses the possible extent of contingent liabilities from SOEs that could affect the central government fiscal stance—either through the budget, debt, or combination of the two.

SOEs' Risk of Distress Must Be Thoroughly Quantified

Because the government's contingent liabilities from SOEs originate in SOEs' financial distress, we begin our analysis of hidden liabilities by quantifying the risk of distress. This part of the analysis is based on the Prowess panel data set of Indian firms.

Our main indicator of distress is based on the interest coverage ratio (ICR): the ratio of earnings (before interest and taxes) to interest payment. We define a firm as being in distress if earnings are not enough to cover interest payments: that is, if the ICR is less than 1. This is a typical measure of distress in the financial literature. We explored other measures, such as those based on debt and other liabilities, with qualitatively similar results.

FIGURE 3.5 **Breakdown of Loss-Making State-Owned Enterprises in India and Pakistan by the Total Number of Years in Which They Made a Loss, 2012–17**

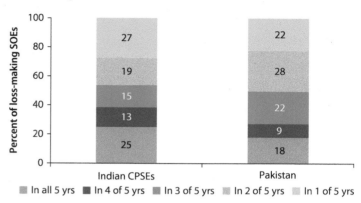

Source: World Bank staff compilations based on data from Prowess and government reports for the five years preceding 2018, various years (see details in annex 3A).
Note: CPSEs = central public sector enterprises; SOEs = state-owned enterprises.

Does owning firms expose governments to risks just like it would any owner—with the only difference being the size and sectoral concentration of government ownership? The answer to this question has implications for how we think about the potential liabilities from SOEs. Thus, we explore the question by using the firm-level data from India and examining whether CPSE distress looks similar to distress among private firms.

CPSEs are more likely to be in distress than similar private firms. Figure 3.7 plots the share of firms in distress in recent years. Between 2004 and 2017, the incidence of distress among CPSEs ranged between 30 percent and 40 percent, compared to between 20 percent and 30 percent for non-SOEs. The gap in the rate of distress between CPSEs and non-SOEs has been narrowing in recent years, but it is too early to say whether this signals a more permanent improvement in the relative performance of CPSEs. Distress among non-SOE Indian firms has been rising consistently since 2010, and until 2015, also rose for CPSEs. For reasons that are not obvious, the distress rate among CPSEs featured in the Prowess database dipped sharply between 2015 and 2017.

The "excess distress rate" of CPSEs—that is, the gap in the incidence of distress between

FIGURE 3.6 **Average Annual Government Support for South Asian State-Owned Enterprises, 2015–17**

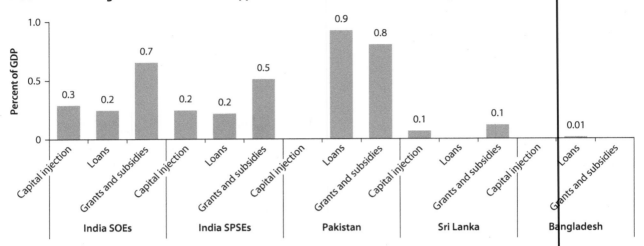

Source: World Bank staff compilations based on data from government reports, averaged over 2015–17 (see details in annex 3A).
Note: Indian SOEs include both CPSEs and SPSEs. CPSEs = central public sector enterprises; SOEs = state-owned enterprises; SPSEs = state public sector enterprises.

FIGURE 3.7 **Share of Distressed Firms in India, 1989–2017**

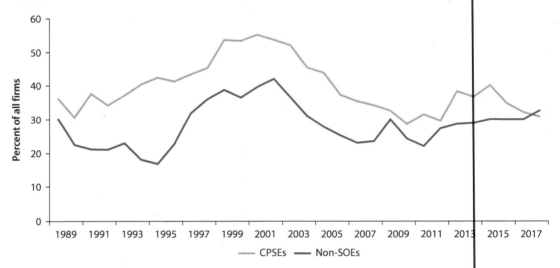

Source: Melecky, Sharma, and Yang 2020.
Note: Firms are considered distressed if their interest coverage ratio (ICR) is less than 1 in a given year. CPSEs = central public sector enterprises; SOEs = state-owned enterprises.

CPSEs and non-SOEs—rises when we consider more persistent distress measures. For example, figure 3.8 presents the share of firms with an ICR below 1 in the three consecutive previous years. Based on this definition, the share of persistently distressed CPSEs has ranged between 10 percent and 20 percent in recent years. The share of persistently distressed non-SOEs has ranged between 5 and 13 percent.

The excess distress among CPSEs is even higher after adjusting for differences in attributes such as size and sector. Table 3B.2 presents estimates of the probability of distress (ICR below 1) in the Prowess panel using ordinary least squares (OLS) regression.

FIGURE 3.8   **Share of Persistently Distressed Firms in India, 1991–2017**

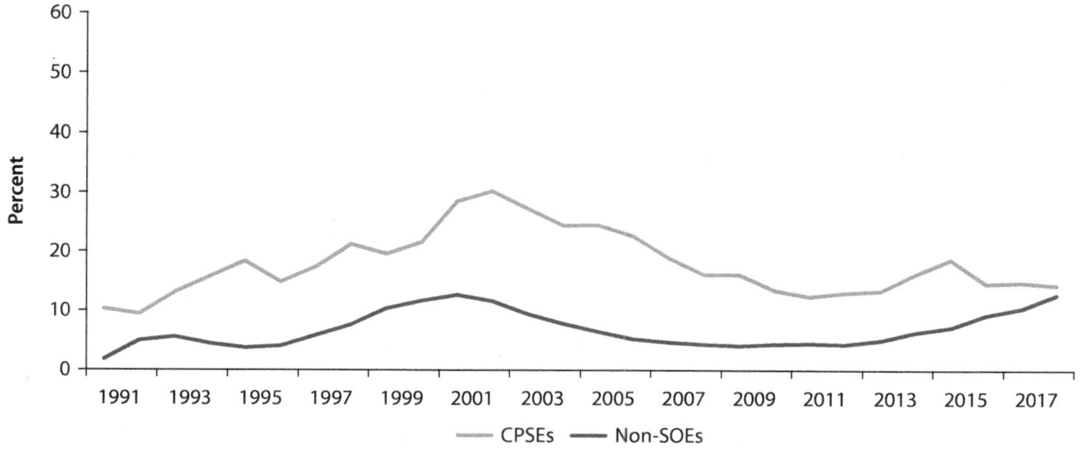

Source: Melecky, Sharma, and Yang 2020.
Note: The excess distress rate is the gap in distress incidence between CPSEs and non-SOEs. The figure shows the percent of firms with an interest coverage ratio (ICR) of less than 1 in three consecutive previous years. CPSEs = central public sector enterprises; SOEs = state-owned enterprises.

The "raw" excess distress rate in CPSE—that is, without adjusting for size and other attributes—is 14.5 percentage points (column 1). This estimate is roughly consistent with figure 3.7. Adding the size control makes a difference, with the CPSE gap in distress incidence rising to 20.7 percentage points. Larger firms tend to have lower distress rates, and hence the CPSE gap becomes larger once we adjust for the fact that CPSEs are larger than the average non-SOEs. While this result does not imply a causal relationship between ownership and distress, it suggests that the higher vulnerability of CPSEs can be explained only by factors other than size, age, and sector.

Next, we interact the CPSE indicator with broad sector dummies to examine whether the excess distress rate of CPSEs is higher in particular sectors (column 4). We find that relative to CPSEs in transport and services (the omitted sector dummy), those in the manufacturing sector are more prone to excess distress, while those in the petroleum industry are less prone.

The patterns shown in table 3B.2 hold true even when we use more persistent distress measures (such as ICR being less than 1 in two or three consecutive years). For

example, controlling for size, age, and sector, CPSEs are 21 percentage points more likely to be in distress in two consecutive years (column 5).

The Likely Magnitude of Contingent (Potential) Liabilities from SOEs Must Be Established

The total liabilities of SOEs are quite large. As shown in figure 3.9, the total liabilities of SOEs in Sri Lanka exceeded 10 percent of GDP and were 20 percent of GDP for SOEs in Pakistan and CPSEs in India in 2017. While the total liabilities of Indian SPSEs are not available for recent years, their total debt (a component of total liabilities) amounted to 4 percent of GDP in 2017. If we assume that their ratio of debt to total liabilities is the same as that of Indian CPSEs, then their total liabilities amount to 8 percent of GDP. The total SOE liabilities in Bangladesh are about 6 percent of GDP, reflecting the smaller size of its SOE sector.

Government guarantees on SOE loans have turned a portion of these liabilities into an explicit contingent liability of South Asian governments. For example, in 2017, the stock of SOE debt with a government guarantee

FIGURE 3.9   **Total Liabilities and Debts for South Asian State-Owned Enterprises, 2017**

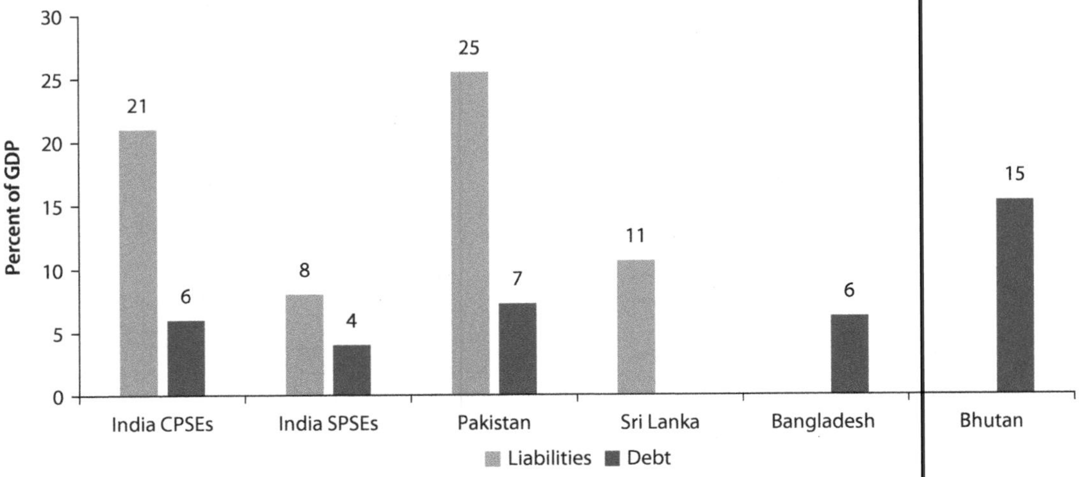

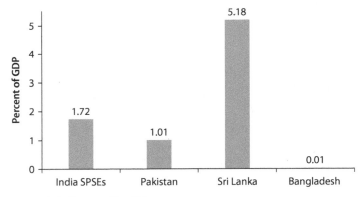

Source: Melecky, Sharma, and Yang 2020 (see details in annex 3A).
Note: CPSEs = central public sector enterprises; SPSEs = state public sector enterprises.

FIGURE 3.10   **Outstanding Government Guarantees to State-Owned Enterprises, 2015–17**

Source: Melecky, Sharma, and Yang 2020.
Note: The outstanding stock of government guarantees to SOEs in Sri Lanka is for the year 2019 and based on Note 33-A (Statement of Bank Guarantees Issued by Central Treasury) of the annual report of the Ministry of Finance. SOEs = state-owned enterprises; SPSEs = state public sector enterprises.

behind it added up to 1 percent of GDP in Pakistan (figure 3.10). Guarantee data on Indian CPSE loans are not available, but loans to SPSEs amounting to 1.7 percent of GDP were guaranteed by the Indian federal government in 2017. In Sri Lanka, the outstanding stock of SOE debt with a government guarantee amounted to approximately 5 percent of GDP in 2019. The corresponding numbers for Bangladesh, as reported in official statistics, are comparatively low (less than 0.1 percent of GDP).

The implicit contingent liabilities from SOE operations are harder to estimate because we do not know what portion of SOE liabilities is implicitly guaranteed and how the guarantee is triggered. Econometric estimation of a country-level model of SOE bailouts is not possible because large bailout events are too infrequent, and there are too few counties in the region, while firm-level data on government financial support to SOEs—which could be used to estimate a firm-level econometric model of bailouts—are not available.[14]

We can get the upper-bound estimates of overall contingent liabilities by examining the total liabilities of SOEs in "distress" in a typical year and assuming that the loss to government is 100 percent of the distressed SOE's liabilities. Figure 3.11 uses Prowess data to plot the total liabilities of Indian CPSEs at high risk of distress from 2000 to 2017. We use four alternative markers to identify CPSEs that are at high risk of distress in a given year: ICR less than 1 in the current year; a loss in the current year; ICR less than 1 in the current and previous two years; and a loss in three out of the preceding five years. The last two measures are more stringent. No matter

FIGURE 3.11   **Total Liabilities of Financially Distressed Central Public Sector Enterprises in India, 2000–17**

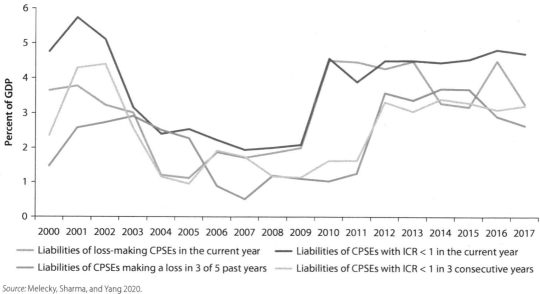

Source: Melecky, Sharma, and Yang 2020.
Note: CPSEs = central public sector enterprises; ICR = interest coverage ratio.

how the risk of distress is identified, the total liabilities in the event of distress have been sizable in the recent years, although they have declined relative to the early 2000s.

Although we cannot measure firm-level distress based on the ICR for other South Asian countries, we can examine the total liabilities of loss-making SOEs using the limited SOE-level data available in Pakistan and Sri Lanka. This is depicted in figure 3.12. In Pakistan, the total liabilities of loss-making SOEs have ranged between 12 percent and 18 percent of GDP in recent years, a remarkably high percentage. If we include only chronic loss-makers—defined as SOEs that made a loss in three out of the five past years—this number remains between 8 percent and 12 percent of GDP. In Sri Lanka, the liabilities of loss-making SOEs have hovered between 4 percent and 5 percent of GDP.

What Drives the Contingent Liabilities from SOEs?

This section analyzes the Prowess panel data to better understand the drivers of SOE distress and debt buildup.

Are SOEs Prone to Distress because They Operate in More Risky Markets?

The excess distress rate of SOEs could reflect the higher risk that SOEs face and not necessarily their inefficiency. Perhaps the developmental mandate of SOEs exposes them to more types of risk or greater risk than other observationally similar firms within the same industry. For example, SOEs could be leading their industry in the exploration of new products, markets, and technologies, and thus may face abnormally high volatility in demand or production costs. Or SOEs engaged in the procurement and distribution of food items and other essential commodities at controlled prices could be particularly vulnerable to exchange rate and commodity price shocks.

We examine this hypothesis by comparing the volatility of firm-level sales across CPSEs and non-SOEs in the Prowess panel. Following Comin and Philippon (2005), we measure the volatility of a variable X (such as annual sales) in firm i in a year t, $Volatility_{xit}$, as the standard deviation of the annual growth rate of X over a 10-year period centered on the year t (that is, between the years $t - 4$ and $t + 5$).

FIGURE 3.12   Total Liabilities of Loss-Making State-Owned Enterprises in India, Pakistan, and Sri Lanka, 2005–17

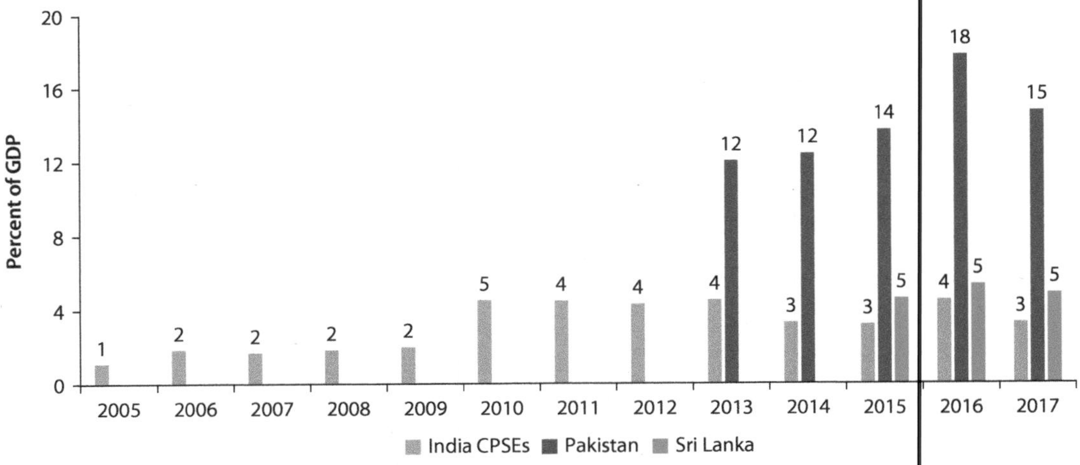

Source: Melecky, Sharma, and Yang 2020 (see details in annex 3A).
Note: CPSEs = central public sector enterprises.

Indian CPSEs are not engaged in inherently more risky activities than private firms. Overall, the results in table 3B.3 show that CPSEs do not have significantly more volatile sales or profits than comparable non-SOEs.[15] Adjusting for size is critical: even though the raw volatility of CPSE sales is significantly lower (column 1), this difference disappears when we include size as a control.

Although individual SOEs do not face more volatile conditions than individual non-SOEs, the SOE sector as a whole could be more volatile because the shocks hitting SOEs are more correlated. But this hypothesis also is not confirmed: The volatility of aggregate CPSE sales has been similar to the aggregate volatility of total sales of private firms in the Prowess database in recent years.

Why Do SOEs Underperform Comparable Private Firms?

Using the same basic regression specification, we next show that SOEs commercially underperform otherwise comparable private sector firms. We regress indicators of performance on the CPSE dummy and controls, such as size, age, and sector-year fixed effects. The results are shown in table 3B.4.

Indian CPSEs overemploy labor and capital. Controlling for size, age, and sector, the revenue-to-wage bill ratio for CPSEs is 85.8 log points lower and their revenue-to-fixed-assets ratio is 21.5 log points lower (columns 2 and 4, respectively).[16] Thus, CPSEs earn less per unit labor cost and per unit capital than comparable private firms. CPSEs also have a higher debt-to-asset ratio than comparable non-SOEs (column 6).

We further compare CPSEs with other firms in terms of revenue-based productivity measures: revenue total factor productivity (TFPR); and the marginal revenue products of capital (MRPK), labor (MRPL), and material inputs (MRPM). The estimates of TFPR, MRPK, MRPL, and MRPM are based on the procedure outlined in Asker et al. (2014), which is based on a model in which firms produce differentiated products using a simple (industry-specific), constant-return Cobb-Douglas production function and face a demand curve that is constantly elastic. The details of the estimation are presented in annex 3C. TFPR measures sales per unit inputs and should not be equated with physical total factor productivity (TFP). Differences in TFPR across firms could reflect distortions such as input adjustment costs, markups, and policy distortions. In a sense, TFPR is similar to the revenue-to-input measures examined in table 3B.4. The difference is that it adjusts for the usage of capital, labor, and raw material by employing industry-specific production function coefficients.[17]

Indian CPSEs are not concentrated in sectors in which profit margins are lower. Table 3B.5 compares the revenue productivity across CPSEs and other firms.[18] The regressions follow the same specifications as those employed in tables 3B.3 and 3B.4. CPSEs have a significantly *higher* TFPR than non-SOEs in the absence of other firm-level controls (column 1). However, this gap becomes statistically insignificant upon introducing controls for size (column 2). Controlling for firm size makes a difference because larger firms have significantly higher TFPR on average, perhaps reflecting higher price markups due to their greater market power. This suggests that CPSEs do not have lower TFPR than comparably large private firms.

Next, we consider the marginal revenue products of labor and capital. CPSEs have significantly lower MRPK and MRPL than non-SOEs (columns 4–8). The gap in MRPL is particularly high (about 83 log points). These results suggest that CPSEs use too much capital and labor—especially the latter—that could be released and efficiently reallocated to private firms with higher marginal returns and capital and labor.

Finally, we observe that CPSEs have a significantly higher marginal revenue product of intermediate inputs (columns 7 and 8). In a sense, CPSEs compensate for the overuse of labor by "underusing" other inputs. For example, SOEs could be using more manual processes, which consume less power.

It has long been argued that SOEs underperform due to internal management problems. It is harder to align the incentives of management and owners in the public sector (see, for example, Ehrlich et al. 1994). The compensation of managers tends to be less strongly linked to the firm's market performance in SOEs (Borisova, Salas, and Zagorchev 2019). A competing hypothesis is that SOEs managers are prevented from

making optimal choices because too many external constraints and conflicting objectives are imposed on them, such as a government mandate leading to excessive hiring (Shleifer and Vishny 1994). The results in tables 3B.4 and 3B.5 are more consistent with the latter theory. In particular, they would seem to favor the hypothesis that SOEs are constrained from adjusting labor use. While internal managerial problems can also lead to inefficient input choices, they are unlikely to cause a systematic and persistent overemployment of an input.

This interpretation is also consistent with recent evidence from a natural experiment involving SOE privatization in India (Baird et al. 2019). This study finds that SOE privatization improved the allocative efficiency of labor across firms by reducing the overemployment of labor in the public sector and reallocating it to private firms with higher marginal returns to labor. Finally, given that we are measuring revenue productivity and not physical productivity, the results could also reflect mandates that prevent SOEs from adjusting prices in response to changes in input costs (Khanna 2012). Some (implicit) mandates could require the SOE to act as an insurance mechanism for volatile prices.

Do SOEs with Better Corporate Governance Perform Better?

Based on the idea that corporate governance reforms could improve SOE performance by enabling better monitoring, greater operational autonomy, and reduced political interference, "corporatization" and corporate governance reforms have taken root in South Asian countries. For example, the Indian government has updated corporate governance guidelines for CPSEs and rates CPSEs on compliance with the guidelines (Government of India 2010). The guidelines relate to the quality and independence of the board of directors, audits, accounting standards, disclosures, and risk management.

To examine whether CPSEs with better corporate governance perform better, we merged data on annual corporate governance (CG) ratings of CPSEs into the Prowess panel. The data are limited because not all CPSEs are rated, but there is some variation in the ratings across CPSEs and over time.[19] This variation allows us to examine the association between the ratings and performance within the subset of CPSEs that have been rated.

Improvements in corporate governance must be complemented by broader reforms in the governing environment around SOEs. The results indicate that a higher corporate governance rating is associated with better performance in the cross-section (table 3B.6). Controlling for sector-year effects, a one-point improvement in the rating (which ranges between 1 and 5) is associated with a 31.4-log point higher revenue-to-wage-bill ratio (column 1). It is also associated with a 5.6-percentage point reduction in the probability of distress (ICR less than 1) (column 7) and a 0.07-point lower debt-to-asset ratio (column 5). However, these correlations are not significant when controlling for firm fixed effects. Because it is possible that the corporate governance rating of CPSEs is correlated with unobserved factors affecting firm performance, the sensitivity of the results to firm fixed effects makes it hard to claim that this regression measures the impact of improved corporate governance. The weak correlation suggests that corporatization alone would not solve the problems of SOE underperformance and financial distress.

The results call for more serious consideration of such reforms as part of package of SOE reforms. The evidence base on corporatization is limited and suggests that corporatization needs to be complemented by even broader reforms of SOE governance and related political economy issues to be effective. Berkowitz, Ma, and Nishioka (2017) argue that part of the positive impact of SOE corporatization in China was due to external changes, such as reduced hiring pressures on SOEs. Corporatization does not necessarily solve the problem of SOEs being captured by politicians or other insiders (Shleifer and Vishny 1994; Qian 1996). For example, there is evidence that the Chinese Communist Party still maintains a high degree of control over corporate SOE boards (Fan, Morck, and Yeung 2011).

Are Soft Loans and Soft Budgets the Root of Contingent Liabilities?

Loans can be used to acquire productive assets, pay for working capital, or cover the occasional loss. The latter course of action is not sustainable if financial markets are competitive and a firm continues to stack up losses. To explore this mechanism, we examine the correlation between the debt-to-asset ratio and accumulated losses in the Prowess panel.

Higher cumulative losses are associated with more indebtedness. Controlling for firm fixed effects and sector-year fixed effects, the estimated β in the specification in table 3B.7 implies that a Rs 1 billion higher accumulated loss is associated with a 0.006 points higher debt-to-asset ratio (column 2). To put these numbers in perspective, the standard deviation of cumulative loss in 2016 is approximately Rs 40 billion. The estimate thus implies that increasing cumulative loss by 1 standard deviation increases the debt-to-asset ratio by 0.24 points. The median debt-to-asset ratio was 0.36. Importantly, this association is significantly stronger among CPSEs. The estimated value of δ (column 4) implies that the additional effect among CPSEs is 0.004 points. This suggests that CPSEs are more likely than other firms to use debt to cover losses.

We explore the soft loan hypothesis—and more broadly, the soft budget constraint hypotheses—further by examining how the financial adjustment to distress and shocks differ among CPSEs and non-SOEs.

Soft loans and implicit guarantees distort the incentives of SOEs to monitor debt levels and act early to improve performance. The results are presented in table 3B.8. Consider first what happens to the average firm on becoming financially distressed (denoted "Enter distress" in the table) (columns 1, 3, and 5). On average, firms that enter distress have a significantly lower growth rate of paid-in capital (equity) and assets (columns 1 and 5). This makes intuitive sense: firms in distress are essentially drawing down their assets. The relationship between distress and the growth rate of debt is positive, but the level of statistical significance is marginal (column 3). Further, this association is not robust to additional firm controls.

The coefficient on the interaction of distress with the CPSE dummy is statistically significant and positive in the case of fixed assets, implying that distress does not hamper CPSEs from acquiring fixed assets to the same extent as it does to non-SOEs. This result is consistent with the soft budget constraint hypothesis. SOEs could also be required to expand they investment to stimulate the economy as the condition of recapitalization or other bailouts—as is the case for the state-owned banks (see chapter 2).

The interaction of distress with the CPSE dummy is statistically insignificant in the case of paid-in capital or debt. This could be because CPSEs adjust through other unobserved channels, such as grants. Another possibility is that our distress measure is too permissive to be able to detect adjustment: as shown earlier, even 20 percent to 30 percent of non-SOEs have an ICR of less than 1 in any given year.

To address these issues, we explore more stringent measures of distress by using large shocks to earnings. We first identify the 10th and 90th percentile of revenue growth rates for every industry in the Prowess panel data. A firm that experiences a revenue growth rate above the 90th percentile of its historical industry norm is classified as experiencing a positive "shock," while a firm that experiences a revenue growth rate below the 10th percentile of its industry norm is classified as experiencing a negative "shock." Our assumption is that these unusual shocks to revenue reflect external market demand factors.[20] Results using similarly defined profit shocks are similar.

Table 3B.9 shows that the raw incidence of negative shocks—that is, not controlling for factors such as firm size—does not vary significantly across CPSEs and non-SOEs

(columns 1 and 4). This result is reassuring because in order to identify the differential adjustment of CPSEs to shocks, we ideally need shocks that are symmetric across CPSEs and other firms. However, controlling for firm-level size, CPSEs have a higher probability of being in a negative shock than other firms (columns 2 and 5). More broadly, the statistically significant coefficients on firm-level variables like CPSE status, size, and age indicate that the shocks as measured are not entirely external to the firm (columns 3 and 6).

The results on the differential adjustment to shocks are presented in table 3B.10. First, considering the regressions without CPSE and shock term interactions (columns 1, 3, and 5), the baseline pattern of adjustment to a shock makes intuitive sense. On average, firms facing a negative (positive) shock have significantly lower (higher) growth rates of debt, paid-in capital, and fixed assets. The most likely explanation is that the availability of funds to finance asset growth is sensitive to revenue shocks because banks and investors see revenue shocks as indicative of repayment capacity.

Next, we observe that the coefficients on the interaction of the CPSE dummy with shocks have consistently a reverse sign to the corresponding baseline shock coefficients (columns 2, 4, and 6) and, in most cases, are statistically significant. This suggests that access to financing—whether through equity or debt—is significantly less sensitive to revenue shocks for CPSEs than for the average firm and that CPSEs do not need to adjust to shocks through assets to the same extent as other firms. Another interpretation is that private firms infer a negative shock as a signal of lower future returns and slow down their borrowing and investment, but SOEs do not behave similarly—suggesting that the latter's decision making is less sensitive to market signals. Overall, the results are consistent with the soft budget constraint hypothesis, which states that the incentives of SOEs to monitor debt levels regularly and act early to improve performance are distorted.

The underperformance of and contigent liabilities stemming from SEOs may not justify blind and unconditional reduction in SOEs across the board. SOEs could still have important roles to play, including through their possible spillovers on the industries in which their operate. We explore the existence of these positive spilovers in the South Asian context next.

The SOE Sector Has a Role to Play in South Asia, Such as through Its Long-Term Investment in R&D and Positive Spillovers on Private Firms

This section explores a major rationale for supporting SOEs: that SOES can complement the private sector by undertaking risky investments with long time horizons. Specifically, this section examines the role of SOEs in undertaking R&D investments. It is well known that investments leading to innovation are underfunded by private investors due to financial market failures (Hall and Lerner 2010). SOEs can help plug this funding gap. For example, in Europe, SOEs tend to invest more than private firms in R&D on sustainable technologies with low commercial returns (Bortolotti, Fotak, and Wolfe 2019).

This analysis is based on Prowess, a panel data set on Indian firms, including CPSEs.

In addition to the availability of panel data, the advantage of studying Indian CPSEs is that they are relatively diverse and can be compared to private sector firms that resemble them in attributes such as size, age, and industry. If this were not the case, it would be difficult to distinguish between ownership (that is, being state owned or private) and other attributes, such as size, age, and sector, when comparing the performance of firms.

The Indian CPSE sector accounts for only about 1 percent of the firms in the Prowess database. Yet, in 2016, 4 of the top 20 Prowess firms in terms of total R&D expenditure were CPSEs. These CPSEs were in aeronautics, heavy machinery, electronics, and oil and gas exploration. Figure 3.13 plots the industry-wise share of CPSEs in total industry fixed assets (x-axis) versus their share in total industry R&D spending (y-axis) in 2016. In most of the industries in which CPSEs have a significant presence (in terms of their share in total fixed assets), their share in R&D spending is disproportionately higher than their share in fixed assets. Indeed, CPSEs account for more than 90 percent of total industry R&D spending in industries such as mining; shipbuilding; manufacturer of aircraft, spacecraft, and related machinery; manufacture of structural metal products; electricity distribution; telecommunications; storage; and transport services.

Table 3B.11 presents regressions comparing R&D spending in CPSEs and non-SOEs. On average, CPSEs have significantly higher R&D spending than other firms (column 1). Note that this estimated R&D gap is robust to including sector-year fixed effects, implying that it is not driven by the concentration of CPSEs in R&D–heavy industries. It is also robust to controlling for firm size and age (columns 2 and 3), although it drops in magnitude upon doing so. In column 4, we interact the CPSE dummy with broad sector dummies to observe that the positive R&D gap between CPSEs and other firms is largely driven by manufacturing.

The regressions presented in table 3B.12 examine the relationship between R&D spending in the public sector and productivity

FIGURE 3.13 **Central Public Sector Enterprise Share of Industry Gross Fixed Assets and Industry Research and Development Expenses in India, 2016**

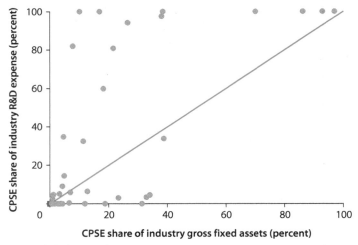

Source: Melecky, Sharma, and Yang 2020.
Note: CPSE = central public sector enterprise; R&D = research and development.

in the private sector. This is to explore whether public sector R&D has any spillovers on the private sector.

We estimate a positive relationship between a firm's own R&D stock and its revenue productivity (as measured by TFPR).[21] Further, an increase in the R&D stock in the CPSE's own industry is also associated with higher revenue per unit input: controlling for firm fixed effects, the estimate of δ is positive and statistically significant at the 10 percent level (column 2). This is not the case with the private R&D stock. The estimate of δ is only marginally sensitive to including controls for the share of the public sector in total industry revenue (column 3).

Given the potential endogeneity of R&D spending, further research would be needed to better establish causation. But these patterns suggest that SOE R&D spending has positive spillovers on private firms in the same industry. This is consistent with the idea that SOEs make long-term investments with positive externalities that would otherwise not be undertaken by the private sector. Any efforts to reduce the state's direct presence in the economy by reducing SOE ownership could thus start with a review to identify those industries in which state presence could be beneficial in the long term, could be needed to create markets, or could expand reach in the medium term and then exit, as opposed to those industries in which state presence is hard to justify.

Only a Combination of Internal and External Policy Reforms Can Help Better Manage Contingent Liabilities from SOEs in South Asia

This chapter has shown that the contingent liabilities arising from SOEs in South Asia can be large but difficult to precisely quantify due to their largely implicit and opaque nature and the lack of data. Governments in South Asia do not track contingent liabilities from SOEs in a systematic manner. Hence, they are ill prepared if those liabilities are triggered. In some cases, it is difficult to quantify even the total liabilities and debt of

SOEs, let alone the contingent liabilities associated with them.

Therefore, the fundamental policy message emerging from this chapter is that it is important for governments to better assess and monitor the fiscal risks from SOEs, incorporate them into their fiscal planning and debt management frameworks, and ensure that adequate provisions have been made for meeting triggered contingent liabilities without disrupting public spending plans. For instance, the government's medium-term fiscal framework (MTFF) should incorporate these contingent liabilities by assessing SOE debt trajectories and their sensitivity to shocks, keeping track of likely government commitments in case of distress (World Bank 2019b).

> Corporate governance guidelines should be strengthened and enforced, and more and better performance contracts should be adopted.

It is also important to mitigate unnecessary contingent liabilities from SOEs. The evidence presented in this chapter suggests that this will entail combining internal, SOE-level reforms to improve their efficiency with external reforms to address the soft budget constraint on SOEs and undue political intrusions into their operations. Internal reforms alone are unlikely to be enough because they seem to work only when SOEs operate in a truly competitive environment (Bartel and Harrison 2005). Global lessons for the World Bank's experience with SOE reforms also suggest that efforts to improve SOE financial performance entail working on several levers, many of which entail efforts to strengthen the broader governance environment of SOEs (World Bank 2019b).

Internal, SOE-Level Reforms: Improving Corporate Governance and Performance Incentives

Corporate governance reforms that professionalize the boards of SOEs, increase their autonomy, and improve financial reporting and external audits can help improve SOE performance by reducing unnecessary costs arising from poor employee or management effort, misaligned incentives, and political interference. This recommendation is supported by the observed positive association between the quality of corporate governance and performance measures in Indian CPSEs (as shown in this analysis) and in India SPSEs (Pargal and Mayer 2014). Although South Asian countries have pursued corporatization of SOEs in recent years, there is still room to strengthen corporate governance guidelines and enforce their full implementation. For example, most state-level power utilities in India comply with the basic corporate governance requirements of the Companies Act, but not with the more stringent guidelines that apply to CPSEs and are recommended for state-owned enterprises (Pargal and Mayer 2014). The formal stringency of financial disclosure and audit requirements appears sound in Indian and Pakistan, but implementation is not well assessed (OECD 2017; Naveed et al. 2018).

Performance contracts could help address SOE underperformance by ameliorating agency problems. A performance contract system typically defines SOE objectives and how they are to be assessed; monitors the achievement of objectives; and creates incentives by linking management rewards to the achievement of objectives. Elements of performance contracting have already been adopted in South Asia. For example, India has introduced a system under which CPSEs sign an annual memorandum of understanding (MOU) with the responsible ministry and get rated on compliance with that MOU. India has also introduced performance-based pay in CPSEs. However, there are doubts about how well this scheme is being implemented (Singh and Mishra 2013).

Overall, we caution that the evidence on the corporatization of SOEs is limited and has been mixed. Our findings on the positive association between CPSE corporate governance and performance are only suggestive. Similarly, evidence on the impacts of performance contracts on SOEs is limited and does not point to encouraging findings (see the survey in Smith and Trebilcock 2001). Relying solely on internal SOE reforms to address the issue of contingent liabilities from SOEs may not be enough.

External Reforms: Addressing the Soft Budget Constraint on SOEs

What *markets* believe about government guarantees to SOEs matters. For instance, in 2015, the Baoding Tianwei Group became the first Chinese central government SOE to default on its debt, shaking the market's faith in the implicit government guarantee behind SOEs. This reduction of implicit guarantees led to a decline in investment and net debt issuance, an increase in cash holdings, and reduced investment efficiency of SOEs in China (Jin, Wang, and Zhang 2018).

Moreover, *political influence* on bank lending to SOEs is a worrying issue in the region. The existence of a large state-owned commercial bank (SOCB) sector in much of South Asia is notable in this regard because "soft" loans of SOCBs to SOEs could be one channel through which governments soften the SOE budget constraints.[22] However, even private sector banks are not immune to this problem. For example, in Pakistan, where banks are largely privatized, preferential lending to politically connected firms has been estimated to cause a significant level of GDP loss through misallocation of capital (Khwaja and Mian 2008). Such banking issues are discussed at length in chapter 2 of this report. Banking sector reform that increases competition and makes banks less susceptible to political influence could help reduce preferential lending to SOEs and discipline their soft budget constraint.

However, reforms to improve the efficiency and competitiveness of the banking sector and financial markets might not end soft loans to SOEs: banks will find SOE loans attractive as long as they believe them to be implicitly guaranteed by the government.

The most urgent and difficult policy issue, therefore, is to address the soft budget constraint by making a credible commitment to not giving unconditional government support to SOEs. The first step toward a credible commitment is to make the objectives of each

SOE clearer and more measurable. In addition to being central to any performance-based management scheme in SOEs, this will allow governments to distinguish between losses incurred because of inefficiencies and losses incurred in efforts to meet socioeconomic objectives.

Making the objectives of every SOE clearer and more measurable will also impose more discipline on the government itself, reducing the temptation to use SOEs as instruments of ever-shifting, short-term policy objectives without due consideration to alternative instruments. The expectation of an implicit, unconditional guarantee to SOEs could arise because financial markets cannot always ascertain whether government support to an SOE is justified by that SOE's mandate, or is simply masking production inefficiency or mismanaged financial risks. Public sector firms should be compensated for excess costs incurred in pursuit of explicit socioeconomic mandates. They should not be compensated for costs arising from inefficiencies to sustain SOEs for political reasons—as is the case with the frequent recapitalization of South Asian public utility companies for losses due to unmetered electricity connections, uncollected energy bills, electricity theft, fraud, and payment evasion (Pargal and Mayer 2014; Zhang 2019).

To introduce greater financial discipline, subsidies for providing public service at affordable (below-market) prices should be channeled through users, to the extent possible, rather than through the obscure financial management systems of SOEs.

Functions and business lines of SOEs should be well aligned with SOE objectives to control possible frivolous diversification and the empire building tendencies of SOE management or their higher-ups.

Governments can also better signal a credible commitment to not giving unconditional support to SOEs by extending them regular support based on previously specified criteria and avoiding bailouts. In 2015, the government of India announced a scheme (Ujwal DISCOM Assurance Yojana, UDAY) under which state governments would take on the debt of loss-making state-owned utility companies in return for a commitment to a charter of reform, which included better metering and reduction in operational losses.[23] Progress on achieving the charter is being monitored through a set of indicators. It is too early to assess the success of the scheme, but the commitment to reform that is required by UDAY is a good idea. It prevents the scheme from devolving into an unconditional bailout. It will be critical for the credibility of this scheme to ensure that the charters are taken seriously by the utilities and state governments. Of course, it would have been even better if the debt of the utilities had not been allowed to build up in the first place.

> To be effective, reforms must signal a credible commitment to not giving unconditional support to SOEs.

Governments must also define clear criteria and methods for determining how to compensate SOEs for costs incurred to meet development objectives. The design of the compensation scheme will depend on the objective of the SOE. For example, SOEs that provide subsidized goods or services should be compensated based on the gap between the price and the marginal cost of provision. The market price gap could be calculated by an independent body, such as a subgroup of the fiscal council. To the extent possible, grants to an SOE should be associated with the specific subsidy programs that it is implementing and kept separate from other balance sheet items. Even better, this subsidy should be channeled through consumers/users of SOE services to install greater financial discipline. Similarly, government loans to fund specific developmental investments should be earmarked as such.

Governments should also adhere to their own rules of SOE compensation and avoid postponing their obligations. For example, subsidies to utilities are not always paid on time. During fiscal 2016, the difference between subsidies booked and subsidies received by state-owned power utilities in India was Rs 24 billion (Zhang 2019). Had the government been paying this compensation on time, there might not have been a need for a scheme like UDAY. Governments should also avoid using circular loans as substitutes for grants when that grant is justified on grounds of a needed social subsidy.

Governments must tie their hands against the possibility of providing unconditional support to SOEs by strengthening internal and external accountability. Internal checks and balances should include strengthened oversight by the central government auditor of government support to SOEs. Distributing the responsibility of regulation, oversight, and policy making related to SOEs is also important. Line ministries are often in charge of all three, potentially creating conflicting priorities. Given that line ministries and finance ministries have limited capacity to monitor SOEs, governments could consider setting up specialized and independent bodies to assess SOE performance at the sector level or to ascertain whether the public intervention is economically justified.

External accountability of government support to SOEs can be strengthened by making data on SOE performance and financial support more transparent and accessible. Some South Asian countries—India, Pakistan, and Sri Lanka—have been publishing SOE-level data in recent years. This is a welcome development. However, as discussed in this chapter, the data are often patchy and not well documented, making it difficult to use them for analysis. Better data would not only help assess and manage risks from SOEs, but also strengthen the credibility of government commitment to tightening the soft budget constraints for SOEs.

Annex 3A. Sources of Data about South Asian SOEs

Bangladesh

Government of Bangladesh, Finance Division, Ministry of Finance. Various years. *Bangladesh Economic Review*.

Bhutan

Government of Bhutan, Ministry of Finance. 2018. *State Enterprises Annual Report*.

India

CMIE (Center for Monitoring the Indian Economy). Various years. Prowess data set. Mumbai.

Government of India, Comptroller and Auditor General of India (CAGI). Various years. *Report of the Comptroller and Auditor General of India on Social, Economic, General, Revenue and General Sectors*.

Government of India, Ministry of Heavy Industries and Public Enterprises, Department of Public Enterprises. Various years. "Public Enterprises Survey."

Government of India, Ministry of Statistics and Programme Implementation. Various years. National Accounts Statistics.

Government of India. 2014. *Annual Report: 2013–14*.

Government of India. 2018. *Annual Report: 2017–18*.

Pakistan

Government of Pakistan, Ministry of Finance, Implementation and Economic Reforms Unit. Various years. *Federal Footprint: SOE Annual Report*.

Sri Lanka

Advocata Institute (Sri Lanka). SOE database (https://www.research.advocata.org/soereform/soe-data/).

Government of Sri Lanka, Ministry of Finance, Department of Public Enterprises. Various years. *Performance Report*.

Government of Sri Lanka, Ministry of Finance. 2019. *Annual Report of the Ministry of Finance*.

TABLE 3A.1   **Definitions/Categorization of State-Owned Enterprises Used in This Report**

Country	Definition/Categorization
Bangladesh	This report follows the classification of nonfinancial public enterprises used by the Finance Division of the Ministry of Finance and also as published in the *Bangladesh Economic Review*, which lists 45 nonfinancial public enterprises.
India (CPSEs)	Central public sector enterprises (CPSEs) are government companies in which more than 50 percent of the equity is held by the central government. (A "government company" is any company in which not less than 51 percent of the paid-up share capital is held by the central government; any state government or governments; or partly by the central government and partly by one or more state governments and includes a company that is a subsidiary company of such a government company.)
Pakistan	This report follows the categorization employed in the Government of Pakistan's *Federal Footprint: SOE Annual Report 2017*, which lists 171 nonfinancial SOEs, including commercial and noncommercial public sector companies and federal authorities.
Sri Lanka	The Ministry of Finance broadly treats any state-controlled institution that is not a department or ministry as a state-owned enterprise (SOE). SOEs could be incorporated by an act of Parliament, or under the Companies Act. SOEs in Sri Lanka include statutory bodies, regulatory agencies, promotional institutions, educational institutions, public corporations, and limited companies. The report generally follows this broad definition of nonfinancial SOEs (which is also followed in the public SOE database published by the Advocata Institute).

Annex 3B. Summary Statistics and Estimations for Indian Enterprises

TABLE 3B.1   **Summary Statistics of Prowess Data for Indian Central Public Sector Enterprises, 2016**

	N	Mean	SD	p25	p50	p75
CPSEs	12,131	0.01	n.a.	n.a.	n.a.	n.a.
Total assets (Rs, million)	12,131	10,795.00	82,738.84	250.30	1,002.80	3,579.20
Sales (Rs, million)	12,131	4,161.56	9,552.77	209.60	929.50	3,103.80
Profit after tax (Rs, million)	12,131	57.19	518.73	−1.60	7.00	69.00
Cumulative loss (Rs, million)	12,131	−2,079.95	43,307.15	−384.00	−37.20	6.00
Interest expense (Rs, million)	12,131	175.17	470.05	3.80	21.50	95.70
R&D expense (Rs, million)	12,131	3.19	14.13	0.00	0.00	0.00
Debt (Rs, million)	12,131	2,208.86	5,984.42	55.90	276.70	1,199.40
Paid-in capital (Rs, million)	12,131	365.60	1,028.03	10.00	51.70	200.00
Gross fixed assets (Rs, million)	12,131	2,421.73	6,481.90	60.70	338.90	1,487.50
Debt-to-asset ratio	12,131	0.41	0.30	0.19	0.36	0.56
Interest coverage ratio (ICR)	12,131	27.71	3,017.92	0.71	1.59	4.00
Wages (Rs, million)	12,131	286.73	680.21	11.90	51.30	203.70
Size of firms (Rs, million)	12,131	6.35	1.86	5.13	6.39	7.55
Age of firms (years)	12,131	17.56	14.19	8.00	14.50	22.00
Corporate governance rating[a]	97	4.00	1.75	4.00	5.00	5.00

Source: World Bank staff calculations based on Prowess data.
Note: Currency unit: Indian rupee (Rs), million. In the last three columns, p25, p50, and p75 refer to 25th, 50th, and 75th percentiles, respectively. CPSEs = central public sector enterprises; R&D = research and development; SD = standard deviation. n.a. = not applicable.
a. Corporate governance performance is rated on a five-point scale, from a low of 1 to a high of 5.

TABLE 3B.2 **Probability of Indian Central Public Sector Enterprises Being Financially Distressed**

	Distress: ICR < 1 in a given year				Distress: ICR < 1 for 2 consecutive years
	(1)	(2)	(3)	(4)	(5)
CPSEs	0.145***	0.207***	0.209***	0.135***	0.211***
	(5.80)	(8.80)	(8.86)	(3.73)	(8.96)
Size		−0.0268***	−0.0265***	−0.0264***	−0.0167***
		(−21.31)	(−20.83)	(−20.60)	(−14.53)
Age			−0.000232	−0.000227	−0.000195
			(−1.64)	(−1.60)	(−1.56)
CPSE × Agriculture				0.0564	
				(0.80)	
CPSE × Mining				−0.0380	
				(−0.37)	
CPSE × Petroleum				−0.174*	
				(−2.07)	
CPSE × Manufacturing				0.144**	
				(2.94)	
Sector-year fixed effects	Yes	Yes	Yes	Yes	Yes
Observations	178,410	178,410	178,410	178,410	178,410
R-squared	0.0341	0.0442	0.0443	0.0448	0.0407

Source: Melecky, Sharma, and Yang 2020.
Note: The table uses the following specification: $Distress_{it} = a + \beta CPSE_i + \gamma X_i + \theta_{jt} + \varepsilon_{it}$, where $Distress_{it}$ is an indicator for a firm i being in distress in year t. The specification controls for X_i, a set of time-invariant firm characteristics such as average size and age in the panel data set. It also controls for sectoral differences and sector-specific shocks though θ_{jt}, a set of sector-year dummies. It is important to control for these factors because SOEs are larger than the typical non-SOEs and concentrate in certain sectors. For column 4, specification is modified to: $Distress_{it} = a + \beta CPSE_i + \gamma X_i + \delta CPSE_i * Sector_j + \theta_{jt} + \varepsilon_{it}$. The standard errors are clustered by firm to account for serial-correlation in shocks. t statistics are in parentheses. . CPSEs = central public sector enterprises; ICR = interest coverage ratio.
*p < 0.05, ** p < 0.01, *** p < 0.001.

TABLE 3B.3 **Volatility of Sales and Profit for Indian Central Public Sector Enterprises**

	Sales volatility			Profit volatility		
	(1)	(2)	(3)	(4)	(5)	(6)
CPSEs	−0.261**	0.0224	0.0538	−1.836***	−0.948*	−0.844
	(−2.71)	(0.22)	(0.54)	(−4.10)	(−2.08)	(−1.84)
Size		−0.147***	−0.137***		−0.466***	−0.435***
		(−10.58)	(−9.88)		(−7.20)	(−6.70)
Age			−0.00681***			−0.0208**
			(−6.19)			(−3.27)
Sector-year fixed effects	Yes	Yes	Yes	Yes	Yes	Yes
Observations	46,165	46,165	46,165	49,495	49,495	49,495
R-squared	0.0642	0.0777	0.0810	0.0170	0.0225	0.0236

Source: Melecky, Sharma, and Yang 2020.
Note: The table uses a specification similar to that used to estimate distress incidence in table 3B.2. Volatility on the indicator for CPSE, controls such as size and age, and sector-year fixed effects are regressed: $Volatility_{xit} = a + \beta CPSE_i + \gamma X_i + \theta_{jt} + \varepsilon_{it}$. Standard errors are clustered at the firm level. t statistics are in parentheses. CPSEs = central public sector enterprises.
*p < 0.05, ** p < 0.01, *** p < 0.001.

TABLE 3B.4   State Ownership and Financial Performance of Indian Central Public Sector Enterprises

	Log(revenue/wage)		Log(revenue/fixed assets)		Debt-to-asset ratio	
	(1)	(2)	(3)	(4)	(5)	(6)
CPSEs	0.753***	−0.858***	−0.183*	−0.215**	0.144***	0.204***
	(7.93)	(−11.81)	(−2.36)	(−2.76)	(4.51)	(6.51)
Size		0.700***		0.0205***		−0.0187***
		(158.22)		(3.94)		(−14.28)
Age		0.000486		−0.00151**		−0.00158***
		(1.13)		(−2.87)		(−11.19)
Sector-year fixed effects	Yes	Yes	Yes	Yes	Yes	Yes
Observations	178,410	178,410	178,410	178,410	178,410	178,410
R-squared	0.132	0.602	0.182	0.183	0.0314	0.0475

Source: Melecky, Sharma, and Yang 2020.
Note: Standard errors are clustered at the firm level. t statistics are in parentheses. CPSEs = central public sector enterprises.
*$p < 0.05$, **$p < 0.01$, ***$p < 0.001$.

TABLE 3B.5   Productivity for Indian Central Public Sector Enterprises and Non-Central Public Sector Enterprises

	TFPR		MRPK		MRPL		MRPM	
	(1)	(2)	(3)	(4)	(5)	(6)	(7)	(8)
CPSEs	0.618***	−0.0156	−0.274**	−0.313**	−0.735***	−0.833***	0.345***	0.287***
	(9.69)	(−0.40)	(−2.88)	(−3.28)	(−9.07)	(−10.86)	(4.69)	(3.92)
Size		0.254***		0.0143*		0.107***		0.00271
		(96.30)		(2.18)		(23.35)		(0.63)
Age		0.00445***		0.000620		−0.0141***		0.00488***
		(16.20)		(1.03)		(−30.79)		(11.01)
Sector-year fixed effects	Yes	Yes	Yes	Yes	Yes	Yes	Yes	Yes
Observations	131,275	131,275	131,275	131,275	131,275	131,275	131,275	131,275
R-squared	0.160	0.464	0.258	0.259	0.0432	0.125	0.0770	0.0861

Source: Melecky, Sharma, and Yang 2020.
Note: Standard errors are clustered at the firm level. t statistics are in parentheses. CPSEs = central public sector enterprises; MRPK = marginal revenue product of capital; MRPL = marginal revenue product of labor; MRPM = marginal revenue product of material inputs; TFPR = revenue total factor productivity.
*$p < 0.05$, **$p < 0.01$, ***$p < 0.001$.

TABLE 3B.6   Corporate Governance Ratings and Financial Performance of Indian Central Public Sector Enterprises

	Log(revenue/ wage)		Log(revenue/ fixed assets)		Debt-to-asset ratio		ICR < 1	
	(1)	**(2)**	**(3)**	**(4)**	**(5)**	**(6)**	**(7)**	**(8)**
Corporate governance rating	0.314***	0.00844	0.0843	0.0283	−0.0747***	0.00403	−0.0565**	0.0163
	(6.06)	(0.26)	(1.48)	(1.31)	(−3.76)	(0.32)	(−3.25)	(0.91)
Firm fixed effects	No	Yes	No	Yes	No	Yes	No	Yes
Sector-year fixed effects	Yes	Yes	Yes	Yes	Yes	Yes	Yes	Yes
Observations	398	398	398	398	398	398	398	398
R-squared	0.392	0.944	0.501	0.959	0.186	0.935	0.249	0.785

Source: Melecky, Sharma, and Yang 2020.
Note: The table uses the following specification: $X_{it} = a + \beta Rating_{it} + \gamma_i + \theta_{it} + \varepsilon_{it}$. Here, X_{it} is a performance measure; $Rating_{it}$ is the firm's annual corporate governance rating; γ_i is a firm fixed effect; and θ_{it} are sector-year fixed effects. Standard errors are clustered at the firm level. t statistics are in parentheses. CPSEs = central public sector enterprises; ICR = interest coverage ratio.
* $p < 0.05$, ** $p < 0.01$, *** $p < 0.001$.

TABLE 3B.7   Cumulative Losses and Debt-to-Asset Ratio of Indian Central Public Sector Enterprises

	Debt-to-asset ratio			
	(1)	**(2)**	**(3)**	**(4)**
Cumulative loss	0.0146***	0.00606***	0.00746***	0.0730***
	(20.77)	(11.59)	(11.41)	(11.16)
CPSEs × Cumulative loss			−0.00593***	0.00425**
			(−7.00)	(2.64)
Firm fixed effects	No	Yes	Yes	Yes
Sector-year fixed effects	Yes	Yes	Yes	Yes
Size × Cumulative loss	No	No	No	Yes
Observations	178,410	178,410	178,410	178,410
R-squared	0.0483	0.692	0.692	0.696

Source: Melecky, Sharma, and Yang 2020.
Note: The table regresses the debt-to-asset ratio of firm i in year t on its cumulative loss, $CLoss_{it}$, firm fixed effects, γ_i, and sector-year fixed effects, θ_{it}, as follows:
$DebtAsset_{it} a = \beta CLoss_{it} + \delta CPSE_i * CLoss_{it} + \theta X_i * CLoss_{it} + \gamma_i + \theta_{it} + \varepsilon_{it}$.
The coefficient on the interaction between the CPSE dummy and cumulative loss, δ, measures how the relationship between cumulative loss and the debt-to-asset-ratio differs for CPSEs compared with the average firm. Knowing that CPSEs are larger than the average firm, the specification also controls for an interaction of size and other attributes with the cumulative loss variable. Cumulative losses are expressed in US$, billion. The debt-to-asset ratio is expressed as a percentage. Standard errors are clustered at the firm level. t statistics are in parentheses. CPSEs = central public sector enterprises.
* $p < 0.05$, ** $p < 0.01$, *** $p < 0.001$.

TABLE 3B.8 **Distress and the Growth Rate of Paid-in Capital, Debt, and Fixed Assets of Indian Central Public Sector Enterprises**

	Growth rate of paid-up capital		Growth rate of debt		Growth rate of gross fixed assets	
	(1)	(2)	(3)	(4)	(5)	(6)
Enter distress	−0.0190***	−0.0200*	0.0126*	−0.0156	−0.00886**	−0.0333**
	(−8.76)	(−2.45)	(2.48)	(−0.86)	(−3.05)	(−3.15)
CPSEs × Enter distress		0.0333		0.0232		0.0511*
		(1.66)		(0.44)		(2.33)
Enter distress × Size		0.0000750		0.00455		0.00387*
		(0.06)		(1.64)		(2.22)
Firm fixed effects	Yes	Yes	Yes	Yes	Yes	Yes
Sector-year fixed effects	Yes	Yes	Yes	Yes	Yes	Yes
Size × Enter distress	No	Yes	No	Yes	No	Yes
Observations	178,410	178,410	178,410	178,410	178,410	178,410
R-squared	0.259	0.259	0.194	0.194	0.297	0.298

Source: Melecky, Sharma, and Yang 2020.
Note: The basic regression is as follows: $Y_{it} = a + \beta Shock_{it} + \delta CPSE_i * Shock_{it} + \theta X_i * Shock_{it} + \gamma_i + \theta_{it} + \varepsilon_{it}$.
The regressions include firm fixed effects, γ_i, and sector-year fixed effects, θ_{it}, as controls. γ_{it} is a measure of financial adjustment (the annual growth rate of debt, paid-up capital, or assets). $Shock_{it}$ is a measure of a firm-level shock. The regression is mainly interested in the interaction term coefficient, δ, which measures the differential adjustment of CPSEs to the shock. The regression first examines what happens when a firm enters distress. In this case, the "shock" measure is a dummy that is equal to 1 when a firm enters distress (switches from ICR of more than 1 in the previous year to ICR of less than 1 in the current year). These estimates should not be interpreted as measuring the causal impact of distress because distress is potentially endogenous to financial decisions. For example, depending on what the borrowed funds are used for, new debt could increase interest payments more rapidly than earnings. "Enter distress" refers to the point at which a firm becomes financially distressed based on ICR. Standard errors are clustered at the firm level. *t* statistics are in parentheses. CPSEs = central public sector enterprises.
* p < 0.05, ** p < 0.01, *** p < 0.001.

TABLE 3B.9 **Probability of Negative Shocks to Sales and Profit for Indian Central Public Sector Enterprises**

	Negative sales shock			Negative profit shock		
	(1)	(2)	(3)	(4)	(5)	(6)
CPSEs	0.00218	0.0380***	0.0403***	−0.00191	0.00851*	0.00921*
	(0.32)	(5.89)	(6.28)	(−0.47)	(2.13)	(2.30)
Size		−0.0156***	−0.0153***		−0.00454***	−0.00444***
		(−35.34)	(−34.47)		(−14.55)	(−14.10)
Age			−0.000287***			−0.0000901**
			(−6.58)			(−2.70)
Sector-year fixed effects	Yes	Yes	Yes	Yes	Yes	Yes
Observations	178,410	178,410	178,410	178,410	178,410	178,410
R-squared	0.0111	0.0223	0.0227	0.00664	0.00787	0.00792

Source: Melecky, Sharma, and Yang 2020.
Note: Standard errors are clustered at the firm level. *t* statistics are in parentheses. CPSEs = central public sector enterprises.
* p < 0.05, ** p < 0.01, *** p < 0.001.

TABLE 3B.10   Sales Shock and the Growth Rate of Paid-up Capital, Debt, and Fixed Assets for Indian Central Public Sector Enterprises

	Growth rate of paid-up capital		Growth rate of debt		Growth rate of gross fixed assets	
	(1)	(2)	(3)	(4)	(5)	(6)
Negative sales shock	−0.0165***	−0.0209*	−0.0538***	−0.0191	−0.0561***	−0.0324**
	(−6.49)	(−2.25)	(−8.38)	(−0.87)	(−18.32)	(−3.00)
Positive sales shock	0.0576***	0.0309*	0.121***	0.0586**	0.0898***	−0.00558
	(17.90)	(2.53)	(21.58)	(2.90)	(24.38)	(−0.41)
CPSEs × Negative sales shock		0.0437*		0.118*		0.0578**
		(2.52)		(2.47)		(3.02)
CPSEs × Positive sales shock		−0.0349		−0.130**		−0.110***
		(−1.76)		(−3.18)		(−4.67)
Negative sales shock × Size		0.000515		−0.00667		−0.00464*
		(0.33)		(−1.80)		(−2.52)
Positive sales shock × Size		0.00442*		0.0105***		0.0158***
		(2.32)		(3.34)		(7.08)
Firm fixed effects	Yes	Yes	Yes	Yes	Yes	Yes
Sector-year fixed effects	Yes	Yes	Yes	Yes	Yes	Yes
Size × Negative shock	No	Yes	No	Yes	No	Yes
Size × Positive shock	No	Yes	No	Yes	No	Yes
Observations	178,410	178,410	178,410	178,410	178,410	178,410
R-squared	0.263	0.263	0.199	0.199	0.307	0.308

Source: Melecky, Sharma, and Yang 2020.
Note: Standard errors are clustered at the firm level. *t* statistics are in parentheses. CPSEs = central public sector enterprises.
*p < 0.05, ** p < 0.01, *** p < 0.001.

TABLE 3B.11   Research and Development Expenditure: Comparing Indian Central Public Sector Enterprises to Other Firms

	R&D expenditure			
	(1)	(2)	(3)	(4)
CPSEs	7.491***	2.896*	2.428	−0.804
	(4.92)	(2.16)	(1.81)	(−0.54)
Size		2.003***	1.935***	1.939***
		(20.51)	(20.57)	(20.62)
Age			0.0598***	0.0600***
			(7.81)	(7.83)
CPSEs × Agriculture				1.554
				(0.24)
CPSEs × Mining				−3.044
				(−1.23)
CPSEs × Petroleum				37.78
				(1.84)
CPSEs × Manufacturing				6.131*
				(2.28)
Sector-year fixed effects	Yes	Yes	Yes	Yes
Observations	178,410	178,410	178,410	178,410
R-squared	0.0695	0.105	0.108	0.109

Source: Melecky, Sharma, and Yang 2020.
Note: The table uses the following specification: $R\&D_{it} = a + \beta CPSE_i + \gamma X_i + \theta_{it} + \varepsilon_{it}$.
$R\&D_{it}$ measures R&D expenditure in a firm i in year t. The regression controls for X_i, a set of time-invariant firm characteristics such as average size and age in the panel data set. Firm size is measured by its total assets (in logs) averaged over the entire panel. The regression also controls for sectoral differences and sector-specific shocks through θ_{it}, a set of sector-year dummies. This is because SOEs are larger than the typical non-SOE and concentrate in certain sectors. The standard errors are clustered by firm to account for serial-correlation in shocks. *t* statistics are in parentheses. CPSEs = central public sector enterprises; R&D = research and development.
*p < 0.05, ** p < 0.01, *** p < 0.001.

TABLE 3B.12   Relationship between Public Sector Research and Development and Private Sector Performance in India

	Revenue total factor productivity (TFPR)		
	(1)	(2)	(3)
Log of R&D stock	0.102***	0.0308***	0.0289***
	(18.15)	(9.66)	(9.42)
Log of private R&D stock	−0.0277*	0.00327	0.00778
	(−2.51)	(0.65)	(1.54)
Log of public R&D stock	0.000722	0.00926*	0.00806
	(0.08)	(1.99)	(1.56)
Private market share			−1.358***
			(−8.38)
Public market share			−1.426***
			(−8.36)
Firm fixed effects	No	Yes	Yes
Year fixed effects	Yes	Yes	Yes
Standard errors clustered at industry level	Yes	Yes	Yes
Observations	128,242	128,242	128,242
R-squared	0.118	0.832	0.835

Source: Melecky, Sharma, and Yang 2020.

Note: The table uses the following basic specification: $X_{it} = a + \beta R\&D\ Stock_{it} + \gamma Public\ R\&D\ Stock_{it} + \gamma Private\ R\&D\ Stock_{it} + \gamma_i + \theta_{it} + \varepsilon_{it}$.
X_{it} is a revenue-based measure of the performance of firm *i* in year *t*. $R\&D\ Stock_{it}$ is a measure of the firm's own R&D stock. The R&D stock is measured as the sum of current and past R&D expenditures, assuming an annual depreciation of 20 percent. For details of measuring the stock of R&D and other intangible investment, please see Dutz et al. (2012). The variable *Public R&D Stock$_{it}$* measures the total R&D stock of all CPSEs in the same 3-digit industry as firm *i*. The variable *Public R&D Stock$_{it}$* measures the total R&D stock of all non-SOEs in the same 3-digit industry as firm *i* (excluding the firm itself). The variable y_i is a firm fixed effect, and θ_{it} are year dummies.
Because the public and private R&D stock variables are time-varying industry-level variables, they are collinear with industry-year dummies, and their effects cannot be identified separately from those of other industry-specific shocks. The regression is mainly interested in δ, which captures the relationship between the aggregate stock of R&D in public sector firms in firm *i*'s industry and firm *i*'s performance.
Because the analysis is interested in spillovers to the private sector, the regression is estimated on the subsample of non–state-owned enterprises (SOEs) in Prowess. In a robustness check, controls were added for the share of the public sector and all private sector firms other than firm *i* in total industry revenue. This is because the public R&D stock variables could be correlated with the size of the public sector, with the latter potentially affecting the revenue of firm *i* through its effect on input and output prices. *t* statistics are in parentheses. R&D = research and development.
*p < 0.05, ** p < 0.01, *** p < 0.001.

Annex 3C. Productivity Estimation

We follow the model and procedure employed in Asker et al. (2014). A firm *i*, in time *t*, produces output Q_{it} using the following technology:

$$Q_{it} = A_{it} K_{it}^{\alpha_K} L_{it}^{\alpha_L} M_{it}^{\alpha_M}, \qquad (3C.1)$$

where K_{it} is the capital input, L_{it} is the labor input, and M_{it} is raw materials. A_{it} is the firm's total factor productivity (TFP).

The production function is assumed to have constant returns to scale (CRS), implying that $\alpha_k + \alpha_L + \alpha_M = 1$.

The firm faces a demand curve with a constant elasticity:

$$Q_{it} = B_{it} P_{it}^{-\epsilon}. \qquad (3C.2)$$

Combining equations (3C.1) and (3C.2), Asker et al. (2014) obtain the expression for the sales-generating production function:

$$S_{it} = \Omega_{it} K_{it}^{\beta_K} L_{it}^{\beta_L} M_{it}^{\beta_M}, \qquad (3C.3)$$

where Ω_{it} is a function of TFP and the parameters of the demand curve, and $\beta_X = \alpha_X \left(1 - \frac{1}{\epsilon}\right)$ for input $X \in \{K, L, M\}$.

Revenue total factor productivity (TFPR) is defined as the log of Ω_{it}. It can be inferred from sales and input values using the sales generating function in equation (3C.3) and taking logs:

$$TFPR_{it} = \log(S)_{it} - \beta_K \log(K)_{it} - \beta_L \log(L)_{it} - \beta_M \log(M)_{it} \qquad (3C.4)$$

Similarly, the marginal revenue product of an input X can be inferred as

$$MRPX_{it} = \log(\beta_X) + \log(S_{it}) - \log(X_{it}) \qquad (3C.5)$$

To estimate the revenue production function input coefficients (the βs), Asker et al. (2014) use the first-order condition for the optimal use of a flexible input in a static model with no frictions or distortions. The condition is that the revenue share of the input's expenditure should equal its revenue function coefficient:

$$\beta_X = \frac{P_{it} X_{it}}{S_{it}}. \qquad (3C.6)$$

Following the procedure in Asker et al. (2014), we use the median expenditure shares of labor and raw materials in every 3-digit industry to estimate β_L and β_M. The medians are calculated using Prowess data pooled over 2000 and 2016. We limit the sample to the same time period in our revenue productivity regressions to avoid any potential biases arising from potential long-term changes in these input coefficients due to demand or technological trends. We estimate β_k as

$$\beta_K = \frac{\epsilon - 1}{\epsilon} - \beta_L - \beta_M, \qquad (3C.7)$$

where ϵ is set equal to 4 following Bloom (2009). To compute TFPR and the marginal revenue products of labor and capital, we plug in the estimated input coefficients into equations (3C.4) and (3C.5).

Notes

1. Unfortunately, data on another measure that would be more appropriate than revenues for comparisons of the share of GDP—value added by the SOE sector—are not available for most South Asian countries.
2. See the Solar Energy Corporation of India Ltd site: http://www.seci.co.in/.
3. The idea of coordination failures goes back to Rosenstein-Rodan's (1943) theory of a "big push" in industrialization. The technology and skills example is from Rodríguez-Clare (2005).
4. See the Rail India Technical and Economic Service Ltd site: https://www.rites.com/index.php?page=page&id=8&name=Profile&mid=8.
5. See https://www.research.advocata.org/sri-lankas-soes-burn-peoples-cash-burden-budgets-undermine-national-savings/, which is based on data from the government of Sri Lanka, Public Enterprises Department.
6. The notion of an implicit government guarantee on SOE debt is not limited to South Asia (see, for example, European Commission 2016).
7. For a review of the global evidence, see Shirley and Walsh (2001). For evidence on India, see Majumdar (1996). For evidence on China, see Li, Lin, and Selover (2014) and Harrison et al. (2019).
8. Similarly, Naveed et al. (2018) suggest that at least in formal terms, SOEs in Pakistan follow clear corporate governance norms related to operational autonomy and financial reporting.
9. It is worth noting that the agency and environmental hypotheses are not mutually exclusive, nor are they necessarily independent of each other.
10. See, for example, S&P Global Ratings, 2017, "SOE Shake-Up: China's Support for Its Ailing Enterprises Will Become More Selective."
11. Our results stay the same if for a given regression we include observations that might be missing other outcome variables but not those relevant to the regression in question. Further, when using Prowess to compute an aggregate statistic for the CPSE sector, we include all observations (except those missing the statistic in question).

12. Although Sri Lanka has 400 SOEs (including subsidiaries), detailed financial data are available for only 42 nonfinancial SOEs, which have been identified by the government as strategically important state-owned business enterprises (SOBEs), based on their importance to the national economy and size.

13. The numbers in this paragraph capture SOE revenues, not value added, as a share of GDP, and as such overstate the contribution of SOEs to GDP. Official public sector reports of South Asian countries often tend to report SOE revenue but not value added. As a result, we could not get comparable and up-to-date value added figures for SOEs across the set of five South Asian countries included in figure 3.1.

14. Even when available, the data do not distinguish between capital investment, grants for developmental purposes, and grants or loans to cover losses.

15. The number of observations is lower than in table 3B.2 because we cannot calculate 10-year centered volatility for the last and first 5 years of the panel, and because only a subset of firms is observed continuously for 10 years.

16. Prowess does not report employment numbers for most firms. We follow prior studies using Prowess (such as Asker, Collard-Wexler, and De Loecker 2014) that have used the wage bill instead of employment.

17. See Hseih and Klenow (2009) for a discussion on the interpretation of revenue-based productivity measures.

18. As explained in more detail in annex 3B, the TFPR calculation involves the estimation of 3-digit industry-specific input coefficients. To lessen the noise in these estimates, we only include 3-digit industries that have at least 10 firms in the panel in 2016. This reduces the sample size compared to the other regressions.

19. Eighty CPSEs were rated in 2010. This number increased to 161 by 2016. The median rating rose from 1.6 to 1.2 (on a five-point scale where 5 is best and 1 is worst) between 2010 and 2017, while the standard deviation increased from 1.0 to 1.3.

20. We cannot claim that these shocks are truly external to the firm because we do not know their underlying causes. In future work, we plan to instrument for these revenue shocks by using more exogenous drivers, such as export market shocks or input cost shocks.

21. TFPR essentially measures sales per unit inputs. Further details about its estimation and interpretation are discussed in this chapter.

22. The lack of access to sufficiently disaggregated lending data, however, makes it difficult to test whether SOCBs make softer loans to SOEs than private banks do in South Asia.

23. See UDAY's official website at https://www.uday.gov.in/home.php.

References

Allen, F., X. Gu, J. Qian, and Y. Qian. 2017. "Implicit Guarantee and Shadow Banking: The Case of Trust Products." Working paper.

Asker, J., A. Collard-Wexler, and J. De Loecker. 2014. "Dynamic Inputs and Resource (Mis) Allocation." *Journal of Political Economy* 122 (5, October): 1013–63.

Baird, M., A. V. Chari, S. Nataraj, A. Rothenberg, S. Telhaj, and L. A. Winters. 2019. "The Public Sector and the Misallocation of Labor: Evidence from a Policy Experiment in India." CEP Discussion Paper 1596, Centre for Economic Performance, London School of Economics and Political Science.

Bartel, A., and A. E. Harrison. 2005. "Ownership versus Environment: Disentangling the Sources of Public-Sector Inefficiency." *Review of Economics and Statistics* 87 (1): 135–47.

BBNL (Bharat Broadband Network Limited). 2019. *Annual Report, 2018–19.* http://www.bbnl.nic.in//admnis/admin/shwimg.aspx?ID=1342.

Berkowitz, D., H. Ma, and S. Nishioka. 2017. "Recasting the Iron Rice Bowl: The Reform of China's State-Owned Enterprises." *Review of Economics and Statistics* 99 (4): 735–47.

Bloom, N. 2009. "The Impact of Uncertainty Shocks." *Econometrica* 77 (3): 623–85.

Borisova, G., J. M. Salas, and A. Zagorchev. 2019. "CEO Compensation and Government Ownership." *Corporate Governance: An International Review* 27 (2): 120–43.

Bortolotti, B., V. Fotak, and B. Wolfe. 2019. "Innovation at State-Owned Enterprises." Working paper, Bocconi University, Milan.

Comin, D., and T. Philippon. 2005. "The Rise in Firm-Level Volatility: Causes and Consequences." In *NBER Macroeconomics Annual 2005*, vol. 20, edited by Mark Gertler and Kenneth Rogoff, 229–312. Cambridge, MA: MIT Press.

Dal Bo, E. 2006. "Regulatory Capture: A Review." *Oxford Review of Economic Policy* 22 (2): 203–25.

Dutz, M. A., S. Kannebley, M. Scarpelli, and S. Sharma. 2012. "Measuring Intangible Assets in an Emerging Market Economy: An Application to Brazil." Policy Research Working Paper 6142, World Bank, Washington, DC.

Ehrlich, I., G. Gallais-Hamonno, Z. Liu, and R. Lutter. 1994. "Productivity Growth and Firm Ownership: An Analytical and Empirical Investigation." *Journal of Political Economy* 102 (October): 1006–38.

European Commission. 2016. "State-Owned Enterprises in the EU: Lessons Learnt and Ways Forwards in a Post Crisis Context." Institutional Paper 31, European Commission, Brussels.

Fan, J., R. Morck, and B. Yeung. 2011. "Capitalizing China." NBER Working Paper 17687, National Bureau of Economic Research, Cambridge, MA.

Government of India, Ministry of Heavy Industries and Public Enterprises. 2010. Corporate Governance Guidelines for CPSEs. https://dpe .gov.in/sites/default/files/gcgcpse10.pdf.

Government of India, Ministry of Heavy Industries and Public Enterprises. 2014. *Annual Report: 2013–14.* Government of India.

Government of India, Ministry of Heavy Industries and Public Enterprises. 2018. *Annual Report: 2017–18.* Government of India.

Government of Pakistan. 2016. *Federal Footprint: SOE Annual Report 2015–16.* Government of Pakistan.

Hall, B. H., and J. Lerner. 2010. "The Financing of R&D and Innovation. In *Handbook of the Economics of Innovation*, vol. 1, edited by Bronwyn H. Hall and Nathan Rosenberg, 609–39. North-Holland, Amsterdam.

Harrison, A., M. Meyer, P. Wang, L. Zhao, and M. Zhao. 2019. "Can a Tiger Change Its Stripes? Reform of Chinese State-Owned Enterprises in the Penumbra of the State." NBER Working Paper 25475, National Bureau of Economic Research, Cambridge, MA.

Hsieh, C-T, and P. J. Klenow. 2009. "Misallocation and Manufacturing TFP in China and India." *Quarterly Journal of Economics* 124 (4, November): 1403–48.

Jensen, M. C. 1986. "Agency Costs of Free Cash Flow, Corporate Finance, and Takeovers." *American Economic Review* 76: 323–29.

Jin, S., W. Wang, and Z. Zhang. 2018. "The Value and Real Effects of Implicit Guarantees." Working paper, Hong Kong University of Science and Technology.

Khanna, S. 2012. "State-Owned Enterprises in India: Restructuring and Growth." *Copenhagen Journal of Asian Studies* 30 (2): 5–28.

Khwaja, A. I., and A. Mian. 2008. "Tracing the Impact of Bank Liquidity Shocks: Evidence from an Emerging Market." *American Economic Review* 98 (4): 1413–42.

Kornai, J. 1986. "The Soft Budget Constraint." *Kyklos* 39: 3–30.

Li, S., Y. C. Lin, and D. Selover. 2014. "Chinese State-Owned Enterprises: Are They Inefficient?" *Chinese Economy* 47 (5–6): 81–115.

Majumdar, S. K. 1996. "Assessing Comparative Efficiency of the State-Owned, Mixed, and Private Sectors in Indian Industry." *Public Choice* 96: 1–24.

Maskin, E., and C. Xu. 2001. "Soft Budget Constraint Theories: From Centralization to the Market." *Economics of Transition* 9: 1–27.

Melecky, M., S. Sharma, and D. Yang. 2020. "State-Owned Enterprises in South Asia: The Distresses, Adjustments, and Fiscal Contingent Liabilities." Background paper for *Hidden Debt*. World Bank, Washington, DC.

Naveed, S., Y. Salman, N. Jabeen, M. Zafar, I. Jadoon, and S. Irfan. 2018. "Governance and Management of SOEs in Pakistan." *Pakistan Economic and Social Review* 56 (1, Summer): 47–66.

OECD (Organisation for Economic Co-operation and Development). 2017. *Disclosure and Transparency in the State-Owned Enterprise Sector in Asia: Stocktaking of National Practices.* Paris: OECD.

Pargal, S., and K. Mayer. 2014. *Governance of Indian State Power Utilities: An Ongoing Journey. Directions in Development–Energy and Mining.* Washington, DC: World Bank.

Peltzman, S. 1976. "Toward a More General Theory of Regulation." *Journal of Law and Economics* 19 (2): 245–48.

Qian, Y. 1996. "Enterprise Reform in China: Agency Problems and Political Control." *Economics of Transition* 4 (2): 427–47.

Richmond, C. J., D. Benedek, E. Cabezon, B. Cegar, P. Dohlman, M. Hassine, B. Jajko, P. Kopyrski, M. Markevych, J. A. Miniane, F. J. Parodi, G. Pula, J. Roaf, M. K. Song, M. Sviderskaya, R. Turk, and S. Weber. 2019. *Reassessing the Role of State-Owned Enterprises in Central, Eastern, and Southeastern Europe*. Washington, DC: International Monetary Fund.

Rodríguez-Clare, A. 2005. "Coordination Failures, Clusters, and Microeconomic Interventions," with comments by F. Rodríguez, R. Hausmann, and J. M. Benaventa. *Economía* 6 (1): 1–42.

Rosenstein-Rodan, P. N. 1943. "Problems of Industrialisation of Eastern and South-Eastern Europe." *Economic Journal* 53 (210/211): 202–11.

Shirley, M. M., and P. Walsh. 2001. "Public vs. Private Ownership: The Current State of the Debate." Policy Research Working Paper 8288, World Bank, Washington, DC.

Shleifer, A., and R. W. Vishny. 1994. "Politicians and Firms." *Quarterly Journal of Economics* 109 (4, November): 995–1025.

Singh, P., and R. K. Mishra. 2013. "Performance-Related Pay in Central Public Sector Enterprises in India." *Indian Journal of Industrial Relations* 49 (2, October): 314–27.

Smith, A., and M. Trebilcock. 2001. "State-Owned Enterprises in Less Developed Countries: Privatization and Alternative Reform Strategies." *European Journal of Law and Economics* 12: 217–52.

Stigler, G. J. 1971. "The Theory of Economic Regulation." *Bell Journal of Economics and Management Science* 2 (1): 3–21.

World Bank. 2019a. "Non-financial State-Owned Enterprises in Bangladesh: Improving Corporate Governance and Financial Performance." World Bank, Washington, DC. Unpublished.

World Bank. 2019b. "Integrated State-Owned Enterprises Framework (iSOEF) Guidance Note Module 2: Assessing the Fiscal Implications of SOE Reform." World Bank, Washington, DC.

Zhang, F. 2019. *In the Dark: How Much Do Power Sector Distortions Cost India?* South Asia Development Forum. Washington, DC: World Bank Group.

Subnational Governments in South Asia: Balancing the Fiscal Risks of Government Decentralization with the Returns | 4

Fiscal decentralization is on the rise around the world, including in South Asia. This chapter investigates subnational fiscal risks and contingent liabilities in South Asia, a region where many countries are already at high risk of debt distress.[1]

The chapter first examines the institutional frameworks across South Asia and relates them to the likelihood of exposure to subnational fiscal risks. An important finding is that central governments in most South Asian countries delegate extremely limited authority to subnational governments to borrow—thus minimizing subnational fiscal risks but also potentially foregoing the benefits of decentralized decision making.

The chapter next studies Pakistan, one of the two countries in South Asia whose institutional framework allows the central government to be exposed to significant subnational fiscal risk. The discussion highlights how a lack of transparency in subnational public debt statistics and guarantees reduces policy makers' accountability and exposes the country to substantial fiscal risks.

The chapter then quantifies contingent liabilities for India—the one country in the region with sufficient data—and examines their impact on fiscal dynamics and the local economy. India's experience is illustrative for the rest of the region, especially for countries such as Pakistan, where provincial borrowing has been expanding, and for Maldives and Nepal, which have started to decentralize fiscal policy.

The chapter concludes by synthesizing the empirical findings, discussing the main drivers of subnational fiscal risks in South Asia, and presenting recommendations to manage them.

The Promise and Risks of Fiscal Decentralization in South Asia

Fiscal decentralization holds great promise for countries, but also carries many risks. On the one hand, because subnational governments (SNGs) are closer to residents and firms, they may have better information about spending needs and citizen demands (Oates 1972, 1999); stronger incentives due to competition among jurisdictions (Keen

---

Note: This chapter draws on the background research paper: Blum, F., and P. S. Yoong. 2020. "The Impact of Subnational Contingent Liability Realizations: Evidence from India." Background paper for *Hidden Debt*. World Bank, Washington, DC.

and Marchand 1997); and greater exposure to higher accountability to make public spending more efficient (Seabright 1996; Persson, Roland, and Tabellini 2000). In turn, the increased efficiency of public spending can crowd in more private investment and spur overall local economic activity and growth. For instance, countries with higher shares of decentralized expenditures tend to experience higher rates of private

FIGURE 4.1 **The Relationship between Private Investment and Fiscal Decentralization**

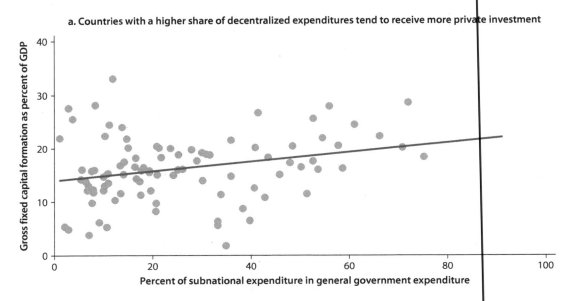

a. Countries with a higher share of decentralized expenditures tend to receive more private investment

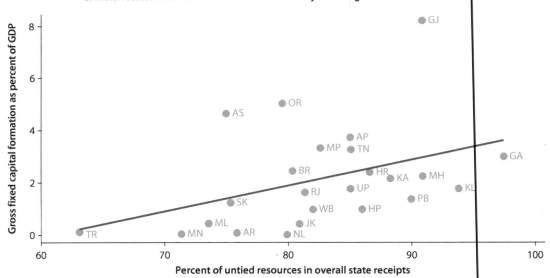

b. Indian states that have more revenue autonomy tend to generate more fixed investment

Sources: IMF 2019a, 2019b, 2019c, 2019d; OECD-UCLG 2019; RBI 2019b; World Bank staff calculations.
Note: Panel a refers to 2017, but similar patterns hold for 2001–16. Untied resources refer to the sum of own-source revenues, tax devolution, and revenue deficit grants. AP = Andhra Pradesh; AR = Arunachal Pradesh; AS = Assam; BR = Bihar; GA = Goa; GJ = Gujarat; HP = Himachal Pradesh; HR = Haryana; JK = Jammu and Kashmir; KA = Karnataka; KL= Kerala; MH = Maharashtra; ML = Meghalaya; MN = Manipur; MP = Madhya Pradesh; NL = Nagaland; OR = Odisha; PB = Punjab; RJ = Rajasthan; SK = Sikkim; TN = Tamil Nadu; TR = Tripura; UP = Uttar Pradesh; WB = West Bengal.

investment (figure 4.1, panel a). In India, states with a greater share of revenue from decentralization—measured by the shares of untied resources in total state revenue—tend to generate greater total investment (figure 4.1, panel b).

On the other hand, fiscal decentralization can also carry risks. Theoretically, fiscal risks can materialize independently of whether they were incurred by the central government or SNGs. For instance, the primary sources of contingent liabilities in Sri Lanka, a highly centralized country, are explicit and implicit guarantees of the central government on the debt of state-owned enterprises (SOEs). These are estimated at 7.1 percent of GDP in 2018 for the largest five SOEs alone. In India, many such SOEs in the electricity sector are owned by SNGs that implicitly guarantee their liabilities, shifting the risks to SNGs but not implying an ad hoc increase in risk.

In practice, however, several factors further amplify the risks when fiscal policy is delegated to SNGs. This amplification may occur because SNGs tend to lack the capacity to monitor and manage these risks. The capacity gaps particularly concern implicit contingent liabilities—such as the likely default of an SOE owned by the SNG—because they are more difficult to identify. Obtaining timely and high-quality data on subnational finances and debt may also be a challenge. Even in several member countries of the Organisation for Economic Co-operation and Development (OECD), such information is available only with a lag, making it difficult for central governments to identify and react quickly to emerging fiscal risks (OECD 2018).

Because SNGs often have explicit or implicit guarantees from the central government to bail them out in case of financial distress, they may also engage in risky borrowing or run higher fiscal deficits—that is, engage in a behavior called *moral hazard*. When subnational fiscal risks materialize, central governments often

have no choice but to rescue the affected localities to reduce spillovers and limit the damage to their own sovereign creditworthiness (Jenker and Liu 2014)—the so-called *soft budget constraint* (Kornai 1986). These repeated bailouts can lead to persistent subnational fiscal problems, as illustrated by the experiences of Argentina and Brazil.[2] In addition, SNGs that rely heavily on transfers from the central government may also be less motivated to raise revenues from their own sources (taxes and fees) because they do not fully internalize the social cost of local public expenditures—the so-called *common pool problem* (Oates 2005; Governatori and Yim 2012; Sow and Razafimahefa 2017).

Moral hazard, the soft budget constraint, and the common pool problem have led to subnational fiscal crises in both advanced and emerging economies. Worldwide, estimates put the cost of unexpected shocks (surprises) to SNGs' debt levels—referred to here as the realization of subnational contingent liabilities or triggered contingent liabilities—at 3.7 percent of GDP on average over 1990–2014 and as much as 15.1 percent of GDP in some SNGs in the extreme (Bova et al. 2016).

Despite these risks, over the last 25 years, the share of subnational expenditure in general government spending has increased substantially, in both advanced and emerging economies (figure 4.2, panel a). South Asia has been no exception to this trend (figure 4.2, panel b). India and Pakistan, which have given significant fiscal autonomy to their states and provinces, respectively, for many years, have continued to devolve a rising share of public resources to SNGs. Nepal has been undergoing a substantial transformation to federalism since a new constitution was finalized in 2015. Bhutan's Twelfth Five-Year Plan (2018–23) proposes the decentralization of significant decision-making power to its local bodies (*Dzongkhags*). Maldives is pursuing a greater decentralization of development and service delivery, including through hub islands.

FIGURE 4.2 **Share of Subnational Expenditure in General Government Expenditure**

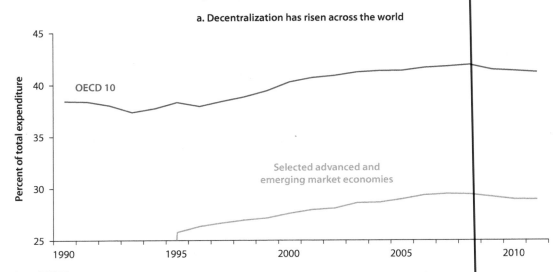

a. Decentralization has risen across the world

Source: IMF 2014.
Note: Percent of total expenditure is an unweighted average of the group. OECD 10 refers to the 10 largest members of the Organisation for Economic Co-operation and Development in terms of GDP.

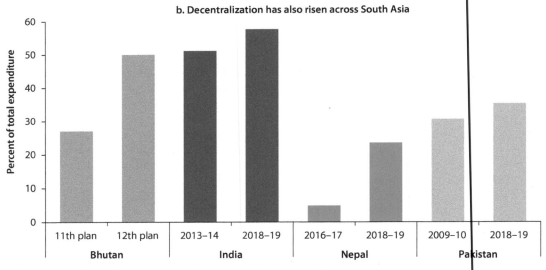

b. Decentralization has also risen across South Asia

Sources: World Bank 2019a; World Bank staff calculations using data from various ministries of finance.

The Unclear Extent of Subnational Fiscal Liabilities and Rising Fiscal Risks in South Asia

From the perspective of a SNG, fiscal risks can emerge from many different sources. Like central governments, SNGs may face liabilities that are *explicit* (specific obligations defined by laws or contracts) or *implicit* (an expected burden stemming from incomplete contracts, public expectations, and political pressures). These risks may also be *direct* (predictable obligations that occur in any case) or *contingent* (obligations that are triggered by a distinct, but uncertain event) (Polackova Brixi and Mody 2002). The degree of fiscal risks depends on the design of fiscal federalism. In some countries, SNGs may not confront such a high level of risk

TABLE 4.1 Categorization of Fiscal Risks at the Subnational Level

	Direct (obligation in any event)	Contingent (obligation if a particular event occurs)
Explicit (liability recognized by a law or contract)	Debt (loans contracted, debt securities issued by the subnational government) Nondiscretionary or legally binding expenditures (such as civil service salaries, pensions)	Guarantees for public and private sector entities (such as firms, publicly owned banks)
Implicit ("moral" or expected obligation)	Social security schemes, future public pensions, future health care financing	Default of a public or private entity on nonguaranteed obligations Natural disasters Recapitalization of publicly owned banks

Source: Adapted from Polackova Brixi and Schick 2002.

from implicit liabilities if these are funded primarily by the central government. Table 4.1 categorizes sources of fiscal risk from the subnational viewpoint.

Subnational explicit liabilities are not an immediate source of fiscal risk in most countries. Across the region, only SNGs in India and Pakistan actively contract loans and issue guarantees. In India, subnational debt amounts to 24.8 percent of GDP,[3] the highest among emerging market federations and toward the high end of federalist countries in general (figure 4.3, panel a).[4] By contrast, in Pakistan, where provincial lending was much more restricted before the approval of the 2010 constitutional amendment, provincial debt is estimated to be 4 percent of GDP (see next section for details).[5] This is toward the lower end of federal countries but higher than the average low- and lower middle-income country (1.9 percent of GDP).[6] A key difference between India and Pakistan is in the composition of lending: while direct borrowing from the market accounts for 54 percent of outstanding state liabilities in India today (figure 4.3, panel b), provincial debt in Pakistan mostly consists of external loans on-lent by the federal government. The move toward market borrowing in India was in part due to the recommendations of the Twelfth Finance Commission of India for greater fiscal autonomy, along with a higher reliance on market discipline among states.

Subnational government borrowing does not occur in practice across most of South Asia. Apart from India and Pakistan, SNGs

> Subnational government borrowing does not occur in practice across most of South Asia.

elsewhere in the region do not raise debt financing or issue guarantees (table 4.2). In some cases—Afghanistan, Bangladesh, and to some extent Bhutan—this is because most SNGs are prohibited from borrowing, likely in the interest of minimizing fiscal risks. However, even when SNGs are legally authorized to borrow—as in the cases of Maldives, Nepal, and Sri Lanka—this does not occur in practice. There are several reasons why this may be the case. First, the limited capacity to formulate fiscal policy at the subnational level and the lack of creditworthiness make autonomous fiscal policy at the subnational level subnational borrowing risky and elevate borrowing costs. Second, in Maldives and Sri Lanka, the high level of indebtedness of the central government makes it difficult for SNGs to justify borrowing independently. Both economies are already at high risk of debt distress as they took on large amounts of non-concessional financing for capital investments in recent years. Third, decentralization is still nascent in the Maldives and Nepal, and virtually nonexistent in Sri Lanka. In the case of Sri Lanka, provincial councils were introduced with the passage of the constitution's 13th amendment (1987), but the central government maintains control over all policies and most of the planning process (Kelly and Gunawardena 2016). As such, only one-tenth of the total budget is

FIGURE 4.3 **India's Subnational Debt in Comparison with Other Federations and Its Growing Access to Market Loans**

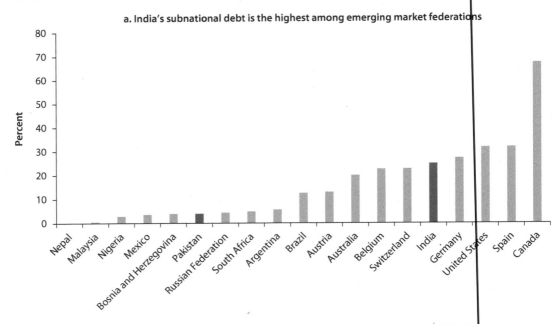

a. India's subnational debt is the highest among emerging market federations

Sources: For India, RBI 2019b; for Pakistan, World Bank staff estimates based on provincial debt bulletins; for other countries, OECD-UCLG 2019.

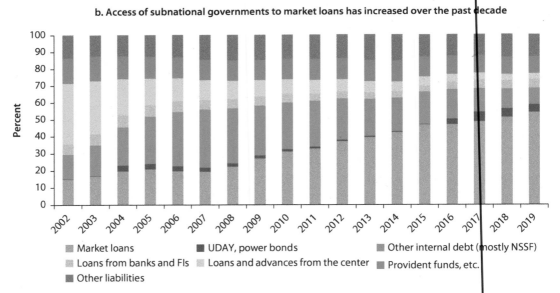

b. Access of subnational governments to market loans has increased over the past decade

Source: RBI 2019b.
Note: FIs = financial institutions; NSSF = National Small Savings Fund; UDAY = Ujwal DISCOM Assurance Yojana scheme.

devolved to provincial and local authorities, which have limited responsibilities for service delivery and capital investment (table 4.3).

Nonetheless, the push toward more decentralized decision making in some South Asian countries suggests that subnational fiscal risks could start to emerge as the requisite legal framework and procedures evolve to enable SNGs to incur liabilities on their own.

TABLE 4.2 Legal Authority for Subnational Governments in South Asia to Borrow and Issue Guarantees

Country	Are subnational governments allowed to borrow and issue guarantees?	Subnational borrowing limits
Afghanistan	No. Municipalities are not allowed to borrow on their own. Cities can only borrow from the central government.	Not applicable
Bangladesh	No. Local governments are not allowed to borrow. In the few instances in which the national government on-lends internally borrowed funds to city corporations for capital spending, these become Treasury liabilities.	Not applicable
Bhutan	Yes. Article 22 of the 2008 constitution and the 2009 Local Government Act empower local governments to "own assets and incur liabilities by borrowing on their own account subject to such limitations as may be provided for by law." However, borrowing does not occur in practice.	Not applicable
India	Yes. Article 293(1) of the constitution empowers states to borrow domestically and issue guarantees within limits set by state legislation (as applicable). Central government consent is required if the state government is indebted to the center, which is currently the case for all states. Municipal corporations are also allowed to borrow with prior approval from the state government.	3 percent of state GDP
Maldives	Yes. The 2010 Decentralization Act and the 2013 Fiscal Responsibility Law permit local councils (city councils, island councils, and atoll councils) to borrow, obtain government guarantees, or seek financing. However, borrowing does not occur in practice.	Up to one-third of the council's income of the previous financial year
Nepal	Yes. With the passing of the 2015 constitution, states can now borrow and receive guarantees from the federal government, while local governments (municipalities and villages) can borrow and receive guarantees from federal and state governments. Internal borrowing does not occur in practice because the requisite legal framework and monetary instruments have not yet been finalized.	Suggested limit for provincial and local government borrowing is 10 percent of the sum of their share of revenues from the value added tax (VAT) and excise taxes
Pakistan	Yes. Provinces are allowed to borrow and issue guarantees up to limits specified by the National Economic Council. All foreign borrowing is on-lent by the central government.	0.85 percent of national GDP for domestic borrowing
Sri Lanka	Yes. Provincial councils are allowed to borrow, as specified in the constitution, but the legal framework for provincial borrowing has not yet been developed.	Not applicable

Sources: Adapted from Ellis and Roberts 2016 and updated using World Bank 2019b for Bangladesh; IMF 2019b for Maldives; IMF 2019c for Nepal.

TABLE 4.3 Vertical Imbalances between Subnational and Central Governments in South Asia

	SNG revenue as share of total GG revenue (percent) (A)	SNG expenditure as share of total GG expenditure (percent) (B)	Estimated fiscal gap (B − A)
Bangladesh	3.8	8.2	4.4
Bhutan	0.8	26.0	25.2
India	52.8	59.0	6.2
Nepal	10.0	36.0	26.0
Pakistan	56.2	39.4	−16.8
Sri Lanka	4.6	10.0	5.4

Sources: World Bank 2019b; Bhutan Ministry of Finance and Royal Audit Authority (FY2016/17); RBI 2019b; Ministry of Finance, Pakistan (FY2018); IMF 2019c; Ministry of Finance, Sri Lanka (FY2018).
Note: Vertical imbalance is defined as the difference between the share of SNG expenditure in total general government (GG) expenditure and the share of SNG revenue in total GG revenue.

Consider Nepal, which recently transitioned to a federalist system. Its 2015 constitution mandates substantial responsibility for the provision of essential public services—such as education, health care, and infrastructure—to provincial and especially local governments, which raise limited revenue.

As a result, the SNGs have a relatively large "fiscal gap"—that is, the difference between the SNGs' revenues from its own resources and its own expenditures, expressed as a share in total general government (GG) expenditures (table 4.3). Although transfers from the center help to finance this fiscal gap, the demand for subnational borrowing could increase as provinces and local governments finance a greater share of functions that were fulfilled by the center. Similarly, the government of Maldives is also taking more concrete steps toward administrative and fiscal decentralization,[7] having recently amended the 2010 Decentralization Act to set aside a share of the state budget for local councils.[8] While Maldives is much further from the prospect of subnational borrowing due to its already elevated public debt, these local councils are legally authorized to borrow and could do so in the future.

Fiscal Responsibility Legislation and Subnational Fiscal Risks

Based on India's experience, fiscal responsibility legislation can help minimize subnational fiscal risks, but only to some extent. In India, enactment of state-level fiscal responsibility legislation began in the early 2000s, following a period of deterioration in states' fiscal indicators. Spurred on by incentives for conditional debt restructuring and interest rate relief provided by the Twelfth Finance Commission, 26 states enacted fiscal responsibility legislation within two years, and all states had adopted them by 2010. The introduction of fiscal responsibility legislation by these states correlates with an improvement of fiscal indicators: while all 17 general category states ran revenue deficits in the early 1990s,[9] 12 recorded revenue surpluses in 2012–13, and almost all states lowered their fiscal deficits (RBI 2015). Most states managed to turn their high primary deficits into surpluses, and the ratio of state debt to gross state domestic product mostly declined. However, most of these positive effects disappear once resources transferred by the central government are excluded from the current deficit (Simone and Topalova 2009), suggesting that fiscal rules do not encourage independent and lasting efforts by states to become fiscally sustainable. Moreover, as our analysis will show, implicit contingent liabilities have served as an escape path from fiscal

rules because the rules focus squarely on explicit liabilities—such as deficit and debt targets, and in some cases, direct contingent liabilities such as guarantees—but do not deal with implicit contingent liabilities.

> Implicit contingent liabilities have served as an escape path from fiscal rules.

The experience with fiscal responsibility legislation at the central government level has been disappointing (table 4.4). Four countries (India, Maldives, Pakistan, Sri Lanka) have budget balance rules, but none of them have consistently adhered to the targets specified in the legislation. Pakistan's public debt (comprising general government and SOE external debt) stood at 86.5 percent of GDP at the end of June 2019—more than 20 percentage points higher than the target specified in the Fiscal Responsibility and Debt Limitation Act (FRDLA) 2005. Similarly, in Maldives and Sri Lanka, public debt ratios are much higher than the targets. In Sri Lanka, the goals have regularly been modified and postponed, diminishing the credibility of the fiscal responsibility act. While there are many reasons why these rules do not "bite," one explanation is that contrary to international best practice, none of the fiscal rules implemented by South Asian countries are formally enforced or monitored by an independent body (Lledó et al. 2017). In addition, only Maldives' and Pakistan's fiscal responsibility legislation have well-specified escape clauses for the case of natural disasters or national security emergencies.[10]

Given that most SNGs in South Asia do not incur liabilities of their own accord, the remainder of this chapter focuses on Pakistan and India, the only two countries in the region where SNGs actively borrow.

Subnational Debt, Data, and Transparency: Lessons from Pakistan

SNGs in Pakistan have significant autonomy to borrow. The constitution enables provinces to borrow both domestically and from abroad

TABLE 4.4 Long-Established Fiscal Rules for the Central Government of Several South Asian Countries

Country (year)	Budget deficit target	Debt target	Treasury guarantees
India (2003)	3% of GDP by 2008; suspended in 2009, reinstated in 2013 with a deadline of 2017–18; in 2016, FRBM committee recommended targeting 3% by FY2020, 2.8% by FY2021, and 2.5% by 2023	None	0.5% of GDP; requires a statement of explicit contingent liabilities in the medium-term expenditure fiscal framework
Sri Lanka (2003)	Less than 5% of GDP by 2006 onward	Less than 85% by 2006 and less than 60% by end-2013 2013 amendment: less than 80% by end-2013 and less than 60% by 2020	Less than 4.5% of GDP; amended to 7.5% in 2013 and 10% in 2016
Pakistan (2005)	Balanced (current) budget by 2008 and surplus thereafter; 2016 amendment imposes limit of 4% of GDP from FY2017/18 to FY2019/20 and 3.5% of GDP thereafter	Debt ratio to be reduced to 60% by 2013; provision maintained by the 2016 amendment until FY2017/18, after which it sets out a transition path toward reducing debt to 50% of GDP	New guarantees to be limited to 2% of GDP
Maldives (2013)	Not exceeding 3.5% of GDP by end-2016 and maintained at that level thereafter; primary balance to be in surplus by end 2016	Debt (including guarantees) ratio to be reduced to 60% by the end of 2016; for 2017–22, required level of debt to be determined by the minister of finance	No specified limits, except that it "should not exceed the amount allocated for loans or guarantees in the national budget"

Source: Adapted from Lledó et al. 2017.
Note: FRBM = Fiscal Responsibility and Budget Management Act (2003, India).

(on-lent through the federal government) and to issue guarantees within limits (if any) imposed by provincial legislature. Provinces also borrow from commercial banks, including those that are state owned, primarily to finance purchases of commodities such as wheat and sugar (termed "commodity operations").

Although official figures are not available, we estimate Pakistan's subnational debt to be at about 4.0 percent of GDP or PRs 1.56 trillion as of the end of June 2019.[11] The relatively low level of subnational debt in Pakistan is in part due to the existence of a hard-budget constraint: prior to passage of the 18th constitutional amendment of 2010, provinces were not authorized to raise new loans if they still held outstanding debt to the federal government.[12] Since all foreign borrowing is on-lent by the federal government to the provincial governments, this meant that provinces were effectively prohibited from borrowing without explicit consent. Since 2010, however, provinces have been authorized to raise financing and extend guarantees within limits specified by the

National Economic Council.[13] Given that the council is primarily composed of provincial policy makers, this amendment may further induce provincial borrowing (Refaqat 2015). Indeed, the National Economic Council raised the cumulative domestic borrowing limit for provinces from 0.5 percent of GDP to 0.85 percent of GDP (approximately PRs 323 billion) in FY2017.[14]

Nonetheless, the bulk of provincial debt consists of foreign multilateral/bilateral loans contracted by the federal government, rather than domestic borrowing.[15] Most of this debt is highly concessionary, with long maturities and fixed interest rates (figure 4.4, panel a). Although provincial governments decide on the interest rate and disbursement mode of each loan, the choice of currency is made by the Economic Affairs division of the federal government (Manoel et al. 2012). Because most of the debt is denominated in foreign currency, primarily in US dollars, provinces are exposed to exchange rate risks (figure 4.4, panel b). In the event of a significant depreciation of the Pakistan rupee with respect to the US dollar, increases in outstanding debt stock

FIGURE 4.4   Composition, Currency Denomination, and Interest Rate Structure of Provincial Debt, Pakistan, 2019

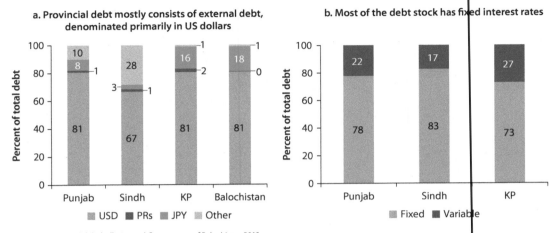

a. Provincial debt mostly consists of external debt, denominated primarily in US dollars

b. Most of the debt stock has fixed interest rates

Sources: Subnational debt bulletins and Government of Balochistan 2019.
Note: Data are as of end-June 2019. KP = Khyber Pakhtunkhwa. JPY = Japanese yen; PRs = Pakistan rupees; USD = US dollars.

and the costs of debt servicing could cause fiscal stress to provinces, which rely solely on foreign exchange management by the federal government to mitigate such risks (Manoel et al. 2012). A 25.5 percent currency depreciation in FY2019 illustrates this risk. It caused the outstanding debt stock for Punjab, Sindh, and Khyber Pakhtunkhwa to jump by 37.7 percent, 25.0 percent, and 20.5 percent, respectively, year-on-year by the end of June 2019.[16]

Poor recording of debt, guarantees, and contingent liabilities elevates the exposure to future fiscal shocks. There is no unified, centrally audited time series of provinces' debt levels on an individual basis (published by each province's Finance Department) or on an aggregate basis (published by the Ministry of Finance or the State Bank of Pakistan). Instead, there are two different sources of provincial debt data. The first source consists of debt bulletins, which are published by all provinces except Balochistan. However, debt information varies in coverage and does not allow for long time series analysis. Punjab's Finance Department publishes the most comprehensive information, offering a compositional analysis of debt by origin, currency, creditor, and risk, but it has done so only

since December 2016, thus limiting the opportunity for time series analysis. Khyber Pakhtunkhwa and Sindh publish a single debt bulletin on their Finance Department websites outlining the composition, currency, and creditor of the most recent debt stock. Budget documents for Sindh have more detailed information, but only as far back as FY2015. Balochistan occasionally publishes debt data in a white paper on the budget (available for FY2020, FY2015, and FY2010).

A second source of debt information is the internal finance account of each province, maintained by the province's Auditor General (AG). These accounts are sent to the AG of Pakistan but are not centrally audited or publicly available. For this report, we have obtained these records for all Pakistani provinces, ranging from FY2008 to FY2018.[17] In general, these provincial debt accounts are constructed based on historical balances, to which payments and receipts to the province's account at the State Bank of Pakistan are added. There are some differences among provinces in how the debt data are accounted for in these reports. For instance, the reports for Sindh do not indicate any buildup of debt stock due to commodity financing, while those for Punjab do. Nevertheless, they are broadly consistent in their classification of debt over a 10-year horizon. Unfortunately, detailed analysis has proven futile due to several issues with the data quality.

First, the AG accounts data are inconsistent with data published in the debt bulletins (figure 4.5, panel a).[18] Figure 4.5, panel b

compares figures for Punjab from the two sources and highlights that while the trajectories are comparable, the AG public debt accounts show a lower level of indebtedness. Similar patterns are observed for Sindh and Khyber Pakhtunkhwa, while the debt levels are similar for Balochistan.

FIGURE 4.5 **Discrepancies and Understatements in the Accounting for Provincial Debt, Pakistan**

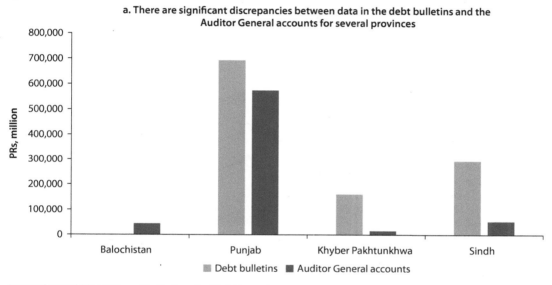

a. There are significant discrepancies between data in the debt bulletins and the Auditor General accounts for several provinces

Sources: Subnational debt bulletins and Auditor General public debt accounts.
Note: Data refer to end-June 2018.

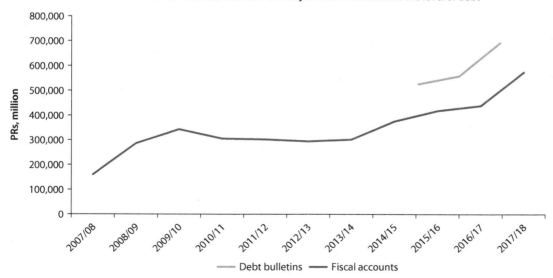

b. Auditor General accounts for Punjab tend to understate the level of debt

Sources: Subnational debt bulletin and Auditor General public debt accounts for Punjab.

Such discrepancies, in turn, may be due to two reasons: first, the AG debt reports compile data on a cash-accounting basis and do not report or account for the depreciation impact in foreign currency loans; and second, not all loans are reported in AG debt reports due to discrepancies in accounting practices, which leads to omission of certain loans and direct third-party payments.

Second, public debt levels—as reported in these AG accounts—turn negative for Balochistan in FY2011 and for Khyber Pakhtunkhwa in FY2017 (figure 4.6, panel a). One possible explanation is that some borrowings were disbursed into other accounts but serviced through the State Bank of Pakistan account, leading to an underestimation of the debt stock.[19]

FIGURE 4.6   Public Debt Levels for Balochistan and Khyber Pakhtunkhwa, 2007/08–2017/18

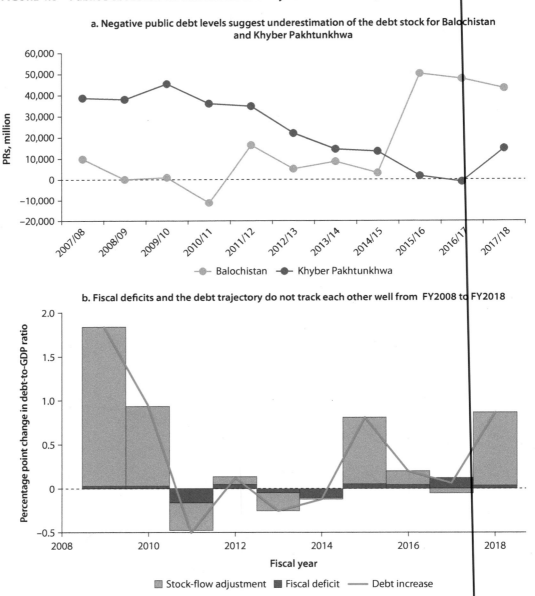

a. Negative public debt levels suggest underestimation of the debt stock for Balochistan and Khyber Pakhtunkhwa

b. Fiscal deficits and the debt trajectory do not track each other well from FY2008 to FY2018

Sources: Provincial Auditor General public debt accounts; World Bank staff calculations.

Finally, there is no apparent relationship between fiscal deficits and the debt trajectory using the AG accounts debt data. Figure 4.6 (panel b) disaggregates the year-on-year change in the debt-to-GDP ratio of aggregate provincial debt into changes in the fiscal deficits and the stock-flow adjustment (SFA)—with the latter measured as the residual. The figure highlights that most of the variation in debt levels cannot be explained by the fiscal deficit.

Apart from public debt, there is also no regular reporting of risks that may arise from guarantees and contingent liabilities at the provincial level. Provinces do not systematically record the amount of guarantees and letters of comfort provided, yet experience shows that contingent liability shocks can exert long-term effects on provincial finances. For example, when the Bank of Punjab suffered some PRs 16.8 billion in losses due to nonperforming loans in FY2008, the government of Punjab—which owned 51 percent of the Bank of Punjab at the time—made capital injections equivalent to PRs 10 billion in FY2010 and PRs 7 billion in FY2011. Subsequently, in FY2015 and FY2017, the government issued two letters of comfort totaling PRs 14.2 billion to the State Bank of Pakistan to guarantee the provisioning requirement against an agreed amount of nonperforming loans. Even though the guarantees have matured and have not been triggered, budgeting for such large contingent liabilities can crowd out public spending on more important and immediate development priorities. It is unclear whether other provincial governments have also lent support to their respective commercial banks,[20] but similar shocks cannot be ruled out in the future.

Unfunded pension liabilities are also a significant source of implicit contingent liabilities for provinces. In Punjab, the government estimates that unfunded accrued pension liabilities stood at PRs 3.8 trillion as of the end of June 2016.[21] Although the Punjab government created the Punjab Pension Fund to partially fund future pension liabilities, the gap between the fund's total assets and projected liabilities remain significant. Similarly, the

General Provident Fund (GPF), available for government employees, is an emerging fiscal risk. In Sindh, it is expected that the unfunded GPF liability will more than double, from PRs 100 billion in FY2014 to PRs 228 billion by 2030, posing significant risk to the sustainability of public finances.[22] The governments of Khyber Paktunkhwa and Balochistan similarly have their own pension and provident investment funds, but had not yet assessed the size of unfunded liabilities at the time of writing.[23] In the case of Khyber Pakhtunkhwa, the provident fund is an exclusive liability of the government because employee contributions are not collected.

Fiscal risks also emanate from the power sector. Although most of the guarantees are provided by the federal government, provincial governments also play a role in financing infrastructure investments in their respective jurisdictions. Out of the PRs 75 billion in guarantees issued by the government of Punjab, for example, PRs 70 billion accrues to the power sector. These guarantees come in the form of (1) credit guarantees of loans issued by special purpose vehicles for the construction of power plants and (2) commitment to financial support in the case of project cost overruns. While these guarantees are part and parcel of financing much-needed capital investments—and do not result in financial outflows unless they are called[24]—delays in the implementation of such projects could pose financial liabilities for the provincial government.[25] Recording and disclosing them regularly would help both the provincial and federal governments better manage potential fiscal risks.

Estimating Contingent Liability Shocks, Adjustment Costs, and Mitigating Factors Using Data for India

Among South Asian nations, India has the longest history and the richest sources of data available to analyze subnational fiscal risks. These data make it possible to implement an econometric framework that estimates (1) the probability of contingent liability shocks;

(2) the adjustments that occur after the shocks; and (3) their impact on relevant economic outcomes such as investment. To this end, this section first lays out the institutional background for subnational borrowing in India before discussing the methodology, data, and results of an econometric analysis of contingent liability shocks.

Institutional Background

Indian states enjoy fiscal autonomy to incur liabilities, either directly domestically or through on-lending of external borrowing by the central government. The Indian institutional framework regulates subnational borrowing through three mechanisms. First, the Finance Commission, a constitutional body primarily tasked with determining the distribution of central funds to states, incentivizes fiscal responsibility through the intergovernmental transfer system. For instance, the Thirteenth Finance Commission proposed a subnational debt relief scheme for subnational loans from the central government that was extended to states that had reduced their fiscal deficit. Second, states' fiscal position and debt levels are also regulated as part of state-level fiscal responsibility laws, following the passing of the central Fiscal Responsibility and Budget Management (FRBM) Act in 2003. These laws typically limit fiscal deficits to less than 3 percent of GDP and in most cases prescribe an overall subnational debt ceiling. Third, SNGs require approval from the central government to incur liabilities whenever they are indebted with the central government—which, in practice, applies to all states.

Indian states borrow through so-called state development loans, which are dated securities issued by state governments. State development loans are auctioned through the Reserve Bank of India (RBI) on a weekly basis, with the issuing states providing the details of envisioned terms and conditions for their borrowing prior to the auction. The RBI also issues notifications in leading newspapers before the auction to assist in marketing. State development loans are valued at a marginal premium over central government securities, and yields vary by state, because there is no explicit central government guarantee on state borrowing. However, the variation in yields across states is limited and only marginally reflects states' fiscal situation, partially owing to the wide-spread perception that state securities enjoy an implicit guarantee by the central government. RBI also manages the borrowing and, through an automated debit mechanism, ensures repayment of states' liabilities.

In 2018, states borrowed primarily from private markets (figure 4.7). In addition, 25.6 percent of subnational debt was owed to pension, savings, and other funds. States also borrow from state-owned banks and enterprises, such as the State Bank of India and the National Bank for Agriculture and Rural Development, which accounted for slightly less than 10 percent of total borrowing in 2018. Loans from the central government, which include states' external borrowing, accounted for 3.8 percent of total borrowing in 2018.

Historically, the development of state debt and fiscal risks over the last two decades can be broadly divided into three subperiods. The first, from the late 1990s to about 2004, was a period of fiscal slippage. In this period, the absence of regulation and central oversight meant that states exposed themselves to significant contingent and noncontingent liabilities, resulting in fiscal deficits and rising debt (figure 4.8, panel a). Fiscal pressure was compounded through the issuance of power bonds by state governments, which increased liabilities by 22.8 percent in FY2004. With concerns about fiscal risks mounting, the central Fiscal Responsibility and Budget Management Act was passed in 2003, and the Twelfth Finance Commission initiated incentives schemes for subnational fiscal responsibility in 2004, which resulted in a second period of gradual consolidation, until about 2012. More recently, states' debt has started increasing again, from about Rs 18 trillion (measured at 2011 prices) in 2012 to Rs 30 trillion in 2018 (figure 4.8, panel a), or about 25 percent of GDP. Jharkhand and Nagaland

FIGURE 4.7   **Indian States' Sources of Borrowing, 2018**

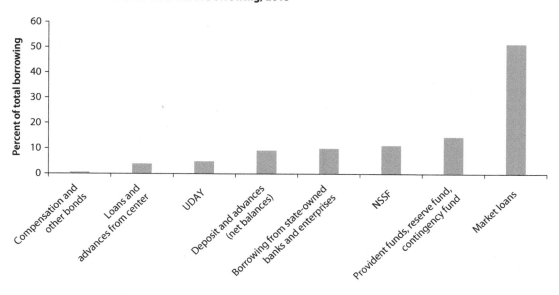

Source: World Bank staff calculations using data from the Reserve Bank of India.
Note: NSSF = National Small Savings Fund; UDAY = Ujwal DISCOM Assurance Yojana scheme.

FIGURE 4.8   **Aggregate Subnational Debt and UDAY Debt, India**

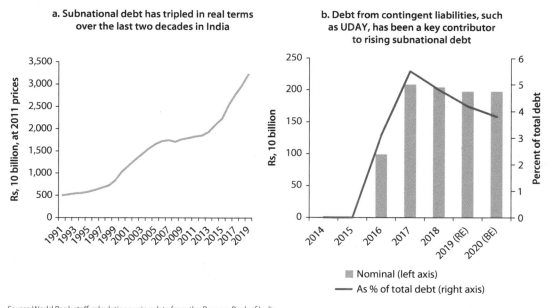

a. Subnational debt has tripled in real terms over the last two decades in India

b. Debt from contingent liabilities, such as UDAY, has been a key contributor to rising subnational debt

Nominal (left axis)
As % of total debt (right axis)

Source: World Bank staff calculations using data from the Reserve Bank of India.
Note: BE = budget estimate; RE = revised estimate; UDAY = Ujwal DISCOM Assurance Yojana debt relief scheme.

have the two highest debt levels, at 49 percent and 44 percent of GDP, respectively, whereas Assam carries the lowest debt burden, at 17 percent of GDP.

The debt dynamics can be driven by direct and contingent liabilities. A key example of a contingent liability is the Ujwal DISCOM Assurance Yojana (UDAY) scheme. As part of this scheme, state governments could take on up to 75 percent of electricity distribution companies' debt starting in FY2016 and repay lenders through the issuance of new bonds. This acquisition of debt occurred "below the line" and thus was not recorded as an expenditure. The participation in UDAY was voluntary, but to date 32 states and union territories have joined the scheme. At the end of FY2018, states had incurred Rs 30.7 billion in debt related to UDAY, accounting for about 5 percent of states' total debt stock (figure 4.8, panel b).

The realization of guarantees presents another source of contingent liabilities. Indian states issue various guarantees, including for loans incurred as part of public-private partnerships (PPPs) or for the borrowing of public sector enterprises. Outstanding guarantees have decreased in recent years, from a peak of 8 percent of GDP in FY2014 to less than 3 percent in FY2018 (figure 4.9, panel a).

To manage such guarantees properly and to buffer their potential impact on the budget, state governments can invest in a Guarantee

FIGURE 4.9 **Outstanding Guarantees and Investment in India's Guarantee Redemption Fund**

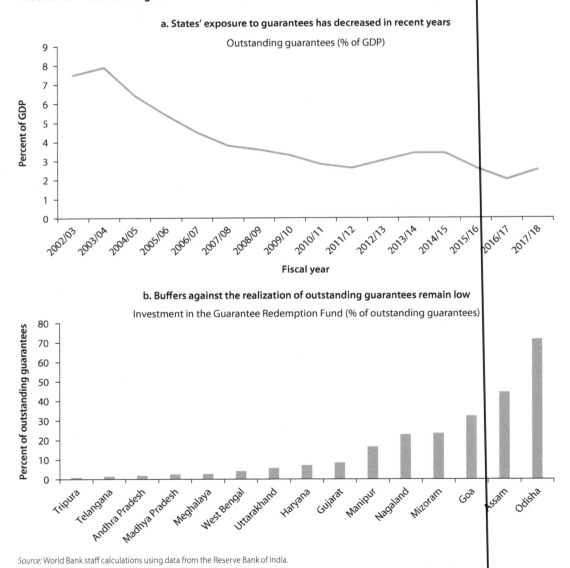

a. States' exposure to guarantees has decreased in recent years

Outstanding guarantees (% of GDP)

b. Buffers against the realization of outstanding guarantees remain low

Investment in the Guarantee Redemption Fund (% of outstanding guarantees)

Source: World Bank staff calculations using data from the Reserve Bank of India.

Redemption Fund (GRF), which is maintained by the RBI. As of June 2018, only 15 of 29 states had invested in the fund. Among those that had invested, the buffers accounted for 16.4 percent of guarantees outstanding (figure 4.9, panel b). States can also buffer for the repayment of liabilities by paying into the Consolidated Sinking Fund (CSF), also maintained by RBI. Contributions to the CSF are higher than those to the GRF and stood at an aggregate of Rs 1,025 billion at the end of June 2018, equivalent to 0.71 percent of GDP. Contributions to the GRF are earmarked to cover payments from the invocation of guarantees, whereas the CSF aims at covering liabilities from market-based borrowing. Investments in both funds can act as collateral to avail of a Special Drawing Facility at the RBI at favorable borrowing rates, which acts as an incentive to invest in the funds.

Indian states face multiple sources of contingent liabilities. A central question is how the triggering of such potential liabilities affects the local economy, both directly and through adjustments made by state governments. To address this question, we performed an economic analysis to quantify the impact of historic contingent liability realization at the subnational level on the real economy, provide evidence on how state and provincial governments adjust to them, and identify mitigating factors.

Data and Methodology

To study contingent liabilities at the subnational level, we constructed a panel data set of Indian states covering a total of 29 states from 1991 to 2018. The primary data source for this investigation was the Reserve Bank of India's State Finances data set (RBI 2015, 2019b). We complemented this data with various other sources: information on budgeted expenditure (by line item), adoption of fiscal rules, and fiscal transparency measures were obtained directly from states' finance departments websites and were hard coded into a comprehensive data set. Detailed information on fiscal transfers by type was obtained from the Finance Commission reports. Data on

states' GDP and gross fixed capital formation was taken from the Reserve Bank of India's "Handbook of Statistics on the Indian Economy" (RBI 2015).

The analysis of subnational debt developments begins with a decomposition of unexpected shocks into those occurring to the budget ("above the line") and those occurring through the SFA ("below the line") (see annex 4A, on methodology). Budgetary (above-the-line) shocks are defined as deviations in the realized fiscal deficit from the budgeted fiscal deficit. In contrast, the SFA (below-the-line) shock captures all changes in the debt stock that are not explained by the fiscal deficit. A positive SFA can arise for two reasons: first, because of below-the-line acquisitions of liabilities and assets (such as due to triggered contingent liabilities); and second, because of changes to the valuation of the existing debt stock. Changing valuations can arise, for instance, because of movements in the exchange rate if debt is denominated in a foreign currency or because of changes to interest rates. While not modeled here explicitly, statistical discrepancies can also be responsible for changes to the SFA.

Figure 4.10 highlights the distribution of the budgetary and SFA shocks through box

FIGURE 4.10 **Distribution of Above-the-Line and Below-the-Line Shocks to Subnational Debt, India**

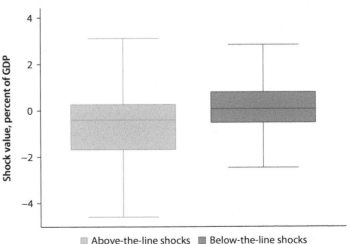

Source: Blum and Yoong 2020.
Note: The figure excludes outside values.

plots. The horizontal line in the middle of the figure represents the median of the pooled distribution of shocks, while the box represents the range between the 75th and 25th percentile. The whiskers show the lower and upper adjacent values, defined as 1.5 times the interquartile range. Figure 4.10 shows that most of the budgetary shocks are negative. Indeed, the median budgetary shock is negative and the 75th percentile of shocks lies just marginally above zero, highlighting that states underspent their budget in many years. Underspending occurs primarily on the capital side, with budget execution rates averaging 77.3 percent between FY2010 and FY2018. By contrast, SFA shocks occur both on the positive and the negative side (right part of the figure). Figure 4.10 shows that more than 50 percent of SFA shocks are positive and thus unexpectedly increase subnational debt. Taken together, the plots in figure 4.10 illustrate that subnational debt shocks in India occur primarily below the line.

Based on this analysis, and consistent with the literature (see, for example, Bova et al. 2016), this chapter identifies contingent liability shocks as positive spikes in the SFA series. This approach is suitable because a significant share of

contingent liabilities materializes below the line (such as the UDAY debt relief scheme). Given the prevalence of cash accounting, this means that this definition captures contingent liabilities that do not go through the budget and thus involve, for instance, bailouts of SOEs or pension funds if governments take over their debt, but not through the payment of subsidies. Similarly, this definition captures the realization of debt guarantees, but not of price guarantees.

Results: Examining the Occurrence of Contingent Liability Shocks

We identify contingent liability shocks as unexpected shocks to the SFA series, standardized by the baseline debt stock. Applying the Kalman filter to the series, we classify observations for which the residual exceeds the predicted mean by more than 1 standard deviation as the contingent liability shock (annex 4B). Figure 4.11 highlights the frequency at which such shocks occur over time. The identified shocks occurred most frequently in Manipur, Meghalaya, Mizoram, Nagaland, and Tripura, with five events occurring in each state between 1991 and 2018. Uttar Pradesh (at no event) as well as Andhra Pradesh and Madhya Pradesh (at one event) have experienced the least frequent occurrence over the same period. The average frequency of contingent liability shocks—as we identify such shocks—is 11.4 percent.

The spikes visible in the figure dovetail with the policy narratives and anecdotal evidence on the realizations of contingent liabilities: The 1990s are generally associated with significant fiscal profligacy by the Indian states, culminating in debt crises and resulting in the gradual adoption of fiscal responsibility legislation in the 2000s.[26] In addition, during this time, borrowings by state-owned public enterprises were removed from the ceiling for state borrowings, leading to a buildup of debt in the SOE sector and associated government bailouts. Furthermore, in 1999, the National Small

FIGURE 4.11   Notable Subnational Shocks in India, 1990–2020

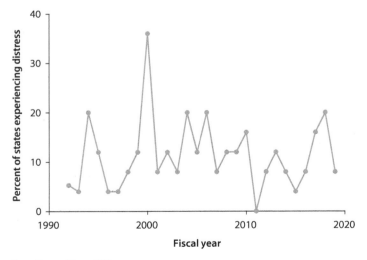

Source: Blum and Yoong 2020.
Note: The relatively sharp changes in 2007–08 occurred during the global financial crisis. The other spikes in 2000 and thereafter can be related to specific policy events.

Savings Fund (NSSF) was established, which invested significantly in state securities. A special feature of NSSF borrowing is that it is unrelated to states' borrowing requirements: because the NSSF is a savings device, states are allocated available funding based on a sharing quota between the central government and the states. As a result of the introduction, the share of NSSF borrowing spiked significantly, from 0 percent in FY1999 to 31 percent the year after, providing a possible explanation for the significant spike visible in 2000 (Rangarajan and Prasad 2012). The spikes in the later 2000s and 2010s can also be linked to specific policy events. In FY2008, India conducted the Agricultural Debt Waiver and Debt Relief Scheme to the tune of Rs 600 billion, which increased public liabilities. From FY2015 onward, states started adopting the UDAY scheme, in which states take on the liabilities of indebted power distribution companies. Finally, in FY2018, eight states provided farm loan waivers amounting to 0.32 percent of GDP.

How Do State Governments Adjust?

Contingent liability realizations are defined as unexpected shocks to SNGs' debt levels.

Such shocks have direct budgetary impacts because they raise borrowing costs and limit fiscal space, thus requiring a fiscal policy adjustment. This adjustment can involve reducing expenditure or increasing revenue. SNGs may also receive assistance from the center, either through increased transfers or by receiving loans.

This section assesses econometrically how Indian states adjust to the realization of contingent liabilities (unexpected shocks to SNGs' debt levels). To this end, we estimate a difference-in-difference regression, comparing states before and after a contingent liability shock to states without a shock in the same year. Figure 4.12 presents the estimated effects of SFA shocks on the key fiscal outcome variables we consider (see also table 4C.1, in annex 4C, for the regression tables). The error bars present 90 percent confidence intervals calculated using the standard errors from the regression estimation.

Figure 4.12 suggests that debt increases mechanically in response to the contingent liability shock. This increase persists for one additional year, with debt increasing by 4.3 percent in the year after the shock, but dissipates thereafter. Governments adjust

FIGURE 4.12 **Estimated Fiscal Adjustments by Indian Subnational Governments to Contingent Liability Shock**

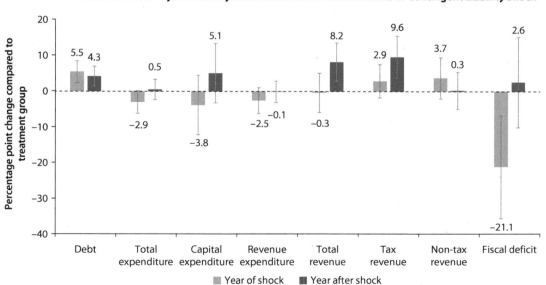

Source: Blum and Yoong 2020.

contemporaneously to a contingent liability shock by reducing expenditure by a statistically insignificant 2.9 percent, with expenditure reverting to trend in the years after. The expenditure adjustment is reflected in both capital and revenue expenditure. The estimates further suggest that governments are unable to increase revenue contemporaneously when a contingent liability shock occurs, but that revenue increases in the subsequent year by 8.2 percent. This effect is driven by an increase in tax revenue. Because of the declining expenditure and only marginally positive response or no response of revenue in the year of the shock, the fiscal deficit decreases by 20 percent. However, the deficit remains unaffected in subsequent years.

Taken together, the results suggest that *the realization of a contingent liability leads state governments to (1) reduce expenditure, split approximately equally between capital and revenue expenditure, and (2) increase revenue through taxes in the subsequent year.*

While Indian states enjoy significant fiscal autonomy, they receive financial support from the central government. A central question is thus whether the central government provides financial assistance when contingent liability shocks occur or whether states are required to manage the fiscal impact independently.

Analyzing this question helps uncover whether the states face hard or soft budget constraints—a factor that is likely to determine fiscal behavior in the longer term. Hence, we estimate the effect of contingent liability realizations on three types of assistance provided by the central government—loans, grants, and tax devolution—again using the difference-in-difference framework. The estimated treatment effects are presented in figure 4.13.

Our results suggest that *states do indeed receive assistance from the central government when a contingent liability shock occurs. This assistance occurs through the provision of loans from the central government and increased tax devolution.* Loans from the central government comprise either external project borrowing—which is typically fixed multiple years in advance—or loan assistance to the states. Our estimates suggest that loans from the center rise by more than 9 percent in the year of a contingent liability shock and the year after, likely driven by loan assistance from the center to the states.

Grants and tax devolution are assigned by the Finance Commission for five-year periods. Grants are assigned in nominal value. Tax devolution is determined based on a formula that considers factors such as

FIGURE 4.13 **Estimated Assistance from the Indian Central Government to Subnational Governments Hit by Contingent Liability Shocks**

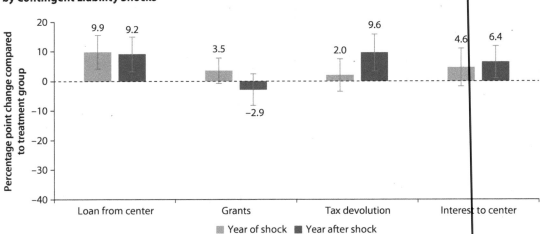

Source: Blum and Yoong 2020; see also table 4C.2 in annex 4C.

population, income, and the gap between the state's income and that of the state with the highest income. These factors, and the weights assigned to them, vary among Finance Commissions. Our estimates suggest that central government support through grants is not affected by the shock. By contrast, tax devolution received from the central government increases by 10 percent in the year after a contingent liability shock.

Why does tax devolution respond but grants do not? This remains somewhat a puzzle. One possible explanation is that grants are fixed in nominal terms by the Finance Commission and are often earmarked and committed to specific projects. Therefore, they provide a limited leeway for responses. By contrast, the central government allegedly enjoys flexibility in the timing of the payout of tax devolution. This flexibility provides a mechanism to counter fiscal shocks at the subnational level. Taken together, the evidence is consistent with an interpretation that states enjoy rather soft budget constraints that partially buffer the impact of realizations of contingent liabilities.

What Are the Economic Costs of Adjustments to Contingent Liability Shocks?

Do debt shocks at the subnational level affect local investments and dampen local economic development? Such negative spillovers could occur for various reasons. For one, debt shocks can reduce public capital expenditure—as we have shown. This reduction, in turn, decreases public capital formation as well as private investment that relies on the execution of public investment (such as connective infrastructure) and that is typically "crowded in" by public investment. In addition, contingent liability shocks can dampen local investments indirectly—for instance, by raising the tax burden, and thus discouraging private capital formation, or by reducing the viability of investment projects, firm creditworthiness, and local lending by banks. For this reason, this section investigates the costs of subnational contingent liability shocks for the local

economy. It does so by reestimating the previous difference-in-difference specification using gross fixed capital formation (GFCF) (in logs) in a given state and year as the outcome variable.

Figure 4.14 reports the results by plotting the estimated treatment effect estimated for five years before and after the occurrence of contingent liability shock. *GFCF in the state falls significantly in the year of a contingent liability shock, continues to decline in the year after, and remains significantly below the trend for three years after the event.* Then, it gradually returns to the trend. Reassuringly, the figure does not a identify significantly diverging trends between affected and unaffected states before the shock, suggesting that the observed divergence in trends is indeed driven by the contingent liability shock.

To quantify the impacts highlighted in figure 4.14, the coefficient estimates in table 4C.3, column 1, in annex 4C, confirm that GFCF falls significantly below its trend following a contingent liability shock. The capital formation experiences a maximum

FIGURE 4.14   **Decreases in Indian Subnational Governments' Gross Fixed Capital Formation following Contingent Liability Shocks**

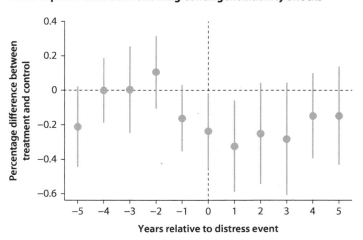

Source: Blum and Yoong 2020.
Note: The figure plots the coefficient estimates β_s of the following regression:

$$Log\,(GFCF)_{it} = \alpha_0 + \sum_{s=-5}^{5}\beta_s CL_{it+s} + \gamma_j + \mu_t + \varepsilon_{it}.$$

Each coefficient measures the relative value of gross fixed capital formation (GFCF, in logs) *s* years before and after a contingent liability shock, compared to states with no such shock. The x-axis plots the time relative to the shock. The y-axis plots the values for the corresponding β_s.

reduction of 32.2 percent in the year after the shock and then returns gradually to trend.

What Factors Can Explain and Mitigate Contingent Liability Shocks?

To guide policy, a central question is which factors explain contingent liability shocks and how these factors can be reformed to mitigate the occurrence and repercussions of these shocks. To investigate this question, we focus on five factors: political incentives during elections, transparency, legal frameworks and fiscal rules, markets, and fiscal capacity and intergovernmental frameworks.

Political Incentives Related to Elections

To identify approaches to mitigating fiscal shocks, it is important to understand whether policy makers can influence the timing of when these shocks occur and whether the shocks are affected by political incentives. To address these questions, we examine the likelihood of contingent liability shocks around elections. We chose elections because they, arguably, shape the main incentives of policy makers. Elections may influence the timing of when contingent liabilities are realized. For instance, policy makers may be prone to adopt a more lenient fiscal policy in the run-up to an election. They can take on debt of state-owned enterprises to secure jobs in the short term. Alternatively, policy makers may instead delay the shock until after elections because the adjustments required in response to a contingent liability realization and the impact on the local economy may cause negative political fallout.

In our data analysis, we focus on state legislative assembly (Vidhan Sabha) elections because they largely determine the state-level governments in India—which hold authority over fiscal policy. The econometric analysis provides evidence of the interrelationship between elections and fiscal policy. Figure 4.15 shows that *the likelihood of a contingent liability shock increases significantly in the year before an election, peaks in the year of and after the election, and then gradually reverts to the trend.* This thus provides direct evidence that contingent liability realizations, as defined here, respond to the political incentives provided by elections.

Transparency

In addition to elections, increasing transparency is an alternative measure to hold policy makers accountable and align their incentives with fiscal responsibility. To assess the effect of transparency measures on contingent liability realizations, we use the gradual adoption of debt transparency measures across Indian states as a case study (figure 4.16). Such measures range from the publication of debt and guarantee data in the annual financial statements and budgets to the publication of dedicated reports analyzing debt and (in some cases) outstanding guarantees.

To systematically assess the effectiveness of increased transparency, we collected information on states' publication of debt and guarantee-related information from the websites

FIGURE 4.15 **Occurrence of Contingent Liability Shocks around Indian State Legislative Assembly Elections**

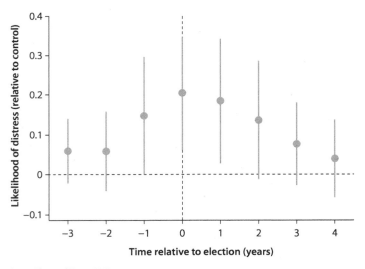

Source: Blum and Yoong 2020.
Note: The figure plots the coefficient estimates β_s of the following regression:

$$CL\ Shock_{it} = \alpha_0 + \sum_{s=-3}^{3} \beta_s Election_{it+s} + \gamma_j + \mu_t + \varepsilon_{it}.$$

Each coefficient measures the relative likelihood of a contingent liability (CL) shock occurring *s* years before and after an election, compared to states with no such election. The x-axis plots the time relative to election, with −1 denoting the year before an election and 1 denoting the year after, for instance. The y-axis plots the values for the corresponding β_s.

of states' finance departments. We differentiated those states publishing information on debt and guarantees in their annual financial statements from those states publishing dedicated debt and guarantee reports. Our data reveal that by the end of FY2019, a total of 22 of the 29 states in the sample had published information on debt and guarantees at least once.

To estimate the effect of these policy measures on the likelihood of contingent liability shocks, we ran difference-in-difference panel regressions that exploit the staggered publication of reports. The regressions compare the change in the likelihood of a contingent liability shock in states that have recently increased transparency to the change in states that have not increased transparency. This approach estimates the effect of policy measures under the assumption that the trajectory of contingent liability shocks in adopting and non-adopting states would have been similar had the policy measures not been implemented. A visualization of the coefficient estimates is shown in figure 4.17. Detailed coefficient estimates are reported in table 4C.4, in annex C.

Our estimates suggest that the publication of debt transparency reports does not reduce the likelihood of contingent liability shocks initially, but does so with a lag of two years (figure 4.17). This effect persists in subsequent years. Therefore, *increased transparency through the publication of debt-related information takes time to become effective but, once it does, it permanently reduces the likelihood of shocks.*[27] Our findings are consistent with other empirical work that finds a negative correlation between transparency and the stock-flow adjustments in a cross-country analysis (Weber 2012).

The Legal Framework and Fiscal Rules

In addition to increased accountability and altered political incentives, the likelihood of contingent liability realizations can also be affected by legislative changes that tie policy makers' hands. To study the effectiveness of such measures, we focus on the adoption of subnational fiscal rules in Indian states.

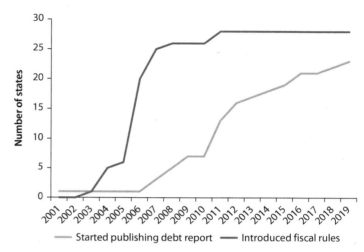

FIGURE 4.16 **Adoption of Transparency Measures and Fiscal Rules by Indian States, 2001–19**

Source: Blum and Yoong 2020.

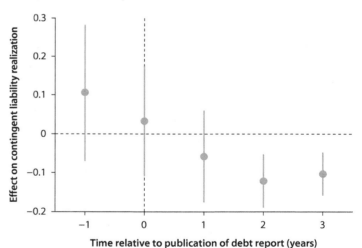

FIGURE 4.17 **Occurrence of Contingent Liability Shocks around the Publication of Debt Reports in India**

Source: Blum and Yoong 2020.

Starting in FY2002, Indian states gradually adopted fiscal responsibility legislation that curbed the fiscal deficit at 3 percent and the revenue deficit at 0 percent, and in some cases, imposed restrictions on debt and guarantees. The adoption of subnational fiscal rules increased rapidly in FY2006, and most states had adopted fiscal rules by FY2011 (figure 4.16). We compiled data from states' finance department websites on the adoption of fiscal rules and used a similar strategy to compare the change in the likelihood of contingent liability shocks for states that had recently adopted a fiscal rule to those who had not. Detailed coefficient estimates are reported in table 4C.4.

Our estimates suggest that the likelihood of a contingent liability shock diminishes significantly in the year before and the current year in which a fiscal rule is adopted (figure 4.18). Although this estimate is statistically significant, results also suggest that it is only temporary, because our estimates do not detect a significant effect of the fiscal rule adoption on the occurrence of contingent liability shocks in subsequent years.

Markets

Our evidence on fiscal rules is consistent with the perception that fiscal rules by themselves are unlikely to be a major driver of fiscal consolidation.[28] This perception is shared by the markets. To validate this market perception, we estimated a panel regression of interest rates paid by states in a given year—calculated as annual interest payments divided by the debt stock—on an indicator of whether a state breached the fiscal deficit rule of 3 percent of GDP. In the estimation, we control for state and year fixed effects. The results suggest that interest rates paid do not respond to the breaching of the fiscal deficit rule by Indian states (figure 4.19). Future research could firm this preliminary finding by using actual current rates on Indian states' debt—either newly issued, debt with floating rates, or debt refinancing.

Fiscal Capacity and the Intergovernmental Framework

The occurrence and impact of contingent liability shocks can also depend on the states' capacity to buffer shocks. For example, some states have lower potential for generating their own revenue, or they depend more on transfers to fund their spending than other states.

To examine this hypothesis, we distinguish between special and general category states in India. India's National Development Council has designated 11 states as special category states, owing to their hilly and difficult terrain, low population density or sizeable share of tribal population, strategic location along borders with neighboring countries, economic and infrastructural backwardness, and/or nonviable nature of state finances (PRS India 2013). This classification has two practical implications. First, given their unique circumstances, special category status can be considered a proxy for low fiscal capacity, thus making special category states more prone to contingent liability shocks and reducing the likelihood that they are able to mitigate the impact on the real economy.

Second, special category states have historically received favorable terms in the allocation of central funding. Until India's Planning Commission was abolished, its funding allocation favored special category states by reserving 30 percent of total funds for them and distributing funds at a ratio of grants to loans of 90 percent to 10 percent, compared to 30 percent to 70 percent for general category states. This favorable treatment ended with the replacement of the Planning Commission by the National Institution for Transforming India (NITI Aayog) in 2015.

FIGURE 4.18   **Occurrence of Contingent Liability Shocks around the Enactment of Fiscal Rule**

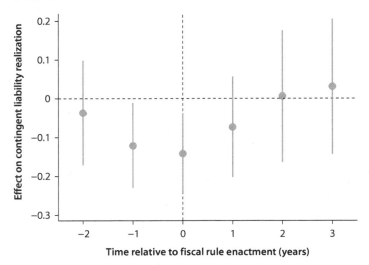

Source: Blum and Yoong 2020.

While central funds transferred through the Finance Commission do not explicitly consider special category status when allocating funds, grants assigned by the Finance Commission implicitly primarily benefit special category states. As such, revenue deficit grants accrue primarily to special category states. Taken together, special category states are thus states that (1) have comparatively weak fiscal capacity to buffer shocks and (2) face softer budget constraints than general category states.

To understand whether low fiscal capacity impacts contingent liability shocks, we repeat the analysis and expand it by differentiating between special and general category states. The estimation results suggest that special and general category states experience contingent liability shocks at comparable frequencies—13 percent of the time for special category states and 10 percent for general category states. However, *low fiscal capacity in special category states implies that contingent liability shocks have a more adverse impact on the local economy of special category states than general category states.* Namely, in general category states, GFCF contracts by only 2.5 percent in the year after a contingent liability shock—an impact not statistically distinguishable from zero. By contrast, in special category states, GFCF contracts by more than 60 percent in the year after a contingent liability shock. Therefore, lower fiscal capacity can leave limited space for subnational governments to buffer contingent liability shocks and can expose the local economy to a more adverse economic impact of contingent liability shocks.

Because special category states enjoy softer budget constraints, measures that enhance policy makers' incentives and harden their budget constraints could be more effective. For instance, in special category states, the introduction of fiscal rules decreases the likelihood of a contingent liability shock in the years after their introduction, unlike in general category states. Moreover, increased transparency through the publication of debt and guarantee

FIGURE 4.19 Breaching the Fiscal Rule: The Effect on Interest Rates Paid by Indian States

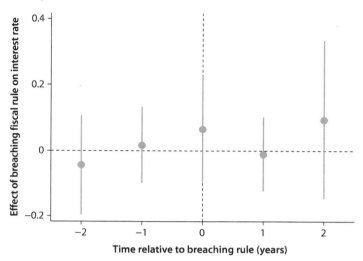

Source: Blum and Yoong 2020.

reports reduces the likelihood of an immediate contingent liability shock in the special category states, compared to a two-year lag in general category states. Taken together, the combination of lower fiscal capacity and softer budget constraints can increase the impact of contingent liability shocks on the local economy. However, the evidence also illustrates how basic institutional measures could effectively mitigate contingent liability shocks in subnational states with initially lower fiscal capacity and softer budget constraints.

Six Takeaways. In sum, our quantitative research into the fiscal stance of Indian states yields six takeaways:

1. Contingent liability shocks—as measured in this report—occur about 11 percent of the time.
2. The contingent liability shock triggers fiscal adjustments through reduced expenditure and increased revenue.
3. States enjoy relatively soft budget constraints because contingent liability shocks trigger support from the center.
4. Contingent liability shocks have material impact on local economic development

because they reduce local investments for multiple years.

5. Shocks do not have purely external sources or origin. Instead, they respond to political incentives, can be mitigated through increased transparency, and their impact depends on states' fiscal capacity.

6. Fiscal rules and markets currently do not impose sufficient discipline on states' finances to mitigate contingent liability shocks.

Improved Transparency and Fiscal Rules, the Disciplining Role of Markets, and Better Intergovernmental Frameworks Are Needed to Achieve Better Subnational Fiscal Outcomes in South Asia

This chapter has reviewed the exposures to subnational fiscal risk across South Asia and has provided new evidence on the adverse effects of contingent liability shocks on fiscal and economic outcomes in India.

It shows that contingent liability shocks occur relatively frequently, trigger fiscal adjustments, and are influenced by policy makers' incentives as shaped by the prospects of election, transparency, fiscal rules, existing fiscal space, and the softness of budget constraints. It also shows that contingent liability shocks significantly affect local economic development: triggered contingent liabilities reduce investment in Indian states for up to four years after the shock and thus dampen local economic activity. India's experience is illustrative for the rest of the region, especially for countries such as Pakistan, where provincial borrowing has been expanding, and for Maldives and Nepal, which have started to decentralize fiscal policy.

Our analysis suggests some pathways to mitigate contingent liability shocks and the associated negative spillovers. For the pathways to be effective, policy makers must understand that the realizations of contingent liabilities are rarely exogenous events. The accrual of contingent liabilities is a policy decision that is shaped by the incentives of

> The accrual of contingent liabilities is a policy decision that is shaped by the incentives of local policy makers and their abilities to manage subnational fiscal risks.

local policy makers and their abilities to manage subnational fiscal risks. Broadly, our analysis has focused on four factors that influence fiscal risks. The first is transparency, which, in an electoral system, is crucial to hold policy makers accountable. The second is a legal framework, including fiscal rules—either self-imposed or imposed by the central government—that limits the ability of subnational decision makers to accrue excessive liabilities. The third is market pricing, which ensures that the debt financing cost incurred by SNGs is commensurate with the subnational fiscal risk. The fourth is fiscal capacity and its reflection in the intergovernmental framework. Based on these considerations, the discussion that follows proposes policy recommendations for governments in South Asia to achieve greater fiscal discipline.

Policy Recommendations

Transparency

The effect of transparency measures on the management of subnational fiscal risks may be slower but more significant and persistently positive than the other factors. Gradually, the Indian states adopted measures to improve transparency and public information on subnational debt and contingent liabilities. The positive effect of these measures took time to materialize, but when they did, the effects appeared significant and lasting. There is no reason why India's positive experience with fiscal transparency at the subnational level could not be replicated more widely in South Asia and beyond.

To increase fiscal transparency across South Asia, central and subnational governments could undertake three measures. A first step would be the adoption of accounting standards that highlight contingent liability risks when they accrue, not when they materialize, to allow for adequate budgeting and decision making. This would require moving from the cash-based standards prevalent in South Asia toward accrual accounting. Second, SNGs should collect and consolidate information on debt and other sources of fiscal risks in a single entity at the subnational level.[29] This unit could be a specialized debt management unit within the finance department that fulfills a back-office function for the entire subnational government. While many Indian states and Pakistani provinces have established debt management offices, information on debt and sources of fiscal risks remain scattered across institutions. Centralizing them into one entity would enable the production of consolidated, whole-of-government financial statements. Third, this information could then be audited, publicized, and analyzed by an independent national agency to ensure its consistency and accuracy. This agency could be an independent fiscal council (see discussion that follows).

While data on state finances in India are more comprehensive and easier to access than those of Pakistan, there are still gaps in reporting that hinder greater fiscal transparency. There are no consolidated financial statements for the whole of government, while audited accounts at both the central and state level take about 10 to 12 months to be produced. Moreover, there are no consolidated accounts on state-owned enterprises. The quality of accounting standards is also uneven across government levels, making it difficult to consolidate information across government jurisdictions. Publishing an integrated, total public debt database that includes explicit and implicit guarantees would help the states and the central government identify threats to fiscal sustainability in a more systematic and timely manner.

Legal Framework and Fiscal Rules

Although many countries have imposed limits on subnational borrowing through fiscal rules, our analysis has shown that these are not always effective in limiting fiscal shocks. Part of the problem is moral hazard. When states are in fiscal distress, the central government transfers more resources to the state through tax devolution. This bailout hurts the central government's finances. It reinforces the states' perception of the "soft budget constraint" that exists in federalist systems and reduces the incentives for states to address underlying sources of fiscal risk.

India has had a mixed experience with subnational fiscal rules. However, other countries in the region should not automatically discard this policy tool. For instance, Pakistan already has a legal limit on domestic borrowing; however, it does not consider that most of its provincial debt comes through external loans that are on-lent from the central government. This practice makes the limit irrelevant. Before Pakistan can start adopting recommendations concerning fiscal rules and other debt limitations, more comprehensive and timely data collection on provincial finances is needed (see box 4.1).

International experience suggests that fiscal rules are most effective when they help reinforce a political commitment to fiscal responsibility. To that end, establishing state-level institutions and strengthening central-level institutions could improve the implementation of fiscal responsibility legislation in India.

Specifically, the recommendation by the Fiscal Responsibility and Budget Management Act (FRBM) Committee for the central government to set up an independent fiscal council could also cover Indian states. This council would be responsible for ensuring compliance of states with the fiscal rule and examining justifications for deviating from expected fiscal targets—rather than arbitrarily evoking "escape clauses" in existing legislation. The independent fiscal council could have powers to punish fiscal laxity and reward subnational fiscal discipline.

In countries with strong public sector governance and high institutional capacity, subnational fiscal councils could also be a solution. For example, in Iceland, the Municipal Fiscal Oversight Committee (MFOC) has the power to impose sanctions on municipalities that breach fiscal rules. While fiscally responsible municipalities have greater autonomy, municipalities with

---

BOX 4.1 Recommendations for Improving Fiscal Reporting and Transparency in Pakistan

Given Pakistan's high debt ratio and general fiscal stress, more attention to monitoring and disclosing subnational fiscal risks is especially warranted. While provincial debt may be under control now, the lack of transparency elevates fiscal risks in the near and medium terms.

In addition to the general recommendations presented in this chapter, the federal government or the Controller General of Accounts could establish some standards about what is considered subnational public debt and mandate a format against which all provinces must report debt stocks. Provincial debt bulletins should provide a clearer breakdown of domestic and external debt figures, especially on (1) commodity financing; (2) debt to the federal government; (3) guarantees by type/sector of institution; and (4) type of creditors. Costs of debt should also be made explicit along with information on redemption schedules. To improve transparency, reporting should be made public on the websites of the province's finance departments and as part of the Debt Policy Coordination Office's (DPCO) publications. Eventually, standardized provincial debt

databases should be institutionalized and aligned with the federal Debt Management and Financial Analysis System (DMFAS).

Pakistani provinces should also endeavor to identify and report on contingent liabilities by reporting on the number and total amount of guarantees explicitly issued to both private and public enterprises on a regular basis. Some discussion of implicit obligations (such as those embedded in contracts for public-private partnerships) should also be included, at least qualitatively, in provincial budget documents. The governments of Punjab and Sindh do this to some extent in their latest white papers on their respective budgets, but do not undertake systematic evaluations of such implicit contingent liabilities. Continuing to improve the functioning of provincial debt management offices and the coherence of debt management strategies would help provinces build the capacity to undertake such an assessment, and in doing so minimize the likelihood of unexpected contingent liability shocks in the future.[a]

a. All provinces except Balochistan have established debt management units.

---

excessive debt must obtain approval from the MFOC for all major revenue, expenditure, and borrowing decisions. The MFOC can also withhold transfers and recommend to the minister of local government that a municipality have its fiscal powers vested in a financial management board.

As subnational fiscal autonomy grows, countries should consider instituting robust guarantee management frameworks and policies. This involves adopting the necessary legislation for the issuance of guarantees, clear procedures for assessing and monitoring such guarantees, and ideally, a register of subnational guarantees maintained at the subnational level and/or central level. In India, state governments impose guarantee fees varying from 0.5 percent to 2 percent of the total guarantee amount, but this is often waived in practice (RBI 2019a). Although several states

have limits on outstanding risk-weighted guarantees, in accordance with their fiscal responsibility legislation, it is important that the states (1) calculate these risk weights accurately; (2) undertake debt sustainability analysis on total public and publicly guaranteed debt; and (3) place limits on guarantees in relation to their credit risks.

Market Pricing

Markets play an important role in influencing the fiscal behavior of subnational governments. When access to debt markets and borrowing costs reflect the likelihood of fiscal stress, policy makers have an incentive to sustain fiscal discipline (de Groot, Holm-Hadulla, and Leiner-Killinger 2015). There is evidence, however, that this mechanism does not function effectively. In India, yields vary too little across states to reflect any fiscal metrics (Saggar and Adki 2017). Our analysis confirms that the response of borrowing costs to the breaches of fiscal rules is limited (figure 4.19). Similar findings in Canada and Germany have been linked to explicit and implicit promises of central bailouts (Schuknecht, Von Hagen, and Wolswijk 2009; Booth, Georgopoulos, and Hejazi 2007).

By contrast, evidence for the United States—whose 11th constitutional amendment prohibits subnational bailouts—shows a link between fiscal deficits and borrowing costs for states. It reinforces the evidence that explicit or implicit support from the center matters (Bayoumi, Goldstein, and Woglom 1995).

Allowing markets to function in South Asia requires the development of competitive sovereign bond and debt markets that accurately price risks. Market signals for subnational borrowing in India and Pakistan are significantly distorted because of (1) implicit guarantees of the central government on subnational debt; (2) on-lending of external debt by the central government that provides an explicit credit risk guarantee; and (3) in the case of India, the joint auctioning of state securities by the RBI that pools subnational fiscal risks across states.

In addition, markets do not price the (non-) transparency in the risk premiums of government bond spreads. Bernoth and Wolff (2008) show that in addition to the level of indebtedness, the increase in the "creative" part of fiscal policy and accounting is punished by markets across the European Union at the national level. Creative accounting should increase risk premiums because if a country is nontransparent, financial markets take gimmickry as a "tip of the iceberg" signal. One concerning result of Bernoth and Wolff's analysis is that the disciplining force of markets may not work in a monetary union. This dovetails with our results for the subnational bond market in India and weakens the hope in market forces to help discipline the fiscal affairs of Indian states. Moreover, Heppke-Falk and Wolff (2008) find evidence of investor moral hazard even in the German subnational bond market in which the larger interest payments-to-revenue ratio of SNGs counterintuitively

lowers risk premiums. As values of the ratio increase, the risk premiums decrease more strongly because a larger ratio increases the likelihood of the SNG receiving a bailout.

Enhancing market signals could involve the following measures (IMF 2018):

- *Improving the quality, coverage, and timeliness of data on states' fiscal health.* For instance, in Brazil, SNG fiscal data on deficits and debt are available on a quarterly basis and disaggregated below the state level. States should also endeavor to provide more complete information on explicit and implicit contingent liabilities.
- *Adopting "no bailout" clauses in intergovernmental arrangements.* In Spain, SNGs that miss fiscal targets may forfeit parts of their fiscal autonomy and are required to submit restructuring plans. Adopting similar measures in Indian states could make subnational fiscal responsibility laws more credible and catalyze reforms toward greater transparency and market discipline.
- *Lowering the statutory liquidity ratio requirement to further liberalize financial markets and improve bond market liquidity.* More liquid markets are more efficient at pricing because of higher trades that mix the preferences of diverse market participants and, in turn, help discover correct prices more effectively.

Fiscal Capacity and the Intergovernmental Framework

The intergovernmental fiscal framework must address a tension between providing incentives and insurance to the subnational governments. On the one hand, higher reliance on central transfers can weaken accountability and impose a soft budget constraint, leading to inefficient spending and fiscal unsustainability. In India, for instance, states that depend more on central government revenues tend to have higher SNG debt (figure 4.20). This is consistent with the notion of a widely documented "flypaper effect," which suggests that greater central grant allocation attracts greater SNG expenditure—sometimes above the sustainable level.[30] On the other hand, fiscal capacity at the subnational level is

FIGURE 4.20   Reliance of Indian States on Central Government Revenues and Share of State Debt, 2017

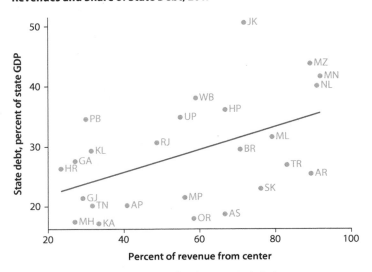

Source: World Bank staff calculations using data from the Reserve Bank of India.
Note: AP = Andhra Pradesh; AR = Arunachal Pradesh; AS = Assam; BR = Bihar; GA = Goa; GJ = Gujarat; HP = Himachal Pradesh; HR = Haryana; JK = Jammu and Kashmir; KA = Karnataka; KL = Kerala; MH = Maharashtra; ML = Meghalaya; MN = Manipur; MP = Madhya Pradesh; MZ = Mizoram; NL = Nagaland; OR = Odisha; PB = Punjab; RJ = Rajasthan; SK = Sikkim; TN = Tamil Nadu; TR = Tripura; UP = Uttar Pradesh; WB = West Bengal.

typically limited, while the central government can collect sizable revenues through direct and indirect taxes. This means that SNGs have limited buffers when they are hit by idiosyncratic shocks. A soft budget constraint and central government support are then needed to prevent a large fiscal adjustment that can negatively affect the local economy.[31] Such support occurs frequently, both in India, as documented in this chapter, and around the world (see, for example, Cordes et al. 2014).[32]

Countries have taken different paths to resolving the trade-off between incentives and insurance. The paths typically contain a mix between providing central bailouts in exceptional cases while maintaining control of subnational financing in normal years. For instance, after the bailouts of regional governments, Spain passed a budget stability law that enhanced transparency and monitoring of subnational budgets through an early warning system. The country also set fiscal rules that contained sanction and enforcement mechanisms. Colombia adopted a formal bankruptcy procedure for SNGs to address debt solvency issues without affecting

the budget. In Argentina, following a subnational pension crisis, the central government absorbed subnational pension liabilities but combined these with reforms to the pension system to support fiscal sustainability going forward.

Annex 4A. Methodology

A quantitative study of contingent liabilities requires a systematic measurement of their effects should they materialize. To this end, it is useful to conceptually define shocks to the debt level as deviations from expectations, defined as follows:

$$Debt_t - E(Debt_t) = Debt_t - (Debt_{t-1} + FD^{Plan})$$
$$= (FD - FD^{Plan}) + SFA_t,$$
$$(4A.1)$$

where $Debt_t$ is the actual subnational debt in year t; $E(Debt_t)$ is the expected debt level in year t; FD is the fiscal deficit; FD^{Plan} is the planned fiscal deficit; and SFA is the stock-flow adjustment.

Equation (4A.1) defines the expected debt level as the amount of liabilities accumulated if the budgeted fiscal deficit had been realized and any debt accumulation had occurred through the budget. The equation also highlights that the actual debt level at time t can differ from its expected value for two reasons: first, because the realized fiscal deficit, FD, can differ from the planned fiscal deficit FD^{Plan}; and second, because of changes that do not go through the budget—that is, changes that happen "below the line" in deficit accounting. The latter is often referred to as the stock-flow adjustment (SFA), defined as the residual of the year-on-year change in debt after accounting for the fiscal deficit:

$$Debt_t - Debt_{t-1} = FD_t + SFA_t. \quad (4A.2)$$

The SFA thus captures all changes in the debt stock that are not explained by the fiscal deficit. To identify the factors that can drive the SFA, it can be useful to consider the government debt stock in year t as consisting of a single representative bond, B_t, priced at rate p_t. Net of the fiscal deficit, the debt stock then evolves as follows:

$$SFA_t = (p_t B_t - p_{t-1} B_{t-1})$$
$$= [p_t (B_t - B_{t-1}) + (p_t - p_{t-1}) B_{t-1}].$$
$$(4A.3)$$

Equation (4A.3) highlights that the SFA can arise for two reasons: first, because of the below-the-line acquisition of liabilities (and assets), holding their valuation constant; and second, because of changes to the valuation of the existing debt stock. Changing valuations can arise, for instance, because of movements in the exchange rate if debt is denominated in a foreign currency or because of changes to interest rates. While not modeled here explicitly, statistical discrepancies can also be responsible for changes to the SFA.[33]

Consistent with the literature (see, for example, Bova et al. 2016), this chapter identifies contingent liability shocks using the SFA because a significant share of contingent liabilities materializes "below the line" (such as the UDAY debt relief scheme in India). "Above-the-line" contingent liability shocks to the fiscal deficit, such as relief expenditures related to natural disasters, are rare in Indian states. Given the prevalence of cash accounting, this means that this definition captures contingent liabilities that do not go through the budget—for instance, bailouts of state-owned enterprises or pension funds if governments take over their debt—but not through the payment of subsidies. Similarly, this definition captures the realization of debt guarantees, but not of price guarantees.

To identify unexpected shocks in the SFA, we apply a Kalman filter to the series. Conceptually, the Kalman filter predicts an expected value of the series for the next period given its historic trajectory. Annex 4B provides a detailed description of the statistical methodology. A contingent liability shock in this application is then defined as a data observation that sufficiently exceeds the predicted expectation. More specifically, outliers are defined by standardizing the Kalman filter residuals and classifying any observation that lies more than 1 standard deviation above the mean as a contingent liability (shock).

Annex 4B. The Kalman Filter

The purpose of filtering is to extract useful information from a signal, removing the noise. The Kalman filter is the best known of these filtering methods. It is a recursive algorithm that estimates unknown variables using imperfect measurements of these variables. In our application, the unknown (state) variable that we are trying to estimate is the underlying level of the stock-flow adjustment (or other public finance series) after we have filtered out the noise from expected expenditures or debt waivers.

In order to estimate this latent variable, we must model how we believe it behaves. Since we are using time-series data, we focus on modeling our series as autoregressive integrated moving average (ARIMA) processes, as they are highly flexible. To select the ARIMA model that best fits our data series for each subnational region, we implement the Hyndman-Khandakar algorithm. This algorithm selects the model that minimizes the Akaike information criterion.

Kalman defined his filter using state-space methods, which simplifies implementation in discrete time. Therefore, we rewrite the best ARIMA model for each subnational entity in its corresponding state-space form and estimate this model using the square-root filter to numerically implement the Kalman filter recursions (De Jong 1991; Durbin and Koopman 2001, sec. 6.3).

When the model is not stationary, the filter is augmented as described by De Jong (1991), De Jong and Chu-Chun-Lin (1994), and Durbin and Koopman (2001, sec. 5.7).

We then estimate the parameters of this linear state-space model by maximum likelihood. The Kalman filter is used to construct the log likelihood, assuming normality and stationarity.

Once we have these parameter estimates, we estimate the underlying states at each time period using previous information from the data series. The data series is predicted by plugging in the estimated states. The residuals are then calculated as the differences between the predicted and the realized data series.

Annex 4C. Regression Tables

TABLE 4C.1 **Effect of Contingent Liability Realizations on Fiscal Variables**

Variables	(1) Debt	(2) Total expenditure	(3) Capital expenditure	(4) Revenue expenditure	(5) Total revenue	(6) Tax revenue	(7) Non-tax revenue	(8) Fiscal deficit
CL shock	0.0550***	−0.0294	−0.0380	−0.0252	−0.00344	0.0290	0.0373	−0.211**
	(0.0185)	(0.0192)	(0.0505)	(0.0220)	(0.0333)	(0.0283)	(0.0350)	(0.0877)
CL shock (t−1)	0.0426**	0.00536	0.0511	−0.000616	0.0821**	0.0960**	0.00263	0.0258
	(0.0170)	(0.0173)	(0.0502)	(0.0184)	(0.0327)	(0.0358)	(0.0315)	(0.0769)
CL shock (t−2)	0.00610	0.0166	0.0366	0.0150	0.0366	0.00839	−0.0220	−0.0360
	(0.0181)	(0.0126)	(0.0474)	(0.0150)	(0.0361)	(0.0383)	(0.0328)	(0.0862)
Observations	644	619	619	619	644	619	644	613
R-squared	0.994	0.994	0.953	0.994	0.981	0.990	0.955	0.916

Source: Blum and Yoong 2020.
Note: The table estimates the following regression: $Y_{it} = \beta_0 + \beta_1 CL\ Shock_{it} + \beta_2 CLShock_{it-1} + \beta_3 CLShock_{it-2} + \gamma_i + \mu_t + \varepsilon_{it}$
Y_{it} denotes the outcome variable of interest, measured in logs. This specification allows for persistent effects of contingent liability shocks by including two lags of the independent variable. The coefficients of interest are β_1, β_2, and β_3, which measure the effect of the contingent liability shock on the outcome variable. These coefficients can be interpreted as causal under the assumption that the trajectory of the outcome variable had been similar in affected and nonaffected states in the absence of the shock. CL = contingent liability. Standard errors clustered at the state level in parentheses. All outcome variables are in logs.
*** $p < 0.01$, ** $p < 0.05$, * $p < 0.1$.

TABLE 4C.2 **Effect of Contingent Liability Realizations on Assistance from the Central Government**

Variables	(1) Loan from center	(2) Grants	(3) Tax devolution	(4) Interest to center
CL shock	0.0985***	0.0354	0.0200	0.0458
	(0.0346)	(0.0258)	(0.0330)	(0.0385)
CL shock (t−1)	0.0916**	−0.0286	0.0956**	0.0640*
	(0.0355)	(0.0323)	(0.0376)	(0.0327)
CL shock (t−2)	0.0491	−0.0249	−0.0136	0.126**
	(0.0386)	(0.0348)	(0.0464)	(0.0503)
Observations	644	619	619	588
R-squared	0.969	0.966	0.981	0.956

Source: Blum and Yoong 2020.
Note: Standard errors clustered at the state level are in parentheses. All outcome variables are in logs. CL = contingent liability.
*** $p < 0.01$, ** $p < 0.05$, * $p < 0.1$.

TABLE 4C.3 **Effects of Contingent Liability Realizations on Gross Fixed Capital Formation**

	Outcome: log(GFCF)		
	Heterogeneity variables		
Variables	**(1)** **All states**	**(2)** **Special category state**	**(3)** **High capital expenditure**
CL shock	−0.196	0.0613	0.362
	(0.146)	(0.124)	(0.272)
CL shock (t−1)	−0.322**	−0.0257	0.130
	(0.140)	(0.0925)	(0.205)
CL shock (t−2)	−0.236	0.133	0.0693
	(0.160)	(0.0973)	(0.192)
CL shock × Heterogeneity variable		−0.612*	−3.419
		(0.302)	(2.156)
CL shock (t−1) × Heterogeneity variable		−0.594***	−2.731*
		(0.210)	(1.454)
CL shock (t−2) × Heterogeneity variable		−0.843***	−1.730
		(0.262)	(1.496)
Observations	532	532	532
R-squared	0.944	0.948	0.946

Source: Blum and Yoong 2020.
Note: CL = contingent liability; GFCF = gross fixed capital formation.
*** $p < 0.01$, ** $p < 0.05$, * $p < 0.1$.

TABLE 4C.4 **Effect of Adoption and Transparency of Fiscal Rules on the Likelihood of Contingent Liability Shocks[a]**

	Outcome: Realization of a contingent liability at time t					
Exogenous variable	**(1)** **Fiscal rule**	**(2)** **Debt report**	**(3)** **Guarantee report**	**(4)** **Fiscal rule**	**(5)** **Debt report**	**(6)** **Guarantee report**
t	−0.104**	0.0220	−0.0550	−0.0962	0.107	−0.0253
	(0.0453)	(0.0814)	(0.0682)	(0.0597)	(0.123)	(0.114)
$t−1$	−0.0424	−0.0747	0.0121	0.0179	−0.0175	0.119
	(0.0713)	(0.0654)	(0.0997)	(0.0967)	(0.0935)	(0.147)
$t−2$	0.0295	−0.133***	−0.107***	0.0663	−0.115**	−0.0909**
	(0.0925)	(0.0391)	(0.0327)	(0.121)	(0.0470)	(0.0402)
$t−3$	0.0478	−0.117***	−0.0830***	0.0299	−0.126***	−0.0892**
	(0.103)	(0.0274)	(0.0252)	(0.123)	(0.0313)	(0.0335)
$t × SCS$				−0.0152	−0.219*	−0.0772
				(0.135)	(0.125)	(0.125)
$(t−1) × SCS$				−0.172*	−0.158	−0.270*
				(0.0925)	(0.0978)	(0.150)
$(t−2) × SCS$				−0.118	−0.0465	−0.0412
				(0.148)	(0.0719)	(0.0631)
$(t−3) × SCS$				0.0268	0.0224	0.0157
				(0.166)	(0.0414)	(0.0391)
Observations	650	650	650	650	650	650
R-squared	0.084	0.087	0.083	0.087	0.091	0.087

Sources: RBI 2019a; Blum and Yoong 2020.
Note: The table presents the results of the following panel regressions:

$$CL\ Shock_{it} = \beta_0 + \beta_1 X_{it} + \beta_2 X_{it−1} + \beta_3 X_{it−2} + \beta_4 X_{it−3} + \delta_i + \mu_t + \varepsilon_{it}$$

The outcome variable is an indicator variable that takes the value 1 for state-year observations in which a contingent liability realization was identified, using the methodology outlined previously. X_{it} denotes the regressor of interest. Depending on the specification, it either takes the value 1 in years in which states adopted fiscal rules or 0 otherwise, or when states began the publication of debt or guarantee reports. State and year fixed effects are further included in the regression. As such, this specification can be interpreted as a difference-in-difference design for a linear probability model, in which the coefficients of interest (β_1 to β_4) estimate the change in probability of a contingent liability shock occurring following the intervention, controlling for state and year specific developments. Standard errors are clustered at the state level in parentheses. SCS = special category state.
a. This analysis focuses on the publication of specialized debt and guarantee reports. The independent variable thus takes the value 0 for instances when debt- and guarantee-related information was only published in annual financial statements.
*** $p < 0.01$, ** $p < 0.05$, * $p < 0.1$.

Notes

1. The most recent joint World Bank–IMF debt sustainability analyses for Afghanistan (IMF 2020a), Maldives (IMF 2020c), Pakistan (IMF 2020b), and Sri Lanka (IMF 2019a) assess these countries as being at high risk of debt distress.
2. Brazil's federal government bailed out subnational governments in 1989, 1993, and 1997–2000 (Manoel, Garson, and Mora 2013).
3. Data are for the end of 2018 (RBI 2019a).
4. China's subnational debt-to-GDP is similarly high (estimated at 20.6 percent), but it has a unitary system.
5. Data are for the end of June 2019 and are estimated by World Bank staff for this study. For more details, see the next section on Pakistan.
6. OECD-UCLG (2019, figure 7.3). Data are for 2016.
7. See Maldives (n.d.).
8. See https://presidency.gov.mv/Press/Article/22833.
9. Eleven states have been designated special category states because of their unique circumstances, such economic and infrastructural backwardness, and nonviable nature of state finances. The remaining 17 states are general category states.
10. Pakistan's fiscal rule can also be suspended if social and poverty-reducing expenditures fall below 4.5 percent of GDP or if health and education spending fail to double in terms of percent of GDP over a 10-year period.
11. This estimate uses data from the latest available debt bulletin of each province except for Balochistan, for which data come from Government of Balochistan (2019).
12. Article 167, Clause (3) states, "A Province may not, without the consent of the Federal Government, raise any loan if there is still outstanding any part of a loan made to the Province by the Federal Government, or in respect of which guarantee has been given by the Federal Government; and consent under this clause may be granted subject to such conditions, if any, as the Federal Government may think fit to impose."
13. Article 167, Clause (4) states, "A Province may raise domestic or international loan or give guarantees on the security of the Provincial Consolidated Fund within such limits and subject to such conditions as may be specified by the National Economic Council."
14. This limit varies for each province according to its share of the national population. For Punjab and Khyber Pakhtunkhwa, for instance, borrowing limits are equal to PRs 143 billion and PRs 44 billion, respectively.
15. In Khyber Pakhtunkhwa and Balochistan as of the end of June 2019, all of the debt is on-lent by the central government. This arrangement exists in part because these state governments do not have a debt management strategy and hence cannot borrow on their own.
16. According to the latest Punjab debt bulletin, 90 percent of the net year-on-year growth in outstanding debt stock was due to rupee depreciation in the previous six months.
17. The Pakistani fiscal year runs from July 1 to June 30.
18. There are also discrepancies between debt stock recorded by the Ministry of Finance and the provincial financial statements in some cases. In Balochistan, for example, the latter understates the debt stock quite substantially.
19. This finding is based on discussions with staff at the Office of the Auditor General of Pakistan.
20. The government of Khyber Pakhtunkhwa, for example, owns 70 percent of the Bank of Khyber and would likely intervene in the case of a crisis.
21. This is a lower-bound estimate given that actual growth in salaries, pensions, and number of employees has been 3 percentage points to 4 percentage points higher than the assumed annual increases in the actuarial valuations. See Government of Punjab (2019, 55–56).
22. World Bank (2017b).
23. See Government of Khyber Pakhtunkhwa (2019).
24. In Sindh, for example, the government provided a sovereign guarantee of $700 million to the Thar coal power plant, which was inaugurated in April 2019.
25. See https://tribune.com.pk/story/2101536/2-pll-sngpl-tussle-threatens-derail-1200mw-project/.
26. See also Government of India (2017).
27. Guarantee reports induce a similar effect (see table 4C.4, col. 3).
28. See Government of India (2018).
29. This contrasts with today's practice in Pakistani provinces. See, for example, World Bank (2017a).
30. See Baicker (2005); Lutz (2010); Litschig and Morrison (2013); Cascio, Gordon, and Reber

31. The one exception is Pakistan, where the division of resources is such that fiscal space lies with the provinces and not with the central government.
32. One interesting international example comes from Spain, where in 2012 the central government provided loans and guarantees to multiple regions to service their debt during the Eurozone crisis, thus preempting a further deterioration of the fiscal crisis while weakening fiscal incentives going forward.
33. For an alternative decomposition of the debt trajectory, see Giavazzi and Missale (2004).

References

Baicker, K. 2005. "Extensive or Intensive Generosity? The Price and Income Effects of Federal Grants." *Review of Economics and Statistics* 87 (2): 371–84.

Bayoumi, T., M. Goldstein, and G. Woglom. 1995. "Do Credit Markets Discipline Sovereign Borrowers? Evidence from US States." *Journal of Money, Credit and Banking* 27 (4): 1046–59.

Bernoth, K., and G. B. Wolff. 2008. "Fool the Markets? Creative Accounting, Fiscal Transparency and Sovereign Risk Premia." *Scottish Journal of Political Economy* 55 (4): 465–87.

Blum, F., and P. S. Yoong. 2020. "The Impact of Subnational Contingent Liability Realizations: Evidence from India." Background paper for *Hidden Debt*. World Bank, Washington, DC.

Booth, L., G. Georgopoulos, and W. Hejazi. 2007. "What Drives Provincial-Canada Yield Spreads?" *Canadian Journal of Economics* 40 (3): 1008–32.

Bova, E., M. Ruiz-Arranz, F. Toscani, and H. Elif Ture. 2016. "The Fiscal Costs of Contingent Liabilities: A New Dataset." IMF Working Paper WP/16/14, International Monetary Fund, Washington, DC.

Cascio, E. U., N. Gordon, and S. Reber. 2013. "Local Responses to Federal Grants: Evidence from the Introduction of Title I in the South." *American Economic Journal: Economic Policy* 5 (3): 126–59.

Cordes, T., M. Guerguil, L. Jaramillo, M. Moreno-Badia, and S. Ylaoutinen. 2014. "Subnational Fiscal Crises." Chapter 6 in *Designing a European Fiscal Union: Lessons from the Experience of Fiscal Federations*, edited by C. Cottarelli and M. Guerguil. London: Routledge.

de Groot, O., F. Holm-Hadulla, and N. Leiner-Killinger. 2015. "Cost of Borrowing Shocks and Fiscal Adjustment." *Journal of International Money and Finance* 59 (C): 23–48.

De Jong, P. 1991. "The Diffuse Kalman Filter." *Annals of Statistics* 19 (2): 1073–83.

De Jong, P., and S. Chu-Chun-Lin. 1994. "Stationary and Non-Stationary State Space Models." *Journal of Time Series Analysis* 15 (2): 151–66.

Durbin, J., and S. J. Koopman. 2001. *Time Series Analysis by State-Space Methods*. Oxford, United Kingdom: Oxford University Press.

Ellis, P., and M. Roberts. 2016. *Leveraging Urbanization in South Asia: Managing Spatial Transformation for Prosperity and Livability*. Washington, DC: World Bank.

Giavazzi, F., and A. Missale. 2004. "Public Debt Management in Brazil." NBER Working Paper 10394, National Bureau of Economic Research, Cambridge, MA.

Governatori, M., and D. Yim. 2012. "Fiscal Decentralization and Fiscal Outcomes." Economic Papers 468, European Commission, Brussels.

Government of Balochistan. 2019. Balochistan Budget White Paper 2019–2020. Government of Balochistan, Pakistan.

Government of India, Ministry of Finance, Department of Economic Affairs, Economic Division. 2017. "Economic Survey 2016–17." Government of India.

Government of India, Ministry of Finance, Department of Economic Affairs, Economic Division. 2018. Economic Survey, 2017–18. Government of India.

Government of Khyber Pakhtunkhwa. 2019. "One Khyber Pakhtunkhwa." White Paper 2019/20 Budget, June. Government of Khyber Pakhtunkhwa, Pakistan.

Government of Maldives. n.d. Strategic Action Plan 2019–2023. President's Office, Republic of Maldives.

Government of Punjab. 2019. White Paper on the Budget FY 2019–20. Government of Punjab, India, June.

Heppke-Falk, K. H., and G. B. Wolff. 2008. "Moral Hazard and Bail-Out in Fiscal Federations: Evidence for the German Länder." *Kyklos* 61 (3): 425–46.

IMF (International Monetary Fund). 2014. "Public Expenditure Reform: Making Difficult Choices." Chapter 2 in *Fiscal Monitor April 2014*. Washington, DC: IMF.

IMF (International Monetary Fund). 2018. "Fiscal Discipline in Indian States: Market-Based and Other Options." Selected Issues, IMF Country Report no. 18/255, International Monetary Fund, Washington, DC, August.

IMF (International Monetary Fund). 2019a. "Sixth Review under the Extended Arrangement under the Extended Fund Facility and Requests for Waiver of Nonobservance and Modification of Performance Criterion–Press Release; Staff Report; and Statement by the Alternate Executive Director for Sri Lanka." International Monetary Fund, Washington, DC.

IMF (International Monetary Fund). 2019b. "Maldives: Technical Assistance Report–Public Investment Management Assessment." Country Report no. 19/102, International Monetary Fund, Washington, DC.

IMF (International Monetary Fund). 2019c. "Selected Issues: Nepal." CR/Issues/2019/02/15 /Nepal-2018-Article-IV-Consultation. International Monetary Fund, Washington, DC.

IMF (International Monetary Fund). 2019d. "Estimating the Stock of Public Capital in 170 Countries. August 2019 Update." International Monetary Fund, Washington, DC.

IMF (International Monetary Fund). 2020a. "Islamic Republic of Afghanistan: Request for Disbursement under the Rapid Credit Facility–Press Release; Staff Report; and Statement by the Executive Director for the Islamic Republic of Afghanistan." International Monetary Fund, Washington, DC, April 17.

IMF (International Monetary Fund). 2020b. "Pakistan: Request for Purchase under the Rapid Financing Instrument–Press Release; Staff Report; and Statement by the Executive Director for Pakistan." International Monetary Fund, Washington, DC, April 17.

IMF (International Monetary Fund). 2020c. "Maldives: Request for Disbursement under the Rapid Credit Facility–Press Release; Staff Report; and Statement by the Executive Director for Maldives." International Monetary Fund, Washington, DC, April 23.

Jenker, E., and Z. Lu. 2014. "Sub-National Credit Risk and Sovereign Bailouts–Who Pays the Premium?" IMF Working Paper WP/14/20, International Monetary Fund, Washington, DC.

Keen, M., and M. Marchand. 1997. "Fiscal Competition and the Pattern of Public Spending." *Journal of Public Economics* 66 (1): 33–53.

Kelly, R., and A. S. Gunawardena. 2016. "Financing Sustainable Urbanization in Sri Lanka." Chapter 7 in *The Sri Lankan Economy: Charting A New Course,* edited by P. Athukorala, E. Ginting, H. Hill, and U. Kumar. Manila: Asian Development Bank.

Kornai, J. 1986. "The Soft Budget Constraint." *Kyklos* 39 (1): 3–30.

Litschig, S., and K. M. Morrison. 2013. "The Impact of Intergovernmental Transfers on Education Outcomes and Poverty Reduction." *American Economic Journal: Applied Economics* 5 (4): 206–40.

Liu, C., and G. Ma. 2016. "Taxation without Representation: Local Fiscal Response to Intergovernmental Transfers in China." *International Tax and Public Finance* 23 (5): 854–74.

Lledó, V., S. Yoon, X. Fang, S. Mbaye, and Y. Kim. 2017. "Fiscal Rules at a Glance." Background Note, International Monetary Fund, Washington, DC.

Lundqvist, H. 2015. "Granting Public or Private Consumption? Effects of Grants on Local Public Spending and Income Taxes." *International Tax and Public Finance* 22 (1): 41–72.

Lutz, B. 2010. "Taxation with Representation: Intergovernmental Grants in a Plebiscite Democracy." *Review of Economics and Statistics* 92 (2): 316–32.

Manoel, A., S. Garson, and M. Mora. 2013. "Brazil: The Subnational Debt Restructuring of the 1990s–Origins, Conditions and Results." In *Until Debt Do Us Part: Subnational Debt, Insolvency, and Markets,* edited by O. Canuto and L. Liu, 33–79. Washington, DC: World Bank.

Manoel, A., S. Refaqat, H. Onder, and M. Ashraf. 2012. "Punjab Debt Sustainability Analysis." World Bank Policy Paper Series on Pakistan 13/12, World Bank, Washington, DC, October.

Oates, W. E. 1972. *Fiscal Federalism.* New York: Harcourt Brace Jovanovich.

Oates, W. E. 1999. "An Essay on Fiscal Federalism." *Journal of Economic Literature* 37 (2): 1120–49.

Oates, W. E. 2005. "Toward A Second Generation Theory of Fiscal Federalism." *International Tax and Public Finance* 12 (4): 349–73.

OECD (Organisation for Economic Co-operation and Development). 2018. Subnational Governments in OECD Countries: Key Data, 2018 edition. https://www.oecd.org/regional/Subnational-governments-in-OECD-Countries-Key-Data-2018.pdf

OECD-UCLG (Organisation for Economic Co-operation and Development–United Cities and Local Governments). 2019. "2019 Report of the World Observatory on Subnational Government Finance and Investment—Key Findings." OECD-UCLG.

Persson, T., G. Roland, and G. Tabellini. 2000. "Comparative Politics and Public Finance." *Journal of Political Economy* 108: 1121–61.

Polackova Brixi, H., and A. Mody. 2002. "Dealing with Fiscal Risk: An Overview." Chapter 1 in *Government at Risk: Contingent Liabilities and Fiscal Risk,* edited by H. Polackova Brixi and A. Schick, 21–58. Washington, DC: World Bank; New York: Oxford University Press.

Polackova Brixi, H., and A. Schick, eds. 2002. *Government at Risk: Contingent Liabilities and Fiscal Risk.* Washington, DC: World Bank; New York: Oxford University Press.

PRS India. 2013. "Special Category Status and Centre-State Finances." PRS India, New Delhi.

Rangarajan, C., and A. Prasad. 2012. "Managing State Debt and Ensuring Solvency: The Indian Experience." Policy Research Working Paper 6039, World Bank, Washington, DC.

Refaqat, S. 2015. "Fiscal Decentralization in Pakistan: A Forgotten Agenda." The World Bank Policy Paper Series on Pakistan. World Bank, Islamabad, June.

RBI (Reserve Bank of India). 2015. "Handbook of Statistics on Indian States." Reserve Bank of India.

RBI (Reserve Bank of India). 2019a. "State Finances: A Study of Budgets." Reserve Bank of India.

RBI (Reserve Bank of India). 2019b. "Handbook of Statistics on Indian States." Reserve Bank of India.

Saggar, S., and M. Adki. 2017. "State Government Yield Spreads–Do Fiscal Metrics Matter?" Mint Street Memo no. 08, Reserve Bank of India.

Schuknecht, L., J. Von Hagen, and G. Wolswijk. 2009. "Government Risk Premiums in the Bond Market: EMU and Canada." *European Journal of Political Economy* 25 (3): 371–84.

Seabright, P. 1996. "Accountability and Decentralisation in Government: An Incomplete Contracts Model." *European Economic Review* 40 (1): 61–89.

Simone, A., and P. Topalova. 2009. "India's Experience with Fiscal Rules: An Evaluation and the Way Forward." IMF Working Paper 09/175, International Monetary Fund, Washington, DC.

Sow, M., and I. Razafimahefa. 2017. "Fiscal Decentralization and Fiscal Policy Performance." IMF Working Paper, 17/64, International Monetary Fund, Washington, DC.

Weber, A. 2012. "Stock-Flow Adjustments and Fiscal Transparency: A Cross-Country Comparison." IMF Working Paper 12/39, International Monetary Fund, Washington, DC.

World Bank. 2017a. "Khyber Pakhtunkhwa Province, Pakistan: Public Financial Management Assessment Report." World Bank, Washington, DC.

World Bank. 2017b. "Sindh Public Expenditure Review." World Bank, Washington, DC.

World Bank. 2019a. *South Asia Economic Focus: Rethinking Decentralization.* Washington, DC: World Bank.

World Bank. 2019b. "Local Government Public Financial Management Assessment for Bangladesh." World Bank, Dhaka.